A Hand Up:

Women Mentoring

Women in Science

A Hand Up:

Women Mentoring
Women in Science

Editor Deborah C. Fort
Project Coordinator Stephanie J. Bird
Executive Director Catherine Jay Didion

THE ASSOCIATION FOR WOMEN IN SCIENCE
WASHINGTON, D.C.

This project was supported by a grant from the Alfred P. Sloan
Foundation.

Library of Congress Catalog Card Number 93-070033

ISBN Number 0-9634590-2-3

Acknowledgments

AWIS thanks women in science everywhere.

The support of the mentoring grant from the Alfred P. Sloan Foundation made possible *A Hand Up: Women Mentoring Women in Science*.

Printed in the United States of America
First Edition

Table of Contents

Preface

The title of this volume, *A Hand Up: Women Mentoring Women in Science*, brings to mind the original mentor. In Homer's *Odyssey*,

Mentor was the wise and faithful counselor, the trusted friend and advisor to whom Odysseus entrusted the education of his son, Telemachus. In Mentor's form, Athena, goddess of wisdom and protectress of the family, helped Telemachus search for his father. After Athena, a long tradition shows women proving to be the best of mentors for men.

Today, as more and more young women pursue odysseys in the form of professional careers, women who have already established themselves professionally are challenged to follow in the footsteps of Athena by serving as inspiring mentors for other women. Mentors offer guidance and friendship to women starting out in their careers. And mentors' advice and support are important today not only to the futures of the young women concerned but also to the future of science and medicine in this country. Why? For this simple reason: Young women are America's future scientists and physicians.

According to the National Center for Education Statistics (1992a, October), in the 1960s women in college were outnumbered by men almost two to one. By 1970, there were two women in college for every three men. In 1979, however, women became the absolute majority in colleges and universities. Today, women are increasingly attracted to higher education. There now are well over a million more women than men studying in colleges and universities nationwide (National Center for Education Statistics, 1992b, December). This pattern also is reflected in earned degrees, including advanced degrees. In absolute numbers, more women are being awarded associate, bachelor's, and master's degrees than men, and it is projected that by the year 2003, about 48 percent of the doctorates will be earned by women. Thus, by the year 2000, most new entrants into the professions and jobs requiring higher education will be women (Bureau of Labor Statistics, 1991).

The general trends in education are mirrored in medicine. Among new entrants to medical school, the number of men has dropped by more than 9 percent in the past 10 years, while the number of women has increased by about the same percentage (American Association of Medical Colleges, 1991a, 1992). Were it not for this trend among women offsetting falling male enrollment, we might face a brainpower shortage in medicine and biomedical research. Similar patterns apply all across science, compensating for what would otherwise be an erosion of the scientific talent base—a talent base that is one of the major ingredients of America's scientific and technological leadership in the world.

A close look reveals that the United States' leadership in these fields may not continue. Recent government reports (Educational Testing Service, 1992a, 1992b, February) suggest that many American students do not receive good science and math educations. According to Karen DeWitt writing in the *New York Times* (1992, March 27), fewer than half of U.S. elementary schools and only about one-third of U.S. high schools make science a priority.

Although we know there are no cognitive differences between boys and girls in their ability to do science, after the fourth grade boys consistently outperform girls, and the gap widens as they progress in school. One explanation for this may be, according to a recent report by the American Association of University Women (1992), that girls and boys do not have equal access to learning. From lack of discussion of women's achievements in textbooks, to teachers giving more attention and encouragement to boys, the report describes a pattern of gender-based bias in our schools.

What happens to most young women as they progress through the higher educational system? According to foundation-funded studies by Joan S. Girgus and Catherine A. Sanderson (1988) and Elaine Seymour and Nancy Hewitt (1992), fewer women than men declare science as a major in college, and a greater proportion of women abandon science for other majors. Studies have shown that, throughout their academic and professional careers in science, women receive more negative treatment than their male counterparts. Jonathan R. Cole and Burton Singer (1991) describe what they refer to as positive and negative kinetic reactions or "kicks" that occur at every stage in a career. Women in science experience far too few positive "kicks"—the rewards and recognition that build the self-confidence needed to conduct research and assume leadership.

Women tend to be paid less, promoted less often, and left in nontenure-track positions. It is not surprising to find that most science faculty members are men. A 1992 report by the National Science Foundation (Table 1-2, p. 8) shows a total of 181,078 men with doctorates teaching in science and engineering departments at four-year colleges and universities, compared with 39,864 women. Fifty-nine percent of the men were tenured, compared with only 36 percent of the women.

The field of medicine mirrors the trends found in science generally. Although women now represent 38 percent of medical students, and their academic performance is virtually indistinguishable from men's, women rarely achieve leadership positions on medical school faculties. Indeed, they represent only 21.5 percent of all medical school faculty members, occupying what might be called an academic ghetto in which 49.8 percent are clustered at the assistant professor level, while only 9.8 percent have achieved the rank of full professor. (Figures from the American Association of Medical Colleges, 1991b.) The glass ceiling remains firmly in place and, at present, often seems shatterproof!

There is some encouraging news for women in the life sciences, however. The inequities in women's career advancement are lowest in biology and greatest in physics, engineering, and mathematics. It is probably no coincidence that more women pursue careers in the biological sciences than in the physical sciences, engineering, or mathematics. Success leads to success. Clearly, one—but not the only—way to help women in all the scientific disciplines is to increase the sheer numbers of women in these fields.

Beyond attracting and retaining more women in the sciences, new strategies to promote equality and ensure advancement for talented women are essential. Institutions must be held accountable for developing sound recruitment, retention, and retraining programs that provide women in science with opportunities for growth at every level. Periodic follow-up studies to evaluate the effectiveness of these programs can ensure that women are not merely brought into the system, but also are given opportunities to achieve their scientific potential.

As a corollary to institutional encouragement, young women need personal mentors, especially during their years of undergraduate and graduate study. While this volume serves as a sort of "paper mentor" for young women in science and mathematics, it cannot be a substitute for flesh-and-blood mentors. It is my hope that the words of wisdom and advice contained within these pages will not only inspire young women embarking on their careers in science but also inspire others to follow in the footsteps of Athena by proving the best of mentors for both men and women.

—Bernadine Healy, M.D.
Director, National Institutes of Health
Washington, D.C., January, 1993

References

American Association of Medical Colleges. (1991a). *Trends in medical school applicants and matriculants, 1981-1990*. Washington, DC: Author.

American Association of Medical Colleges. (1991b). *U.S medical school faculty*. Washington, DC: Author.

American Association of Medical Colleges. (1992). *American Association of Medical Colleges data book: Statistical information related to medical education*. Washington, DC: Author.

The American Association of University Women. (1992). *How schools shortchange girls*. Washington, DC: Author.

Bureau of Labor Statistics. (1991, November). *New entrants to the labor force, 1990-2005*. Washington, DC: Author.

Cole, Jonathan R., and Singer, Burton. (1991). A theory of limited differences: Explaining the productivity by puzzle in science. In Harriet Zuckerman, Cole, and John T. Bruer. (Eds). *The outer circle: Women in the scientific community* (pp. 277-310). New York: Norton.

Education Testing Service. (1992a, February). *Learning mathematics* [A report prepared for the National Center for Education Statistics and the National Science Foundation]. Princeton, NJ: Author.

Education Testing Service. (1992b, February). *Learning science* [A report prepared for the National Center for Education Statistics and the National Science Foundation]. Princeton, NJ: Author.

Girgus, Joan S., and Catherine A. Sanderson. (1988, September). *Women and science: An alliance gone awry* [Discussion paper prepared for the Science Advisory Committee, Pew Science Program in Undergraduate Education]. Philadelphia: Pew Charitable Trusts.

National Center for Education Statistics. (1992a, October). *Digest of Education Statistics*. Washington, DC: Author.

National Center for Education Statistics. (1992b, December). *Projection of Education Statistics to 2003*. Washington, DC: Author.

National Science Foundation. (1992). *Women and minorities in science and engineering: An update*. Washington, DC: Author.

Seymour, Elaine, and Hewitt, Nancy. (1992). *Factors contributing to high attrition rates among science and engineering undergraduate majors* [Report prepared for the Alfred P. Sloan Foundation]. New York: Alfred P. Sloan Foundation.

Foreword

The Association for Women in Science (AWIS), is an organization dedicated both to the advancement of women in science and technology and to the encouragement of girls and women in the study of mathematics and science. Our membership includes practitioners, teachers, and policy-makers from all branches of science and spans the range of seniority from students to members of the National Academy of Sciences. Our members, employed in industry, academia, and government, include women of color and represent a wide range of ethnic groups.

In 1990, the Alfred P. Sloan Foundation gave AWIS a three-year grant to facilitate development and enhancement of activities designed to increase the number of women in science. Mentors help undergraduate and graduate science students identify the best paths for their academic and professional careers by advising them on everything from courses, thesis topics, and authorship issues to job interviewing skills to balancing family and career. *A Hand Up* is one component of the AWIS Mentoring Project. We very much appreciate the generosity of the Sloan Foundation in funding the project and we hope that this publication will extend its impact.

This volume highlights the way in which women in science form a community in the best sense. *A Hand Up* is designed to serve as a source of support for women interested in pursuing careers in science, however geographically or socially isolated they may feel. Because not all of us are in supportive communities with existing mentoring networks, it is our hope that *A Hand Up* will serve as a "paper mentor" to all in need. While it cannot, nor does it seek to replace the vitality of human interaction, it should inspire and advise women in a wide range of careers in science.

We see *A Hand Up* as a tool for women today as they pursue their dreams. This publication is a starting point—not a destination—and can be used to discover many possible avenues of exploration.

Like advice from any mentor, the suggestions, ideas, and interpretations of life experience provided by the contributors to *A Hand Up* need to be considered and evaluated critically. Each of us has a unique perspective that reflects the cultural context of our lives; the people we have known and dealt with; our hopes, dreams, expectations, and disappointments; what we have learned, rightly or wrongly, intentionally or by necessity. The ideas presented within these pages are not infallible, but they detail lessons learned that may—or may not—be applicable to you. You alone have to decide.

We wish you a rich, interesting, productive, and rewarding life. May *A Hand Up* in some way help to make that possible.

—Stephanie J. Bird, Ph.D.
Mentoring Project Coordinator

—Catherine Jay Didion
Executive Director
January, 1993

Introduction

A Hand Up comes into *your* hands at an exciting point for women in science in the United States. While women make up a majority of the total population, they continue to be a decided minority in science—1988 National Science Foundation figures show that overall only 16 percent of scientists and engineers are women (1992, p. 4). The climate, however, is changing, and the contributors to this book—women who are succeeding in science, mathematics, or engineering and female students who are moving toward scientific careers in the near future—are part of the impetus. Another push is the widely accepted prediction that women and minority group members will make up about two-thirds of the new entrants to the workforce around the turn of the century (Bureau of Labor Statistics, 1991), along with the recognition that, to be effective, this new workforce must be well-educated in general and in particular in science and technology.

Many women in science are recognizing that not only should the *numbers* change but also the field itself. Science, long dominated by male metaphors as well as by men, must at least become gender neutral in numbers and method, or, better, incorporate the best that masculine and feminine approaches offer.

As the male scientists and students who have overwhelmingly populated science in the past know well, one of the factors that can make or break a career commitment to science is the presence at certain crucial points of a mentor. Lucky children are guided by sensitive and friendly adults, happy youth by inspired and committed teachers, and fortunate adults by experienced colleagues and friends. All these are mentoring relationships. Because of the make-up of the field, in the past mentors for both men and women in science have been overwhelmingly male.

But, as women become a larger presence among students and faculty and among research, industrial, and academic scientists and mathematicians, female mentors also have an increasingly important role to play. *A Hand Up: Women Mentoring Women in Science* provides guidelines, resources, advice, and networks, both for those seeking mentors and for those willing to serve as guides. In these pages, nearly 60 women provide their insights, advice, and assistance to those who would become a woman in science or to those already there who would, if they could, become less isolated.

A Hand Up comprises four sections.

I. The Interviews

The first part of *A Hand Up*, **Individual Voices,** contains interviews with 37 women scientists, postdoctoral fellows, and students.* Each offers her personal view of what helped her enter the sciences, what she found there, and what helped her to stay in atmospheres often virtually devoid of women, or, worse, hostile toward them.†

AWIS has aimed at a wide cross-section of scientists and students from a number of fields, professional and educational levels, and ethnic and racial backgrounds. For various reasons, the scientists tend to cluster in the East, and the students in the West; four of the students attend two California universities with carefully constructed support groups for those made minority by gender, race, or ethnicity. The interviews, subdivided into those by practicing scientists (among them, research, academic, industrial, and managerial specialists) and students, are otherwise arranged alphabetically. Every woman interviewed has offered herself as a resource for women thinking of entering science and for women already in the

---

*About a third of the interviews (as indicated) follow up earlier conversations, mostly conducted with Barbara Mandula, Nancy M. Tooney, Diane Ross, and Edna Kunkel, which originally appeared in the *AWIS Newsletter/Magazine* between 1977 and 1991. Many of this volume's new interviews were originally conducted in 1991-1992 by Kim Austin and Melissa Blouin. We are also grateful for the most recent surveys conducted by Mary Ann Borchert, Mecca B. Carpenter, and Diane Wallender.

†AWIS hopes to publish a comprehensive list of mentor networks in the near future. As a beginning, however, readers are invited to consult three useful collections of mentoring resources geared to different audiences from widely varying sources. *Exemplars: Women in Science, Engineering, and Mathematics* is a university-based list of mentors for girls in junior high school and high school available from the Ohio Academy of Science, 445 King Avenue, Columbus, OH 43201. *Northwest Women in Science: Women Making a Difference, A Role Model Guide Book,* a federal (Department of Energy) publication that lists women willing to be mentors also for the precollege group, is available through the Northwest College and University Association for Science, Washington State University—Tri Cities, 100 Sprout Road, Richland, WA 99352 ([509] 375-3090). Students leaving college needing career guidance and help from a mentor may turn to the listings in *The Student Pugwash USA Mentorship Guide: A Directory of Resource People and Advisors in Social Change* (Brent Hopkins and Jeff McIntyre, Eds.), which is available through Student Pugwash USA, 1638 R Street, NW, Suite 32, Washington, DC 20009 ([202] 328-6555).

field needing support (each interview includes contact information). Readers are invited to approach the first section by reading through it as a whole, to seek respondents in their particular fields through the table of contents, or to use the index to find women dealing with issues of particular interest to them individually.

II. The Overview

The next section, **The Consensus,** offers a brief cross sectional approach to the views and advice provided in part I. Several patterns of response emerged.

Women scientists and science students shared their views of what and who first interested them in science and explained what it is and was like starting out in new fields, describing their experiences in college and beyond, in fellowships, and on their first jobs. Many went on to tell of their life in the workplace—how it began, how it changed, how they organized their professional priorities. Other themes numerous women touched are

◆ the value of networks

◆ the need to balance personal and career commitments

◆ the ways to survive on the job

◆ the importance of gender: From feminism, to sexual harassment, to the difference between male and female approaches to certain issues, tasks, and views

✔ While these thematic trends came up frequently, the women themselves offer quirky, unique insights that defy generalization and emerge only from a reading of each of the individual interviews.

III. Advice

Following the overview of the interviews comes part III, a collection of 20 short papers by women scientists, educators, and philosophers, gathered as **Advice From the Field.** These originative thinkers in the field of gender and science discuss a number of concerns central to all women in science.

Papers in the opening section of part III consider the broad *philosophic questions* raised by women about their responsibilities to their work, to their families, to their gender, and to science. Lorraine J. Daston opens the discussion by showing us that there are many paths to understanding, that concepts of "true" and "wrong" are by no means simple or, always, even useful in science or in life. Sheila Tobias defines and applies some of her concepts about feminism and patriarchy to the world of science, playing off several of the ideas explicated and opened by Evelyn Fox Keller in the conversation with Bill Moyers that concludes this section. Earlier, Lynn Margulis considers a theme raised often by the individual voices of part I, the relationship of personal and familial to career priorities.

The second section offers five papers that focus on *education**— from Betty P. Preece's piece on the need to advise young girls about how to find the place in science that can be theirs to Virginia Walbot's advice on how to succeed in graduate school and beyond. Shirley M. Malcom and Barbara Furin Sloat define important ways in which colleges and universities can become more welcoming, more nurturing to the underrepresented (and, at times, under-prepared), who are often women and/or minorities. Student Lisa A. Zuccarelli provides concrete advice to fellow graduate students on making their studies both fulfilling and profitable.

In the third section of part III, five more papers shed light on *professional matters* likely to need explication and advice for women in science at many levels. Stephanie J. Bird opens the section with an essay defining the specific responsibilities that women embrace as scientists, responsibilities that go beyond those of other adults, parents, and citizens. Barbara Filner provides concrete advice on applying for grants and fellowships, and Marian G. Glenn, Dorie Monroe, and Judith Lamont, along with Heidi B. Hammel, discuss the importance of women's speaking at meetings—and doing so effectively. Florence P. Haseltine concludes this section with some concrete and idiosyncratic thoughts on balancing career and personal needs, demands, and desires.

The fourth section collects four papers on *gender issues,* which have, of course, formed an active subtext throughout the volume. The section opens with an unsigned piece, written 15 years ago, whose warning to women to avoid disguised sexism is still, unfortunately, relevant: The author's desire for anonymity, alas, remains sensibly unchanged. The anonymous paper is followed by that of Anne M. Briscoe, who weaves an account of her work as AWIS' affirmative action advisor into her analysis of the continuing problem of sexual harassment. Her paper dovetails with that of Radcliffe president Linda S. Wilson's discussion of the national as well as personal toll of discrimination and harassment of women in male-

---

*The subject of what keeps most of the young—boys somewhat less than girls—out of science in the first place is the subject for another book.

dominated occupations. Finally, Sheela Mierson and Francie Chew discuss the sad result when lowered self-esteem turns anti-female sentiment inward, causing women to undervalue other women and themselves.

Part III concludes with a second essential theme—this one, however, overriding and entirely positive—of *A Hand Up: Women Mentoring Women in Science.* Betty M. Vetter and Bernice Resnick Sandler conclude the volume proper with thoughtful and far ranging essays on the importance of mentors for women in general and women in science in particular.

IV. For Further Help

Part IV, **Resources,** wraps up with an extensive listing of national and federal organizations made up and/or supportive of women in science. Compiled by AWIS staff member Susan E. DeLay, this list includes organizations, contact persons, addresses, telephone numbers, and relevant publications. Also appearing here is an updated, revised version of an advice piece on the job search from the Association of Women in Cell Biology. Finally, AWIS reprints its widely praised feature on letters of recommendation—how to gather, analyze, and check them.

* * * *

According to a number of thinkers, many women are more drawn to collaboration than to competition. This preference helps make the process of women mentoring other women attractive, feasible, and effective. Cooperation among AWIS staff and members has certainly been essential in bringing this volume—which includes 37 separate interviews from 28 scientists and 9 students, 20 individual papers, 3 appendixes, and several overviews—to fruition.

Without mentors working within the educational "system" and outside it in the field, without hands joined to help, support, and guide, forming a network of colleagues and companions, the status of women in science would have been worse in the past, less promising now, and not as certain to improve in the future. And, without the help of national AWIS staff and generous AWIS members, *A Hand Up* would be hands down.

I would particularly like to acknowledge the firm leadership of AWIS' executive director Catherine Jay Didion, the wisdom and guidance of AWIS' mentoring project coordinator Stephanie J. Bird, and the advice and succor of long-time AWIS leader Barbara Filner. In addition, my gratitude goes to AWIS' intern Heather Anne Herring and to research associate Elizabeth Niewoehner for her dedicated, careful, efficient, and tireless work in the final stages of *A Hand Up* and her extensive contributions to the index.

My final expression of gratitude goes to *my* mentor, Paul F. Brandwein, writer, editor, scientist, publisher, and teacher, and man of grace, wisdom, humanity, humor, and unfailing courtesy.

Thanks to all. Hands Up!

—Deborah C. Fort, Ph.D.
Editor
January, 1993

References

Bureau of Labor Statistics. (1991, November). *New entrants to the labor force, 1990-2005*. Washington, DC: Author.

National Science Foundation. (1992, January). *Women and minorities in science and engineering: An update*. Washington, DC: Author.

Part I
Individual Voices

Scientists

Juanita J. Anders, Ph.D.
Associate Professor of Anatomy

B.A. in biology, Wilkes College   1969
M.S. in zoology, Pennsylvania State University   1972
Ph.D. in anatomy, University of Maryland   1976

Anders' interest in science was fostered by her father, her early years on a Pennsylvania farm, and her high school teachers. At Uniformed Services

University of the Health Sciences School of Medicine, Maryland, she combines her interest in basic and applied science in her research on the potential of low-energy lasers in medical treatments. She also teaches anatomy courses and encourages several students, predominately women, working in her laboratory.

Anders says she received excellent laboratory training as an undergraduate. During her doctoral studies, Anders says, she "fell in love with the nervous system."

She married Anthony A. Anders in 1970.

AWIS: *What is difficult about being a woman in medicine? Are there any advantages?*
ANDERS: I get teased because I often have an all woman lab. I do make an effort to encourage young women in my laboratory. I often find extremely talented women in the lab who don't have confidence in themselves. I try to change that. But, as women, you're not part of the club, and you're always treated a little bit separately. Even at meetings there's a social wall. I think that's still one of the hardest things to face.

AWIS: *What would be your advice to a young woman thinking of embarking on a scientific career?*
ANDERS: We are having trouble across the country getting people into graduate programs. Women can use that under-enrollment to their advantage, and I'd like to see more women come into the field of anatomy. I tell the women in my lab that, if they want to teach at

3

a medical school and do medical research, they should go into medicine and not just go for their Ph.D.s.

I was naive about my opportunities, fearing, "If I get an M.D., I'll just be a clinician." I wasn't aware of the greater freedom of options with the M.D. versus the Ph.D. If you want to be in the medical sciences or medical research, an M.D. is the way to go. You get a higher salary right off the bat, if you come out with an M.D. The top research jobs, laboratory heads, and institute directors go to M.D.s. A woman M.D. [Bernadine Healy—see her preface to this book on pages ix–xi] recently became the head of the National Institutes of Health.

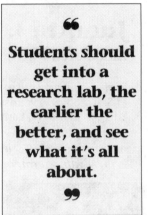

66
Students should get into a research lab, the earlier the better, and see what it's all about.
99

AWIS: Is there a single pattern that a woman interested in a research career in science should best follow?
ANDERS: A big concern is balancing things. You read a lot of articles that say, "You can't have it all." That may be true, but there are a lot of options where you can have a great deal. You shouldn't get discouraged because you're not "super." You can do a lot.

Students should get into a research lab, the earlier the better, and see what it's all about. Students often think that science is black and white. It's not: I often suggest an experiment where outcomes may or may not be successful. I just tell students, "Let's see what happens this week and we'll design it from there." That is what makes science exciting, but also at times what makes it frustrating. I advise students to get into research labs and to get hands-on experience.

AWIS: What is the value of professional associations?
ANDERS: I often suggest that students join women's organizations. My own participation in the National Organization of Women was an informative and formative time for me, changing both how I viewed myself and how I saw other women. From that experience, I made important decisions about helping other women. I think women should be encouraged to take part in such organizations.

AWIS: What are the major obstacles keeping girls from going into science?
ANDERS: The biggest obstacle is within the girls themselves, with their self-esteem. Somewhere early on girls have to have encouragement, something to help them to believe in themselves. It can come through their parents, teachers, or someone else, but it has to come. You have to have that "I can do it!" feeling.

AWIS: May women starting out in your field contact you for guidance?
ANDERS: I'd love to be contacted. I have tried to support young women—and occasionally young men—at both the graduate and undergraduate levels in my lab. As director of graduate programs at the University, I also frequently counsel students—usually in favor of the M.D. degree. Students may call me at (301) 295-3200 during working hours or write me at USUHS, Department of Anatomy and Cell Biology, 4301 Jones Bridge Road, Bethesda, MD 20814.

AWIS: What (or who) was the greatest help in turning you toward science?
ANDERS: My sister, older by 16 years. She is a nurse who wishes she had continued in her studies rather than stopping with the R.N.

AWIS: What (or who) was the greatest help in keeping you in the field?
ANDERS: My undergraduate premed course at Wilkes College was wonderful. During my sophomore year in college, I worked in Robert Ogren's lab, did hands-on experiments, and—with his guidance—had a paper published before I graduated.

AWIS: What (or who) was the worst hurdle in entering science? How did you overcome this barrier?
ANDERS: This isn't exactly a hurdle because I just shrugged it off. But, when I decided to do a master's in zoology at Penn State University, the chairman told me that I had been awarded my half-time teaching assistantship only because the young man who should have had it was fighting in Vietnam.

What a jerk, I thought [of the chairman]. I'm here, and that's what matters.

Pamela Tatiana Anikeeff, Ph.D.
Psychologist

B.A. in psychology, University of California, Berkeley	1970
M.A. in psychology, University of Akron	1972
Ph.D. in psychology, Ohio State University	1977

Anikeeff says her undergraduate experience embodied intellectual freedom. There were periods in her career, however, that were not marked with such latitude. She has met with many of the difficulties with which women scientists must deal all too frequently: Stolen ideas, sexual harassment, inequitable salaries, and lack of job mobility. At one point, a discrimination suit she filed was settled out of court.

Anikeeff has worked for the federal government for 15 years.

Her primary areas of concentration are experimental and applied social psychology, organizational behavior, and the application of learning the-

ory and motivation to social problems. A licensed psychologist, she is also a painter and a photographer.

AWIS: *How did you decide to be a psychologist?*
ANIKEEFF: I have two different loves: Art and science. A major question that almost everyone asks: "What do I want to do when I grow up?" Someone pointed out to me that it's easier to be a scientist who is also an artist than to be an artist who practices science.

AWIS: *What are the most important characteristics for which to search in mentors or other advisors?*
ANIKEEFF: Sometimes your mentor is not your faculty advisor. A senior faculty member may be ideal, especially someone who is accomplished, recognized, and has nothing to win or lose by your downfall. Some people will use your ideas to their own benefit, and who needs that? Senior faculty members can give you information. Junior faculty members can become colleagues and provide moral support.

AWIS: *Have you ever experienced gender discrimination as a woman in science?*
ANIKEEFF: Yes. And, unfortunately, it manifests itself in more than one way.

If you are being discriminated against by male administrators because of your competence in a world that is unfriendly to strong women, if you are being unequally paid for equal work, for example, you are facing one kind of injustice that many women face.

What are some signs of this kind of discrimination? One clue is if you are given mysterious deadlines that don't seem necessary or real. Or deadlines may be suddenly moved forward. Or there may be comments such as, "Don't apply; it's not time yet." Or "Maybe this grant shouldn't be yours but should go through someone else." Or "Maybe it's not time for you to be independent yet."

But there are other kinds, and, in one of the most distressing, certain women collude with *their* harassers, who will also become *your* harassers by creating a hostile sexual environment. If a man in power indicates that he'll make a woman's professional life easier if she indulges in flirtatious behavior—whether actually consummated or not—it can be very disturbing for serious female staff.

In one instance, a colluding woman brought pornographic marzipan cookies—shaped like breasts and penises—to an office party celebrating the marriage of a male colleague. He was appalled, and I was appalled, but the highest-level supervisor was delighted, sporting the "breasts" by holding them on his chest and leering at his captive audience.

The recent suit won by Securities and Exchange Commission attorney Catherine Broderick was a landmark case against the kind of hostile sexual environment such behavior exemplifies. Broderick wasn't participating in these adventures, but she saw them happening around her and rejected the message—"This is the way to advance."

There are also the cases of internalized sexism, the result of the Queen Bee syndrome. (See also pages 4, 37, 47, 138, 142, 154, 155, 261–266.)

AWIS: How should women scientists cope with gender discrimination?
ANIKEEFF: I encourage speaking out against harassment, but you must be aware of the possible ramifications. You may be unpopular with your colleagues, and road blocks may be placed in your way. Before you accept a position, make sure that it is part of a cultural environment where you feel comfortable and where you think that your views and research would be encouraged and rewarded.

In any case, it is good to talk to someone who has seen discrimination before and can make suggestions.

During almost any case of discrimination—against women or men for whatever reason—at some point, the victim is likely to have had enough and say, "That's it." In my case, I came to feel strongly that I was not going to let this nonsense go on, and I took action.

AWIS: What advice would you give a woman going through a lawsuit?
ANIKEEFF:

◆ Presume that no one will be on your side.

◆ If you engage an attorney, people will try to discredit your work and categorize you as insubordinate. You have to rise above this, which is very hard. You must remain polite.

◆ Rely on women's and labor organizations. Speak to someone who has been through a harassment suit or to a feminist lawyer. These individuals can provide support and let you know what you should expect.

◆ Find "safe havens"—remove yourself from the negative atmosphere (you may feel depressed—this is normal under the circumstances).

◆ Have outside interests, exercise, and friends. In experiences like this, many people end up feeling diminished, but you need to be able to counter these feelings.

◆ Consider seeing a counselor to help you deal with your rage and the psychological abuse that you may encounter.

◆ And remember, in the words of Shelley, "O wind if winter comes, can spring be far behind?"

AWIS: What would be your advice to a young woman thinking of embarking on a scientific career?
ANIKEEFF: Gravitate toward people who have bad attitudes. That means they are *thinking*—Darwin, Freud, the Curies, and Pasteur all were asking disturbing questions.

AWIS: May women starting out in your field contact you for guidance?
ANIKEEFF: Yes. Please ask them to call me at the office (202) 366-2754 or at home (202) 363-7897. I am more than pleased to offer a safe reality check for women worried about the possibility that they may be experiencing gender discrimination on their jobs.

AWIS: What (or who) was the greatest help in turning you toward science?
ANIKEEFF: My family. My father is also a psychologist, and my whole family has been supportive of my interests. As children, our curiosity about the world, nature, living things—life—was always encouraged and valued.

AWIS: What (or who) was the greatest help in keeping you in the field?
ANIKEEFF: My own interest and my family.

AWIS: What (or who) was the worst hurdle in entering science? How did you overcome this barrier?
ANIKEEFF: There was no barrier to entering science, but in advancing, I found numerous men, and unfortunately also a number of women, who had difficulty with dealing with women who were comfortable with themselves—with their own intelligence and giftedness.

Jean Elnora Brenchley, Ph.D.

Microbiologist and Biotechnologist

B.S. in biology, Mansfield University of Pennsylvania   1965
M.S. in marine microbiology, University of California, San Diego   1967
Ph.D. in microbial physiology and genetics, University of
   California, Davis   1970

Raised on a small farm in Pennsylvania, Brenchley was not originally encouraged to go to college. "*I was supposed to get married and move onto the farm next door," *she explained. Without really understanding*

why, she decided to continue her education beyond high school and went on to the only kind of postsecondary institution considered appropriate for a woman—a nearby teacher's college. There, she excelled in biology, only to find her professors pushing her toward an available high school teaching job rather than graduate school.

Although she was unsure as to what graduate school entailed, Brenchley decided that she, like a fellow male student with a lesser record, wanted to try it. But while Mansfield faculty members were pushing hard to get him into Cornell, she had to persuade her way into graduate school on the West coast. "It wasn't that I rejected teaching," *she emphasized. She honors it. But, like the men students, she wanted to explore all her options, not follow someone else's choices.*

In spite of her professors' lack of enthusiasm, she earned a master's and then a Ph.D. from the California university system and went on to postdoctoral work.

Brenchley began her academic career as an assistant professor of microbiology at Pennsylvania State University; next, she took a post as a professor of biology at Purdue University. In 1981, Brenchley joined the Genex Corporation, a biotechnology company, as research director. In 1984, she returned to Penn State as department head of molecular and cell biology and director of the newly organized Biotechnology Institute.

In 1987, she took on the Institute directorship full time; three years later, she embarked on a new career in research and teaching, investigating in

---

*This interview follows up on an earlier discussion with Brenchley appearing in the 1984, December/1985, January *AWIS Newsletter*, *13*(6), 10–13.

depth some of the problems in biotechnology that she had uncovered earlier.

Brenchley married Bernard Asbell in 1990.

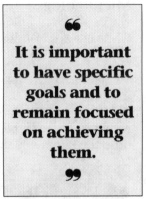

66

It is important to have specific goals and to remain focused on achieving them.

99

AWIS: *What is the relationship between academic and industrial sciences?*
BRENCHLEY: At Genex, I was in charge of research in the microbial biochemistry department. I helped develop research techniques to apply to producing chemicals in different microorganisms. I already had a lot of management experience, since I had developed my own research program. Also, my experience on university committees and with outside professional activities provided a useful background.

AWIS: *How do you manage to keep track of your varied activities?*
BRENCHLEY: I'm a list maker. I keep a list of things I want to do and try to cross off as many as possible. It is important to have specific goals and to remain focused on achieving them.

AWIS: *Why did you leave industry?*
BRENCHLEY: My return to an academic position does not reflect dissatisfaction with industry. I enjoyed the excitement at Genex and greatly valued the opportunity there for professional growth that the work provided. One of the most important aspects of my experience was the discovery that I enjoyed both the academic and industrial environments and that I could have a career in either area.

My decision to return to Penn State as department head and biotechnology director was difficult. I had planned to remain at Genex longer and had declined other offers because I was not interested in leaving. Several factors made this situation unique, however. First, Penn State is special to me because it's where I started my independent research. In addition to this loyalty was the recognition of the huge potential that exists at a large, comprehensive university. Another important component in my decision was the commitment by the president of Penn State and the governor of Pennsylvania to develop a biotechnology institute to bring Penn State to the forefront in biotechnology.

AWIS: *What did you like about working for a biotechnology company? What did you dislike?*
BRENCHLEY: For me, the positive effects centered on the work as an important learning experience. For others, the positive aspects

might include the excitement of being involved in a rapidly developing industry and seeing their work applied. The disadvantages most often cited are the loss of independence and the need to meet specific goals within a short time frame.

AWIS: What kind of career opportunities have you found in biotechnology? What kind of training do you recommend?
BRENCHLEY: As we learn to apply more biological systems to solve industrial problems, biotechnology as a field will continue to grow. There is no substitute for superior training in the traditional sciences, including microbiology, biochemistry, molecular biology, and chemical engineering. Some additional courses in biotechnology that illustrate the complications associated with process development and production would also be important training for molecular biologists. Also, courses designed to give process engineers some familiarity with molecular biology and microbial physiology would help them better understand the organisms they are using to produce substances of commercial interest.

AWIS: What career opportunities has your background afforded you?
BRENCHLEY: One of the important consequences of my work in industry was that I discovered a whole new range of interests. I was amazed to find that there were so many new careers that I could enjoy. We should be careful not to limit ourselves because we haven't looked at career alternatives. It is important to take risks occasionally to continue to learn and to be challenged.

AWIS: Have you ever experienced gender discrimination as a woman in science?
BRENCHLEY: I doubt that any woman could have entered science at the time I did and not have faced special challenges. Almost every situation presents new problems to be solved, but these are exciting times that also present many opportunities. I'm aware that I'm usually one of a very small number of women when at meetings, but the numbers are growing, and that makes it better for all of us.

The problems, however, remain. Many difficulties formerly overt are now merely buried.

AWIS: What is the value of professional associations?
BRENCHLEY: It is important to work within our professional societies to see that women scientists have opportunities to pursue their careers.

AWIS: *May women starting out in your field contact you for guidance?*
BRENCHLEY: Yes. They may call at (814) 863-7794 during working hours or write to me at 209 South Frear, Pennsylvania State University, University Park, PA 16802.

AWIS: *What (or who) was the greatest help in turning you toward science?*
BRENCHLEY: There's no *who* responsible, but the *what* is growing up on a small dairy farm—that taught me the value of self-discipline and hard work, as well as exposing me to nature.

AWIS: *What (or who) was the greatest help in keeping you in the field?*
BRENCHLEY: There are two parts to that question. The *who* is John Ingraham, my advisor at the University of California, Davis. The *what* is my own determination to rise above hurdles and challenges.

AWIS: *What (or who) was the worst hurdle in entering science?*
BRENCHLEY: There were many; all were male; and all were worsts. When I started, there were never any women in positions to help or hinder my career. At the time that I started studying, it was much against the grain for women to continue. We were supposed to stop with our bachelors' degrees and go off and teach. Science was not seen as a reasonable course of action for a young woman.

Audrey B. Champagne, Ph.D.
Science Educator and Chemist

B.S. in chemistry, State University of New York at Albany	1957
M.S. in chemistry, State University of New York at Albany	1958
M.A. in science education, Harvard University	1961
Ph.D. in curriculum education, University of Pittsburgh	1970

Champagne's enthusiasm for science was sparked by her grandfather and an imaginative kindergarten teacher.* Mrs. Schiller did hands-on science experiments with familiar objects long before the term had been coined; Champagne's grandfather assigned her household and garden science projects and illuminated the role of science in the everyday world. These

*This interview follows up on an earlier discussion with Champagne appearing in the 1985, August/September *AWIS Newsletter*, *14*(4), 12–14.

influences overshadowed later messages she received at school. "Just being given the confidence as a girl that I could do things like lay tile and fix electrical switches was important when I got to school,"

Champagne said. "There, the environment wasn't so warm for a little girl who was interested in mechanical and scientific things."

Champagne's graduate studies, briefly interrupted by the birth of her two sons in 1963 and 1965, led her to focus upon science education.

After earning her doctorate, Champagne joined the staff of the University of Pittsburgh, where she remained until 1984. There, she was a senior scientist in the Learning Development Center working on a National Institute of Education-funded project to improve learning in public education. In 1985, she was appointed program manager at the American Association for the Advancement of Science's National Forum for School Science, a project originally funded by the Carnegie Corporation and now continuing under the Association's auspices. Under her leadership, the Forum began annually publishing This Year in School Science. *She now holds a joint appointment in the department of chemistry and the school of education at the State University of New York at Albany. Champagne also currently chairs the National Research Council's Working Group on Science Education Assessment Standards (one of the three prongs of its ongoing project on developing national standards for pre-college science).*

Throughout her career, she has studied the dynamics of science teaching to try to improve education in public schools. In her research, Champagne asks, "How can educators spark a child's interest in science and keep that spark burning?"

Champagne is married to David W. Champagne.

AWIS: *What would you like to see change about preparation for the science profession today?*

CHAMPAGNE: When I was in school in the 1940s and 1950s, science was considered something that boys did and not girls. High school was a little bit better, but junior high, which is where I think kids really get turned on or off, wasn't very supportive. Ironically, it was a woman teacher that had the "boys only" rule for science club. To some extent we still have this kind of problem.

One of the biggest problems we're seeing now in school science education is the fact that junior high school is often just a wasteland. There are a lot of people teaching junior high school who have elementary school certification. Most states don't certify middle school teachers, just high school and elementary. And heaven forbid that a well-prepared high school science teacher would go down to junior high! Typically, the preparation of elementary school science teachers doesn't include any "wet" science, and maybe not *any* science at all. So you have a lot of good, well-meaning teachers who end up turning kids off to science pretty rapidly.

In the high schools, many students take just one science course, usually biology, and only the college-bound kids take more. So we have a real problem—we in education and you in science, too.

AWIS: Do you recommend that women intending careers in science hold tutoring jobs or teaching assistantships while they are in graduate school?
CHAMPAGNE: Teaching or tutoring is a good way to get a clearer understanding of subject matter, to understand thoroughly things you may have glossed over before. Many students who get graduate degrees in chemistry don't want teaching assistantships: They want to get right to the bench. That is unfortunate in terms of their own understanding of science.

AWIS: What are the prospects for increasing the numbers of women scientists?
CHAMPAGNE: I'm pessimistic. Many factors make it particularly difficult for women in academe and industry. The "good old boy" network still operates and is a potent force that propels men through the system. Many women professionals are working to develop similar networks, and that's the only way we're going to make it. There is still the Queen Bee syndrome that we have to watch out for: The women who "make it" by being like men are not particularly nurturing of women coming into the profession.

There's another factor we're only beginning to recognize: Women work differently than men do. I'm not sure that the cultures of industry or academe are hospitable to a woman's perspective. Women tend to run very open shops. Information is accessible—everybody knows what's going on. Men see information as power, and they share it only grudgingly. These factors must be better understood, for they are critical in getting women into positions of power.

AWIS: Have you any advice for a Ph.D. interested in science teaching versus "hard science"?
CHAMPAGNE: Scientists have a high regard for researchers. When scientists go into education, communication, or policy, they're not really thought of as scientists anymore. When scientists who have "made it" in their scientific disciplines decide to make pronouncements about science education, the science community listens to

14

them. If scholars get Ph.D.s in science and go straight into education, they should have their eyes open. There's not as much prestige in education as there is in being a research scientist.

It's very easy for scientists to be critical of what's going on in the public schools in terms of science teaching, but when you get right down to it, the quality of science teaching in our colleges and universities isn't all that great either.

AWIS: How have you balanced your personal and professional commitments?

CHAMPAGNE: It's not easy, but it has been worth it to me because I enjoy what I do, and I don't see it as "work" work. My husband has been very supportive. If I had stayed home and not worked, my two kids would probably have become basket cases, given my energy level and need to organize and direct things. My sons have survived their working mother very well. Out of necessity, both have become excellent cooks, and they can wash their own clothes. I think it's helped make them much more independent.

AWIS: May women starting out in your field contact you for guidance?

CHAMPAGNE: Yes. They may write me at ED 119, State University of New York at Albany, 1400 Washington Avenue, Albany, NY 12222.

AWIS: What (or who) was the greatest help in turning you toward science?

CHAMPAGNE: My family and my schooling—my grandfather, my husband and sons, my kindergarten teacher, my professors at Albany.

AWIS: What (or who) was the greatest help in keeping you in the field?

CHAMPAGNE: First, what I would call my own delayed social development. I went into science because I didn't get the picture that the field wasn't a warm and cuddly place for women. This happened partially because of the strong encouragement my professors at Albany gave me to go immediately for a Ph.D. in chemistry.

Second, my own inner-directedness. People differ in the degree to which they respond to internal versus external pressures. I tend to ignore negative messages.

AWIS: What (or who) was the worst hurdle in entering science? How did you overcome this barrier?

CHAMPAGNE: When I went from SUNY at Albany to other institutions, I finally noticed that there were no other young women as students, and that the society as a whole was primarily male.

There was no overt hostility—nothing was ever said—but the assumption was that I would eventually give up my profession for marriage and children.

Jewel Plummer Cobb, Ph.D.
University President Emerita and Trustee Professor

B.A. in biology, Talladega College	1944
M.S. in cell physiology, New York University	1947
Ph.D. in cell physiology, New York University	1950

Cobb was heavily influenced by her father, a physician whose dinnertime science talks "opened up a whole new world."* She also recalls a "great experience with a microscope" during a biology lab in high

school, which inspired her to want to become a biology teacher. Cobb believes herself fortunate in being encouraged throughout her education to pursue scientific interests, even in a period when women, especially minority women, were usually not expected to become scientists. She is especially grateful for the support she received at New York University.

As well as her administrative work, Cobb has done research, has published, and has taught. She began her career teaching and doing research in medical settings in Illinois and New York.

Before assuming the presidency at California State University, Fullerton, (from which she retired in 1990), Cobb filled a number of other prestigious positions. She held a senior faculty appointment at Sarah Lawrence College, where—with National Science Foundation support—she encouraged undergraduates to work in her lab, and deanships at Connecticut College and Douglass College of Rutgers University. Cobb has received 18 honorary doctorates. She is currently trustee professor at California State University, Los Angeles.

Cobb has worked throughout her career to improve the status of women and minorities in science. In the 1970s, as a member of the National

*This interview follows up on an earlier discussion with Cobb appearing in the 1990, March/April *AWIS Newsletter, 19*(2), 10–13.

Science Board, the policy body of the National Science Foundation, she chaired the Task Force on Women and Minorities.

Along with her research, publishing, teaching, and administrative responsibilities, Cobb, who was divorced in the mid-1960s, shared with her former husband the rearing of their son.

She defines herself as a black woman scientist who cares about what happens to the young, particularly to women going into science.

AWIS: *What would you like to see change about preparation for the science profession today?*
COBB: What disappoints me is that there were so few black college students at my former institution majoring in science in general or in biology in particular. The reasons are complex and involve social negatives, including economic issues.

We still have a crisis in science education in terms of the image of science as a male subject with few women interested in the field. And we still have a dearth of minorities, particularly blacks and Hispanics, entering science careers.

AWIS: *What, so far, do you see as the most rewarding aspect of your career?*
COBB: I think that would have to be the postbaccalaureate program for premed minority students that I developed and ran at Connecticut College. This program enrolled minority students who had demonstrated undergraduate learning skills in college but had decided late in their college careers that they wanted to go to medical, dental, or veterinary school. They received a year's tuition, room, and board at Connecticut College, while they were brought up-to-date in the science courses that they had not taken as undergraduates.

AWIS: *Do you have any advice for women pursuing their doctorates?*
COBB: I would say that every woman who is now doing doctoral work in science should hang in there and work hard to finish up the research and the dissertation. She should consciously develop a network of referrals, which by necessity will be primarily male— that's still the make-up of the science world: She should, for example, talk to a number of people in various laboratories and give papers at professional meetings. Working her schedule around the timetables of annual meetings that appear in various journals will help her meet publication deadlines.

While attending meetings, she should become acquainted with scientists whose work she respects and whose laboratories seem interesting.

17

AWIS: *How about postdoctoral strategies for women?*
COBB: Once you have your degree, quickly get that dissertation published either as a whole piece or by breaking it down into smaller articles. Many people believe that the first 10 years after the Ph.D. are the most productive of a scholar's life. I believe that is certainly the case in science. Women, especially in the life sciences and related fields, tend to stay in postdocs much longer than men do: Be careful of that.

AWIS: *Is there a single pattern that a woman interested in a research career in science should best follow?*
COBB: No. A number of exciting possibilities are available and one of them need not exclude the others. For those in the life sciences, there are at least three paths open.

1. You can, if you care very deeply about teaching, go to an undergraduate liberal arts college and do your research in relative isolation or with a small group. You will have the stimulating experience of teaching undergraduates, and you can spend your summers in concentrated research either on your campus or at some special government laboratory or biological station.

2. You can also join a major research university or the research wing of a hospital, however, and become part of a large group of scientists. With this choice, you are more likely to be closely allied with fast-moving changes in that discipline.

3. You can join a pharmaceutical house. There's good money, steady work, and good experience, but you are rarely able to publish your results. Personally, I wanted credit for my research.

AWIS: *May women starting out in your field contact you for guidance?*
COBB: Yes indeed. Please write to me at Administration 815, California State University, Los Angeles, 5151 State University Drive, Los Angeles, CA 90032-8500.

AWIS: *What (or who) was the greatest help in turning you toward science?*
COBB: A high school biology teacher.

AWIS: *What (or who) was the greatest help in keeping you in the field?*
COBB: My teachers and my parents.

AWIS: *What (or who) was the worst hurdle in entering science? How did you overcome this barrier?*
COBB: There were no barriers, so I had no trouble overcoming them.

18

Rita R. Colwell, Ph.D.

Marine Microbiologist and Biotechnologist

B.S. in bacteriology, Purdue University	1956
M.S. in genetics, Purdue University	1958
Ph.D. marine microbiology, University of Washington	1961

Venturing far from the small town in Massachusetts where she was born, Colwell now works worldwide. She lectures in Europe; she does cholera research in Mali; she serves on the National Science Board. In spite of

discouragement from her high school chemistry teacher and others about embarking on a career in science, she became a marine microbiologist and molecular biologist.

Colwell was a pioneer in environmental microbiology with her work on cholera. She was one of the first scientists in the U.S. to use computers in microbiology (a practice usually now considered a necessity).

Founder and president of the University of Maryland's extensive Biotechnology Institute, scientist, wife of physicist Jack H. Colwell, and the mother of two daughters born in 1963 and 1965, Colwell says she has a "wonderful life."

AWIS: *Was your path into science smooth?*
COLWELL: My chemistry class in college had about 1,000 people in it, and I didn't do very well. I earned only a *B*, but I stayed in science. I kept my options open, taking chemistry, algebra, calculus, and physics, but, by my third year in college, I was fed up with missing out on a broad education in other areas such as art and literature. I dropped out of science and took courses in literature. One of my roommates, however, was enthusiastic about a bacteriology course she was taking from a woman professor, so I took the course, and that's what did it. I switched my major to bacteriology, graduated in bacteriology and premed, and was accepted to medical school.

AWIS: *Have you ever experienced gender discrimination as a woman in science?*
COLWELL: The prejudice is still there: It's just underground. There is kind of a "snicker-snicker" pretense that administrators practice— they have to act as if they were open and giving women opportuni-

ties. This is a generalization, and perhaps it's unfair, but some male researchers use women graduate students as technicians, no matter what the detriment to the women's careers.

That's changing, but what I often see is women getting stuck at low academic levels. There is a glass ceiling, and it needs to be smashed. It's going to take a lot of persistence, because women are recognized as good assistant professors and laboratory technicians, but they don't get promoted as readily as their male counterparts. There aren't very many women senior professors.

There aren't many women in most science departments in most universities, and that is the result of sheer prejudice. Jobs are scarce now; therefore, any excuse is used to cut someone out, and a "different" person is the one they cut.

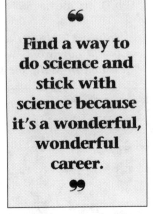

> **Find a way to do science and stick with science because it's a wonderful, wonderful career.**

AWIS: How do you cope with discrimination?
COLWELL: I just get angry internally and become more determined than ever externally.

AWIS: How have you balanced your personal and professional commitments?
COLWELL: I had no intention of having children until I was in a position to be able to afford child care. I wanted my children to have opportunities that I didn't have. For example, I worked my way through school, with help from scholarships. That was hard. My husband and I wanted to be able to pay for our daughters' education, and we have done so. One is earning her M.D.; the other, an M.D. and a Ph.D.

AWIS: Do you notice differences between the way men and women approach a research task?
COLWELL: One of the differences I've noticed between female and male graduate students is this: When women enter the lab, they are likely to ask, "May I use this? May I do that?" Men tend to say to their fellow students, "Get out of my way. I need space. I need this. I need that." That's changing: Women are still more inhibited, but they are also more directed. I am pleased that they have aspirations.

AWIS: What would be your advice to a young woman thinking of embarking on a scientific career?
COLWELL: Stay the course. Put up with whatever is necessary to get through first your degree and then into your first job. Find a way

to do science and stick with science because it's a wonderful, wonderful career. I travel a lot; I am involved in varied and exciting research; I do administration; I give talks; I publish papers.

I love what I'm doing.

AWIS: Is there a single pattern that a woman interested in a research career in the life sciences should best follow?
COLWELL: Get a bachelor's degree in microbiology or zoology or botany and go on from there. I don't advise a baccalaureate in an interdisciplinary science. I think it's important to get the rigor of a disciplinary science. Get as much math as possible, up to calculus at the minimum. Any person with scores of 600 or more on the analytic and quantitative sections of the Scholastic Aptitude Test or the Graduate Record Examination should be able to handle calculus.

Don't be put off. If you're good at science, you'll find a way to break through the barriers, and high salaries and advancement will be your rewards.

AWIS: May women starting out in your field contact you for guidance?
COLWELL: Yes. They should write to me at the Office of the President, Maryland Biotechnology Institute, 4321 Hardwick Road, Fifth Floor, University of Maryland, College Park, MD 20740.

AWIS: What (or who) was the greatest help in turning you toward science?
COLWELL: That's hard to say. I worked part time when in high school at some jobs I did not want as a career. More positively, while I was growing up, my brothers and sisters were in college, and our house was full of interesting, energetic people, most of them scientists. My sister is an artist, but her husband is a scientist, and my two brothers are engineers.

AWIS: What (or who) was the greatest help in keeping you in the field?
COLWELL: I was in a very fortunate mix of people in my university years. My undergraduate advisor, a geneticist, my scientist husband, and my Ph.D. advisor were all extremely supportive.

AWIS: What (or who) was the worst hurdle in entering science? How did you overcome this barrier?
COLWELL: That would be the department chairman at Purdue. I had been accepted into medical school. Then, as a married student, I asked the chair for a fellowship, so that I could stay on another year while my husband and I finished our masters' degrees. He said,

"No," explaining that the department didn't waste fellowships on women.

My advisor, however, gave me a research assistantship in his laboratory, and I did a master's in genetics.

Then my husband and I both left Purdue University together to do our Ph.D.s in the more supportive environment of the University of Washington at Seattle.

Geraldine Anne Vang Cox, Ph.D.

Environmental Scientist and Vice President

B.A. in biology, Drexel University	1966
M.A. in environmental sciences, Drexel University	1967
Ph.D. in environmental sciences, Drexel University	1970

As a girl, Cox was interested in how things work. Fascinated by the processes of nature, she remembers a visit, made during elementary school to nearby caverns, that fueled her interest in rocks. She majored in biology

in college, however, because her mother told her that geology was "no profession for a woman." Cox taught high school for a while and liked it but left teaching to finish her graduate work in science. While at the University, Cox supported herself as a food technician, an accountant, a beer tester, and a lecturer in anatomy and physiology.

Since then, her career has been in the applied sciences. She worked at Raytheon Oceanographic and Environmental Services in Portsmouth, Rhode Island, from 1970–1976, before moving to Washington, D.C., where she accepted a one-year White House Fellowship and then worked for a year and a half at the American Petroleum Institute. She next took a 12-year post as vice president and technical director of the Chemical Manufacturer's Association. In 1991, Cox became vice president of Fluor Daniel, Inc., an engineering and construction company.

Cox is married to Walter George Cox.

AWIS: Have you ever experienced gender discrimination as a woman in science?

COX: At the first meeting on water control I attended as a graduate student, I was told that the women registered upstairs. "Isn't that the registration for the spouses?" I asked. "Yes," conference organizers replied. "Well, I'm a participant. You had better make me up a name tag," I returned.

It took some haggling, but I finally attended on my terms, not theirs.

I recommend that women deal with harassment through humor. People who dwell on discrimination problems may have trouble progressing. Elect to ignore the perpetrators and go beyond them. There's no limit to what you can achieve.

AWIS: How should women scientists cope with gender discrimination?
COX: Don't role-play: Be yourself. Learn to ignore a lot. Ask yourself, "If I get involved in this, will it help me further my goal?"

AWIS: How have you balanced your personal and professional commitments?

COX: I married as an undergraduate and might not have gone on for higher degrees without my husband's support. The last year of my graduate program, he went to graduate school in Rhode Island. After I finished my Ph.D. and had worked for 6 years, I received a White House Fellowship in Washington, D.C., and my husband remained in Rhode Island. We spent the next 10 years in a commuting marriage, but for the past 6, we have been together in Washington.

We had big telephone bills, but we were both very involved in our research at the time, and the arrangement worked out.

AWIS: What would be your advice to a young woman thinking of embarking on a scientific career?

COX: Environmental science is a combination of many fields, so it makes you sort of a "trained generalist." I don't recommend a bachelor's degree in environmental science, though, because you don't learn enough to be comfortable in any field. A strong foundation in chemical engineering would serve a better purpose: It has good practical applications. I recommend that students get at minimum a master's degree in their field.

AWIS: May women starting out in your field contact you for guidance?
COX: Yes, many already do, and they may in the future. They may write to me at Fluor Daniel, Inc., 800 Connecticut Avenue, NW, Suite 600, Washington, DC 20006.

AWIS: *What (or who) was the greatest help in turning you toward science?*
COX: A realization that if you wanted to manage anything, you had to know what you were managing.

AWIS: *What (or who) was the greatest help in keeping you in the field?*
COX: My husband.

AWIS: *What (or who) was the worst hurdle in entering science? How did you overcome this barrier?*
COX: My mother, who could not understand that I did not want to be the *wife* of a vice president—I wanted to *be* the vice president. I could overcome her opposition only through a total break with her for a couple of years. This rift was only partially rectified.

Jane R. Dillehay, Ph.D.
Professor of Biology

B.S. in biology, Allegheny College	1971
Ph.D. in molecular biology, Carnegie Mellon University	1980

Dillehay, a successful scientist and professor, was born deaf.* Since 1980, she has taught biology at Gallaudet College, a university for deaf students located in Washington, D.C., where she currently chairs the biology department.

When she was a child, her interest in science was piqued by scientific discussions around the family dinner table, discussions she followed by lipreading—her family was hearing. Dillehay remembered talking about "why water goes clockwise down a drain in the Northern hemisphere and counterclockwise south of the equator." *In addition, Dillehay sought out science courses in school. Overcoming the difficulties posed by her deafness, she was educated in mainstream schools and universities.*

*This interview follows up on an earlier discussion with Dillehay appearing in the 1987, July/August *AWIS Newsletter, 16*(4), 6–9.

After earning her baccalaureate, Dillehay supported herself during graduate school as a research assistant in microbiology and phage genetics. She has worked throughout her career both to help deaf students and to increase awareness about their particular problems.

AWIS: *What special difficulties arose for you because of your disability?*
DILLEHAY: I was really expected to behave like a hearing person. That was hard: I had to deny myself. I had to pretend I could hear.

Most deaf women scientists, unlike me, were born hearing and became deaf later in life. Very few go into the physical sciences. (More go into psychology or sociology.) It's almost impossible for a deaf woman to get a Ph.D. without good oral skills.

There are a lot of subtle difficulties if you're deaf in a hearing world. While nobody says, "We don't want you here," nobody encourages you to stay, nobody talks to you, nobody offers you a place in his or her lab. It's hard to fit in socially, and that makes it difficult for our graduates to go on for advanced degrees.

A deaf scientist can't keep up with research by telephoning people. I have to ask someone else to phone, or write a letter. It's not the same as getting an immediate answer.

Communication is a major problem, even with interpreters. For example, I can't take part in scientific meetings the way I want to. First, it is hard to be accepted at a meeting. Second, no matter how well qualified, the interpreters don't understand the technical aspects of the topic, which makes it hard to understand what they're signing. Third, there's a barrier between you and the speaker, so it's hard to participate in discussions. At one meeting I went to about 10 years ago, the lecturer didn't want the interpreter there and asked us to leave. He grudgingly let us stay.

The interpreter is also a social barrier. If the deaf person looks at the interpreter, the hearing person may think (even unconsciously) that he or she is not being listened to. And communication with facial expressions and other gestures is missed because the deaf person is watching the interpreter.

AWIS: *How important are mentors and role models?*
DILLEHAY: Very important. I teach a section of introductory biology, and so do two hearing women. More students in my section become majors, because the students see me—a deaf woman—being a scientist and think they can become one also.

I was always encouraged by my teachers. My Ph.D. advisor was sarcastic but also supportive. You need to get support to keep going, and that's very hard to do through interpreters: You need one-on-one conversation.

25

AWIS: *What problems and inhibitors do deaf children face?*

DILLEHAY: All through their education, deaf students are trying to catch up. They start losing the day they're born. My three-year old son picked up phrases and sentences by listening to TV and to me talking to my husband. A deaf child can do nothing like that. When I was three, I had a vocabulary of two words—*up* and *apple*. Besides being behind in language, a deaf child starts school with almost no understanding of the social world s/he lives in.

Deaf children of deaf parents seem to have fewer problems because the children and parents communicate in similar ways.

AWIS: *How have you balanced your personal and professional commitments?*

DILLEHAY: When I was the mother of two boys under three, I found it difficult to manage both family and a career in teaching and research. At that point, I reduced my involvement in research because of the demands on my time and energy. Since then, I have become involved in researching effective teaching strategies in science education. I am currently preparing a paper on the results of teaching reading strategies to students in our introductory biology course. I am also studying the effect of cooperative learning groups on student motivation and academic performance in biology courses.

Research in science education is essentially a compromise for me. The demands on my time and energy as chairperson, professor, wife, and mother, along with the lack of adequate research facilities, make it extremely difficult to pursue my original interests in molecular biology. My desire to do research finds an outlet in science education.

I still have not abandoned my dreams of microbiological research with student researchers. Our building is being renovated, and within a year we should have better facilities. In addition, I hope to take advantage of a number of programs at places such as the National Institutes of Health and the Department of the Interior's Fish and Wildlife Service to develop an environmental research program at Gallaudet College.

AWIS: *Have you any advice for a woman interested in teaching as well as research?*

DILLEHAY: As a graduate student, I enjoyed teaching undergraduates at Carnegie Mellon University. After completing my doctoral work, I decided I wanted to teach for a while. I went to Gallaudet because I wanted the chance to get to know other deaf people. (I had been completely isolated from the deaf community all my life.)

26

I find teaching very stimulating. It is rewarding to work with students and see them develop laboratory and research skills. At the same time, the load of paperwork and the task of teaching students who are uninterested or poorly prepared in math and English can be very frustrating.

AWIS: What do you like best about your job?
DILLEHAY: I enjoy working in the lab with other people, once they understand that I need to see their faces when they talk to me. I enjoy research, discussions, developing ideas and experiments, all the usual things. The problem is facing strangers who are not used to deaf women functioning as scientists. You have to go through the whole process of educating them each time.

We're working on expanding the use of computers. It removes communication barriers: You can't tell if a person is deaf on the computer. Also, with computer networks being set up on many college campuses, our students can contact other students and faculty. We hope to work with deaf students across the country.

AWIS: May women starting out in your field contact you for guidance?
DILLEHAY: Yes. They may write me at the Biology Department, Gallaudet University, 800 Florida Avenue, NE, Washington, DC 20002-3695, or, better still, if they have E-mail and BITNET, they may contact me at JRDILLEHAY@GALLUA.

AWIS: What (or who) was the greatest help in turning you toward science?
DILLEHAY: First, my family's interest in science and support of my aspirations to become a scientist. Second, my own determination to succeed in college and graduate school. Third, my faculty advisor in my major and my graduate advisor gave me support.

AWIS: What (or who) was the greatest help in keeping you in the field?
DILLEHAY: I think that day-to-day interaction with my advisor, other graduate students, and lab technicians kept me motivated. At the time, I was a graduate student, there were only two female faculty, and they were busy with their own students and labs.

AWIS: What (or who) was the worst hurdle in entering science? How did you overcome this barrier?
DILLEHAY: My communications difficulties were the most serious hurdle. Basically, I handled that problem by establishing one-to-one

communication with the people I needed to work with or get information from. But again, I had to initiate contacts and think up ways around barriers—I always felt that it was my responsibility to come up with solutions, that the hearing world was willing to meet with me, but I had to do all the work.

Anne Ritger Douglass, Ph.D.
Astrophysicist

B.A. in physics, Trinity College	1971
M.S. in physics, University of Minnesota	1975
Ph.D. in physics, Iowa State University	1980

Douglass proves it is possible simultaneously to earn a Ph.D., raise a family, and be a scientist.* She has five children and a satisfying job at the National Aeronautics and Space Administration's Goddard Space Flight Center in Maryland. At Goddard, she specializes in stratospheric science and studies the ozone layer.

Douglass' original interest in mathematics was inspired by a high school teacher, a nun, whose influence encouraged a number of her classmates to study for advanced degrees. As an undergraduate, Douglass encountered some young women Ph.D.s who encouraged her interest in physics and suggested that she work on a doctorate. Their choices exemplified the possibility of combining career and family. After earning her baccalaureate, she married Charles H. Douglass in 1971 and had her first child the same year, returning to school part-time to earn first a master's degree and then a doctorate. During her eight and a half years of graduate studies, she had three more children—in 1974, 1976, and 1978—and a fifth in 1983 after she started work at Goddard.

At Goddard, Douglass works as an astrophysicist. Her parental responsibilities have lightened somewhat as her children have grown older, and she now travels professionally and gives talks.

*This interview follows up on an earlier discussion with Douglass appearing in the 1991, March/April AWIS Magazine, 20(2), 6–10.

AWIS: *How have you balanced your personal and professional commitments?*

DOUGLASS: A lot of people think they should go to school and get established professionally and then think about having a baby about mid-career. It worked out fine for me to delay the start of my career. By going to school part-time I was never *completely* out of the field, and I had time for my children. Being a student is easier than working: You set your own hours, and your time is your own.

I took classes in the daytime and I had a sitter, but I arranged my schedule so I had at least one whole day at home and a couple of afternoons. I had an assistantship—teaching labs—and the schools all helped me arrange the schedule.

A lot of people thought I wasn't serious, but the people in power were helpful. I had to prove myself. The first few weeks I was at Minnesota, the department head hesitated over my lab teaching schedule, but when the student evaluations came in, I had some of the highest marks. Since none of my students complained, and the professors I worked with were happy, I had no more problems.

After I finished my doctorate at Iowa State, my husband gave up his tenured position at Drake University, and we went on the two-job search in one place. That place turned out to be the Washington, D.C., area.

> **66**
>
> **Work on things you're going to be proud of, but don't keep overextending yourself in the name of your career because then you end up doing too many things and none of them well.**
>
> **99**

Not only could we not survive on one paycheck but also I *wanted* to work.

AWIS: *Have you ever experienced gender discrimination as a woman in science?*

DOUGLASS: When I started graduate work at Minnesota, there were no other women enrolled in graduate school in physics at any level. That was intimidating. You have to develop a rapport with the men with whom you work over time, and I didn't really succeed in graduate school. I had a few close friends, but I didn't go to study groups or stay up late doing problems and drinking beer. That was more the male experience.

Things have improved since them. There are not many of us women, but there is very little evidence of discrimination. The field of atmospheric science is experiencing such growth and expansion. I think that bright newcomers are welcome.

AWIS: *What are the most important characteristics for which to search in mentors or other advisors?*

DOUGLASS: Find someone who will treat you like any other graduate student. You don't want to spend the first six months proving yourself.

When you're looking for an advisor, have him/her talk to you about what the job opportunities are. Some people only want to do the science that interests them the most and are detached from the reality that, eventually, their students will have to get a job. A lot of professors in school have tenure. They don't have anything to worry about, and they want to have students working on their research interests: You, however, need employment.

AWIS: *What would be your advice to a young woman thinking of embarking on a scientific career?*

DOUGLASS: Look realistically at what you're doing. That I didn't want to work for the defense department was one reason I gravitated towards environmental science. I know a scientist who worked in low-temperature, solid-state physics and who was distressed to find that many of the job opportunities in that field were in weapons research. Think about such things before you commit yourself.

If a woman is aiming at a career in atmospheric sciences, she should major in chemistry, physics, or math, rather than in meteorology or atmospheric sciences. It's better to have an undergraduate background in one of the fundamental sciences. My background was in physics, and I learned the chemistry later. If you have a strong background in one science, you can learn what you need to from the other fields.

Mentors can be essential in helping students get good placements. The National Research Council offers postdocs, and we place a number of fellows at Goddard.

Since I've been here, only one person has been appointed whose major professor did not have connections here. The professors call up and say they have a student coming out who is looking for a postdoc and who is interested in this, this, and this. And somebody says, "that sounds great," and then the student has a job here.

If your professor never makes that call, you don't have much of a chance to do a postdoc here.

AWIS: *Are there other avenues into good postdoctoral positions?*

DOUGLASS: One candidate wrote a letter to virtually everyone in our branch. Our organization puts out a directory of research and technology. This student read the directory, looked for people who had interests that matched his, and wrote letters to all of these people. You have to work a lot harder, however, if you're not connected.

AWIS: *If you had the chance to start over, what would you do differently?*
DOUGLASS: I'd be more relaxed about the opportunities that would still be available when my children were grown up. Sometimes I got depressed, when other people were presenting my work, and I felt as if that were going to go on forever. As soon as I was ready, everybody was glad I was on my own.

AWIS: *Is there a single pattern that a woman interested in a research career in science should best follow?*
DOUGLASS: Work on things you're going to be proud of, but don't keep overextending yourself in the name of your career because then you end up doing too many things and none of them well. That's true for science and anything else.

AWIS: *May women starting out in your field contact you for guidance?*
DOUGLASS: Yes. Please write to me at Code 916, NASA/Goddard Space Flight Center, Greenbelt MD 20771.

AWIS: *What (or who) was the greatest help in turning you toward science?*
DOUGLASS: My high school math teacher, Sr. Barbara Garland.

AWIS: *What (or who) was the greatest help in keeping you in the field?*
DOUGLASS: My many women teachers at Trinity College [a women's college in Washington, D.C.] and my own determination. I simply decided: "I'll show those guys."

AWIS: *What (or who) was the worst hurdle in entering science? How did you overcome this barrier?*
DOUGLASS: After I left school—the children. I had simultaneously to balance my responsibilities to them and convince my colleagues that I could make a contribution. (Still, I didn't work full time until my youngest started kindergarten.)

Male coworkers thought that it was impossible to have a child and be a woman and be a scientist.

They're all my friends now. They don't think that any more!

31

Barbara Filner, Ph.D.
Grants Program Officer

B.S. in biology, Queens College   1962
Ph.D. in biology, Brandeis University   1967

Filner's specialties are plant physiology, developmental biology, and molecular biology.* She began her career in academia as an assistant professor at Columbia University, where she remained six years enjoying

"terrific" students and her National Science Foundation-sponsored research. After a brief stint at Kalamazoo College (Michigan), Filner switched to public policy at the National Academy of Sciences' Institute of Medicine. Hired as a staff officer, she became director of the Division of Health Sciences Policy. She now serves as a program officer for graduate education and international programs in the Office of Grants and Special Programs of the Howard Hughes Medical Institute.

Filner has long been an active member of AWIS, mentoring and aiding women scientists and working for their general advancement. At AWIS, Filner has served in the past as president and newsletter editor and is currently on the board of directors.

Filner married Harry M. Rosenberg in 1984.

AWIS: *Were there any advantages to starting your career as an unmarried woman?*
FILNER: Being single had two major advantages. First, I had to take my job seriously. My income determined my standard of living, and I had to rely on myself. Maybe that fact helped others take me seriously as well. Also, I could take any job opportunity that seemed attractive. I didn't have to think about a job for my spouse or schools for my children.

My married friends budgeted their time carefully and were much more efficient than I was. There is a mystique in science about long hours—into the night and on weekends—but I don't believe that is necessary to be productive.

*This interview follows up on an earlier discussion with Filner appearing in the December, 1985/January, 1986 AWIS Newsletter, 14(6), 10–13. See also Filner's paper, pages 219–225.

Marrying at 43 didn't have the same impact on my career as marrying younger would have had. I would guess that most of the big complications of a dual-career marriage occur early in one's career. My husband is a real asset at this point—providing emotional support and practical advice. And we share household responsibilities, so I do less of that kind of work than when I was single.

AWIS: Have you ever experienced gender discrimination as a woman in science?

FILNER: I was certainly aware of inequities all through graduate school and later, but I didn't think about it systematically until I was at Columbia. Until then, I viewed a given episode as the stupidity of the person who was discriminating. . . In the mid-1960s, it was quite socially acceptable to make outrageous stereotyping comments about women. I often heard that "women shouldn't be scientists." It also was cute, indeed complimentary, to sexually harass a women student. This was something a professor would boast about, and the department would make jokes about.

My experiences in the 1970s as an assistant professor at Columbia University opened my eyes. It was next to impossible to talk science with my fellow faculty. They instead discussed cars, Chinese restaurants, and the latest mugging. This was not the case when I was a graduate student or a postdoc, but I thought somehow it was my fault. Then we appointed another woman to the department. She interacted with people differently than I did . . . but she had the same communication problems with colleagues in the department. She had been in the department as a postdoc and was well-respected there as a scientist. But once she was an assistant professor, a peer, all of that changed. It seemed to me that as long as a man was validating you, things were fine, but academic science couldn't quite cope with an independent woman.

AWIS: What would be your advice to a young woman thinking of embarking on a scientific career?

FILNER: Many young women take for granted newly won career opportunities, and I'm glad. Their confidence will help assure that we don't revert: It will help them have even greater expectations. I hope it spurs them to action rather than closed-mouth acceptance when they do encounter inequities, as I believe they inevitably will.

Young women need to be confident about their own value. There are two corollaries to that: First, get out of bad situations. If a career step doesn't work, search for a situation where your qualifications will allow you to thrive. Don't be narrow in what you think of as a possible job.

Second, don't be afraid to volunteer for projects that interest you, even if you have little experience. You'll learn as you go.

I would also advise young women to ask colleagues for critiques of drafts of papers and grant proposals. The final product will be better and the interaction may provide the start of an important working relationship.

AWIS: What is the value of professional associations?
FILNER: My involvement with AWIS, and especially editing the newsletter for 10 years, really did change my life. It taught me that I enjoyed writing and editing and that I did it well. That became the basis for an informed change in career direction. It also provided me with credentials. I used the newsletter to show that I could write clearly on nontechnical topics, that I could edit other authors, and that I could meet a deadline.

AWIS has also provided me with some of my most precious friends and advisors.

AWIS: May women starting out in your field contact you for guidance?
FILNER: Write to me at the Howard Hughes Medical Institute, 4000 Jones Bridge Road, Chevy Chase, MD 20815-6789 or call during working hours (301) 215-8884.

AWIS: What (or who) was the greatest help in turning you toward science?
FILNER: My own interest was the most important—math and science were my best subject areas in school, and I was especially fascinated with biology. Perhaps I should also credit my parents and teachers, none of whom tried to keep me away from science.

AWIS: What (or who) was the greatest help in keeping you in the field?
FILNER: My friends in graduate school and my brother, who is a scientist too.

AWIS: What (or who) was the worst hurdle in entering science? How did you overcome this barrier?
FILNER: That's a *really* hard question, because it *wasn't* hard. It was the path of least resistance, the subject matter with which I felt most comfortable.

34

Maria Cordero Hardy, Ph.D.
Professor Emerita of Biological Sciences

B.S. in biology, Midland Lutheran College	1952
M.S. physiology, Fordham University	1956
Ph.D. in physiology, Fordham University	1958

At 16, Hardy came to the United States from a Puerto Rico girl's school to enter college in Nebraska. There, she encountered one of her first role models, a woman professor who inspired her to alter her career plans. "I

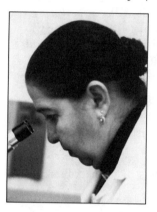

decided medical school was not what I wanted," Hardy said. "I wanted to be a Madame Curie," she explained. She nonetheless worked as a technician in a New York hospital, where she first became involved in research, and then went on to earn her master's and doctoral degrees in four years.

Since her doctorate, Hardy has held professorships at Rutgers University and Louisiana State University, where she headed the medical technology program until 1986 and did other administrative work. Retired since 1988, she continues to write. At her students' request, she is preparing her lecture series for publication. She is also writing a cookbook and is active in women's issues in Carteret County, North Carolina.

Hardy married Anthony Michael Hardy in 1962. They have two adult children (born 1963 and 1964).

AWIS: *What are the most important characteristics for which to search in mentors or other advisors?*
HARDY: See if s/he is interested in the things that interest you. You have to know a little about what you want to do. Don't rush into this relationship because it's going to make an impact for the rest of your life.

Watch how your prospective mentor treats the students and how much time s/he allocates to them. If the expert uses students to do work published under his/her name, choose someone else! Such a person is probably more concerned about his/her career than about developing the potential of students.

AWIS: *What would be your advice to a young woman thinking of embarking on a scientific career?*

HARDY: When choosing a career, make certain that there is a market for it, because many areas are already overcrowded. Make sure there are opportunities available for you.

Beyond that:

◆ Do the best you can.

◆ Know your limitations, learn what is involved, what the choices are, and go for the prize.

◆ I hate to say it, but learn to play the game. Know the system and work within it to effect change.

◆ Don't use your femininity as a tool because it will come back to haunt you. You don't have to be one of the boys either. Just be the best you can be: Get the best possible credentials, acquire good communication skills, and remember that you have to make decisions continuously.

◆ You are not superwoman. You can not be all things to all people. You cannot excel as a mother, a scientist, and a teacher all at once. Something will have to give, so get your priorities straight. Decide what you really want most.

◆ Share your commonality. Listen to the needs of your colleagues and be there for them.

◆ Keep your sense of humor!

AWIS: Is there a single pattern that a woman interested in a research career in science should best follow?
HARDY: If you do not get your hands dirty, analyze the results, and make deductions, you can't be a scientist. The sooner you get into the lab the better.

AWIS: How have you balanced your personal and professional commitments?
HARDY: My husband received a very good promotion, and we moved to Louisiana from New Jersey. I had a choice between my career at Rutgers and living in the same city as my husband, and I put my marriage first. I had not done much publishing, so I feared I wouldn't be able to get a good university position.

I had been an associate professor at Rutgers. I had been teaching for almost 20 years, and I had sponsored graduate students. When an administrator in Louisiana offered me an assistant professorship at $18,000 a year, I said, "You are wasting my time, and furthermore, I find that insulting."

"Well, what *do* you want?" I was asked.

"No less than what I was making before and an associate professorship," I replied.

I got both.

AWIS: *How important are mentors and role models?*
HARDY: At Louisiana State I served as a role model to young women. I also had men in my labs, and I thought: Here is a perfect opportunity to sensitize future male scientists to the needs of female scientists. I helped these young men realize the problems that women go through, the allowances we have to make for each other.

AWIS: *Are women scientists' difficulties entirely the result of men's sexism?*
HARDY: No. There is a lot of infighting among women also. This sets us back because the pie is so small. We are all fighting for a bit of it instead of trying to make the pie bigger.

AWIS: *May women starting out in your field contact you for guidance?*
HARDY: Yes. They may write me at PO Box 4173, Emerald Island, NC 28594.

AWIS: *What (or who) was the greatest help in turning you toward science?*
HARDY: That's a very difficult question—there were a series of reasons and influences. But I think the most important thing was working on nature badges in the Girl Scouts.

AWIS: *What (or who) was the greatest help in keeping you in the field?*
HARDY: My professor at Midland College, a woman named Marguerite Jesserich. She was a neurologist. I was the only girl in the class, and at the time, I was still a raw recruit from Puerto Rico. My spoken English was not too good, although I could read it fine. She let me work in the lab; she had me to her home for conversation and tea. She was a very warm and supportive person.

AWIS: *What (or who) was the worst hurdle in entering science? How did you overcome this barrier?*
HARDY: While in graduate school, I broke my jaw. That set me back six months. Most of my professors were actually supportive, and I faced no major obstacles in graduate school. The real barrier was my family, except for my mother who was always encouraging. The rest of my family felt that I was in a man's world—and I was! When I graduated, however, even my grandfather came around.

37

Florence P. Haseltine, Ph.D., M.D.

Gynecologist and Administrator

B.A. in biophysics, University of California, Berkeley	1964
Ph.D. in biophysics, Massachusetts Institute of Technology	1969
M.D., Albert Einstein School of Medicine	1972

At age 6, Haseltine planned to earn her Ph.D. in physics (from the Massachusetts Institute of Technology); at 12, she decided she also wanted an M.D.* In spite of "fairly severe" *dyslexia, which kept her from*

reading until she was 11 but turned her interests to mathematics, she achieved both goals. "Everybody thought I was stupid," *said Haseltine,* "but for some reason I figured I'd make it in science anyway. I guess I didn't understand what *stupid* meant," *she explained.*

After earning her medical degree, Haseltine did a one-year internship at the University of Pennsylvania, followed by three years of residency at Harvard University. From 1976–1985, she was at Yale University, first on a fellowship training in genetics and infertility, then as supervisor of its Human In-Vitro Fertilization Laboratory. She is presently the Director of the National Institutes of Health's Center for Population Research in Maryland. There, she summarizes, her overall responsibility is to "watch over and nurture reproductive biology."

Haseltine is a strong proponent of raising the numbers of women in science, particularly in her own field of research, gynecology, where there is a dearth of women scientists. She works hard to help women scientists break the "glass ceiling" *and attain their goals.*

Haseltine is married to Alan Chodos. They have two daughters, born in 1979 and 1981.

AWIS: *What are the most important characteristics for which to search in mentors or other advisors?*
HASELTINE: If you find a mentor, be sure that the women s/he has trained have succeeded. Look at the track record. If the mentor's

---

*This interview follows up on an earlier discussion with Haseltine appearing in the 1989, March/April *AWIS Newsletter, 18*(2), 8–10. See also Haseltine's paper, pages 237–241.

students have not done well, it could be the mentor's fault even if every student blames herself, excuses herself with explanations such as "I decided to have kids," or "I decided to teach."

This is not an attack on either of these activities—both of which I have practiced myself. But they do not tend to produce tenure, and the effective mentor will let the student know this.

Also, find mentors who have daughters!

AWIS: How have you balanced your personal and professional commitments?
HASELTINE: You can't do everything, so I've had full-time child care from the time my children were born. You have to delegate the basic care of the kids to someone else if you can't do it. It costs money. It's very hard.

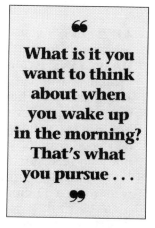

What is it you want to think about when you wake up in the morning? That's what you pursue ...

I think that child care should be part of the whole package that people get once they finish their basic training for any profession. I don't think people have to have kids in their 20s. They should probably have them in their early 30s after preparing for their careers.

After my medical training was complete and my schedule became my own, I decided to get pregnant. I kept miscarrying, but eventually had two successful pregnancies (at ages 38 and 40). My second delivery was to be a repeat C-section scheduled either for December 28 or 30, 1981. I knew that Elizabeth, the first in-vitro fertilization baby conceived in the United States, was going to be delivered on December 28, and the romantic in me opted for my daughter, also Elizabeth, to share that birthday.

Although we had tried a year earlier to get the Yale In-Vitro Fertilization Lab established, after my daughter Elizabeth was born, I fought more aggressively—this time successfully. Our lab's first successful pregnancy began in October, 1982. The day I learned of the pregnancy, I went out and got the license plate that I still have on my car: *EGGDOC.*

Part of every job package should be day care. Our nation needs children, but day care is often unavailable for people who need to work. Day care should be part of the working environment, like having safe water to drink.

Although my daughters live in New Haven with my husband, who also works full-time, and we have a live-in couple who help with the children, I do not think I have missed important events in our girls' lives. I've never been interested in attending things such as

39

Parent-Teachers' Association meetings and school plays. I keep in touch with my children in other ways. For example, I routinely take one of my children to every meeting I attend, every talk I give, and I respond quickly to their messages.

AWIS: Have you any advice for a Ph.D. interested in science teaching versus "hard science"?

HASELTINE: Women are usually good teachers. Chairmen say "You're so wonderful with the students, I want you to continue." The trick is not to be good at it: The person who wins the teacher-of-the-year award never gets tenure at the more prestigious schools. You also can't believe the chairman who tells you that you need to be a good team player: The man who is a lousy team player is the one who gets promoted.

There's nothing the matter with teaching, but if that's what you want to do, you should go to a school that rewards teaching.

AWIS: Do you notice differences between the way men and women approach a task?

HASELTINE: Yes. But when you come into a job, you initially come into their world, and you often have to succeed on their terms before you can change things. You have to get inside before you can change things, and you can't even always make inroads then.

AWIS: You have earned both an M.D. and a Ph.D. Why?

HASELTINE: The Ph.D. teaches you to think and allows you to add to knowledge through your research. The M.D. gives you an entrée into a world that you don't have with the Ph.D. alone.

Which you choose (if you choose) depends on what you want to do. If you want to deal with human medicine, having an M.D. is invaluable, but for research, the Ph.D. helps. For unorganized people like me, both were the answer.

M.D./Ph.D. programs are now very good, but back in 1969 they were just getting started, and their heads weren't letting women in. Administrators told me they weren't going to give money to women, and almost no one back then thought the statement was unreasonable.

AWIS: What is difficult about being a woman working in medicine?

HASELTINE: The brutal thing now is that medical schools are so expensive. We're training people who can't go into research careers. You don't earn a lot of money in research: You have to enjoy it. I earn enough, but if I had a huge debt I wouldn't have enough to make ends meet. Students are driven into clinical practices and specialties that make a lot of money.

AWIS: *Are there any advantages?*

HASELTINE: I may be one of the only people for whom Affirmative Action has worked. After I was hired, I heard how I was chosen.

The job had been vacant for months, but no one within the government could meet all the criteria required for the position. The government's affirmative action policy required that a woman be evaluated, and the search committee required a board certified gynecologist. They also wanted someone with National Institutes of Health and managerial experience—both of which I had. Only two women's names came out of the search, and I was chosen.

As an administrator, I think it's very important to promote women. Everyone knows that that's among the many things I was hired to do. But I am tough on women, and I sometimes take advantage of them because when I give a young woman a responsibility, I count on her to exercise it responsibly and produce. Women are always trying to prove themselves. As for men, in fact I have probably helped more men than women.

AWIS: *What would be your advice to a young woman thinking of embarking on a scientific career?*

HASELTINE: Don't take no for an answer and remember: If somebody else can do it, so can you.

What is it you want to think about when you wake up in the morning? That's what you pursue, because no matter what you do, some of it will be boring. You should be able to enjoy most of it.

AWIS: *May women starting out in your field contact you for guidance?*

HASELTINE: Yes. They may write at Center for Population Research, National Institutes of Health, 10500 Rockville Pike, #1226, Rockville, MD 20852, or call during business hours at (301) 496-1101.

AWIS: *What (or who) was the greatest help in turning you toward science?*

HASELTINE: I grew up in a science community. My mom encouraged me in math—she said I could always get a job if I knew math and did not know how to type.

AWIS: *What (or who) was the greatest help in keeping you in the field?*

HASELTINE: I didn't have any choice—once I made the decision, I was in to stay.

AWIS: *What (or who) was the worst hurdle in entering science? How did you overcome this barrier?*

HASELTINE: My teachers in high school and college who didn't want to give As to girls and who thought girls didn't belong in physics classes. Also, certain boyfriends who didn't want to date a girl in science—but they weren't really important: I got rid of those generic jerks immediately.

Esther Arvilla Harrison Hopkins, Ph.D., J.D.
Chemist, Patent Attorney, and Deputy General Counsel

A.B. in chemistry, Boston University	1947
M.S. in chemistry, Howard University	1949
M.S. in biophysical chemistry, Yale University	1963
Ph.D. in biochemistry, Yale University	1967
J.D., Suffolk University Law School	1977

One of the few women in America to have a doctorate in science and a license to practice before the U.S. Patents and Trademark office, Hopkins majored in chemistry in college.* After graduation, she hoped to go to

medical school, but when she wasn't admitted to the university of her choice, she continued in chemistry. "The school I wanted had a quota," *Hopkins explained.* "It was right after the war, and it had filled its two minority slots with one veteran and one black woman with a master's degree. I didn't fit.

"Admission to graduate and medical school was not what it is today," *she continued.* "Very few places after World War II would take women."

After earning her master's, Hopkins worked at Howard University's medical school and then taught chemistry to non-majors at Virginia State College. "That was frustrating," *she admitted.* "At that time, the public schools were promoting everyone: Some were prepared; many had not had the proper background."

Leaving Virginia, Hopkins moved back to New England, where she worked first as a control chemist and then in a research lab. She found, however, that her work was "not leading anywhere. So my husband and I

---

*This interview follows up on an earlier discussion with Hopkins appearing in the 1978, September/October *AWIS Newsletter,* 7(5), 10–12.

decided that I should get the 'union card,' that is, the Ph.D," *and she went back to school at Yale University, which was then admitting only a very few women into its graduate programs (and none as undergraduates).*

"My son and I were Yale's oddest couple—he, in nursery school and I, in graduate school. My son would sit on my lap while I was studying thermodynamics," *she remembered.* "Yale was an odd situation," *she summarized,* "strengthening me, in a way. I became tough through it, and the experience helped when I left. When you make it in an environment unfriendly to women, you do so with a sword and shield, fending off dangers with the sword and protecting yourself with the shield."

After graduation, Hopkins took a job as a research chemist at Polaroid, where she remained for 22 years. There, she became familiar with and interested in the work of the patent department. Her concern about the potential health hazards of the chemicals with which she was working broadened her interest into questions beyond the purely scientific. Like a colleague who was studying law, she entered law school at night and became an attorney as well as a scientist.

Since 1989, Hopkins has been deputy general counsel in the Massachusetts Department of Environmental Protection. She is fiscal and administrative counsel.

Hopkins' life reflects her view that obstacles need not preclude accomplishment and that it is possible to remain sensitive to others' needs while achieving professional recognition. Her path also reflects the faith of her mother, who left school after fourth grade, in the power of formal education. When Hopkins' mother was told that her daughter, who studied hard and did well in school, had been given a low grade because it was the teacher's habit to give black students poor marks, she was "furious," Hopkins said. "My mother believed in women's lib before it became fashionable."

Committed to the women's movement, Hopkins cares deeply about the difficulties women and minorities have encountered in both science and industry. She acknowledges with gratitude the support throughout her career provided by her husband Ewell Hopkins and her children (born in 1953 and 1959).

AWIS: How have your race and gender affected your career?
HOPKINS: I have never been able to separate the effects of being black from the effects of being a woman. I was aware of racism, of the feeling you can't afford to fail because others will have a problem because of your failure. I also knew that there were boys who resented girls who did better than boys. Each individual must make

43

her place in the world. It helps to know that paths have been made. People have survived, and you can also. There are people who are supportive. I wish there were better ways that women could support one another, so each woman could do what was right for her.

Many years ago, I listened to women who were supposedly successes and felt that many had paid a dreadful personal price for their professional achievements, a price that men need not pay. Women should be able to choose whether or not to buy into the male game.

Basically, unfortunately, things have remained much the same since then. I still see young women not getting all the chances they should, but I see some doing well. When people put 110 percent of their effort into what they are doing at work, however, something suffers.

AWIS: **How do you relate your view of science to your concept of the law?**
HOPKINS: My description of the role of patent attorney is very personal. It springs from the way I see my function.

The inventive concept springs from the mind of a person, not a machine. A chemist uncovers a new compound, a useful one that no one has made previously. Like parents their offspring, chemists want to display their findings to the world, yet protect them. The inventor explores in words her ideas, describes them, and defends them to me—a person who understands them, who is neither a competitor nor a detractor, who recognizes the joy of discovery, the beauty of an elegant solution.

The patent attorney takes this description down in a logical, scientific, legal, and candid form by interacting personally with a unique mind operating at the forefront of science and has an opportunity . . . to write the words that flesh out the child.

Having written the appropriate document, the patent attorney presents the invention to the U.S. Patent and Trademark Office and acts as its advocate, pointing out where it meets society's requirements for its 17-year protection.

When the patent has been awarded, the patent attorney shares with the inventor the pride in having a piece of intellectual property that is valued.

AWIS: **You began your career as a research scientist. Now your work's emphasis has changed. Has its essence also altered?**
HOPKINS: No, my work to protect the environment is not a change in concept or motivation from my work as a chemist or as a patent attorney.

Environmental protection—preserving air and water—is as vital and as fascinating as patent work. The central question is this: How can we give our children a clean world?

One way of working to do so is to organize and regulate and respond to emergencies. "Clean-up" is a very important part of it.

Women care a lot about these issues, and more than half of the lawyers in my office are women. So are many environmental scientists. Women scientists, technologists, lawyers—all should look to the environment.

The only people who can't find a niche working to save the environment are those who want to make lots and lots of money! (They need to look for work some place else.)

AWIS: How have you balanced your personal and professional commitments?

HOPKINS: I don't see how I could have survived without my family's support. A person is lucky if encouragement comes from within a family, but I think it can be found outside too. I could not have attended law school while working full-time if my husband had not approved. And both my son and my daughter grew up knowing that washing machines and dish washers are not aware of the user's gender.

It is unrealistic and unwise to split one's life into personal and professional priorities. They need to be complementary.

AWIS: What would be your advice to a young woman thinking of embarking on a scientific career?

HOPKINS: There's no use saying that you should have done something sooner, or that it's too late now.

AWIS: May women starting out in your field contact you for guidance?

HOPKINS: Yes. During working hours, they may call at (617) 292-5928, or they may write me at 1550 Worcester, Number 524, Framingham, MA 01701. Because I believe in the essential importance of this kind of networking, I have been serving for a number of years as a career consultant for the American Chemical Society. A group of about 40 of us—males and females, blacks and whites— have made this commitment.

AWIS: What (or who) was the greatest help in turning you toward science?

HOPKINS: Mentors and role models are very important. There was a white woman doctor in my hometown named Madeline Fisk, a marvelous person doing such important things, and I thought she was wonderful. I wanted to emulate her. She went to Boston University, so I did too. Now, I am a trustee on its board.

AWIS: What (or who) was the greatest help in keeping you in the field?
HOPKINS: My husband, a man who helps people see what they can do and then sees how he can help them do it.

AWIS: What (or who) was the worst hurdle in entering science? How did you overcome this barrier?
HOPKINS: There were certain diligent people in guidance in high school who looked at my parents' educational background and tried hard to steer me away from a career in science—or one demanding any postsecondary study.

Judith Kantor, Ph.D.

Cancer Expert

B.S. in biology, Allegheny College	1964
M.S. in radiation physics, University of Pittsburgh	1967
Ph.D. in biochemical genetics, George Washington University	1974

Kantor's scientific curiosity was initially roused in high school by two excellent teachers: one in biology, the other in chemistry. Following her marriage to Falk Kantor and completion of her master's degree, she moved

from Pittsburgh to the Washington, D.C., area, where she transferred to George Washington University. Kantor now does gene regulation research pertaining to genetic diseases and tumor-associated antigens. She conducts her work at the National Institutes of Health, where she heads her laboratory.

While pursuing her doctoral studies at George Washington University, she had the opportunity to work at the National Institutes of Health under the guidance of eminent geneticist French Anderson. After receiving her Ph.D., Kantor taught at Georgetown University. Yet she preferred research, despite its commitments and frequent frustrations, so she returned to the National Institutes of Health. She says many people can't handle the slow pace. "A bricklayer lays a wall," says Kantor, "and after eight hours you can see progress. I have been trying to clone one gene for four years."

AWIS: *What made you decide to go into science? Into your particular field?*

KANTOR: It was a challenge. English and history came easily to me, but I had to work to understand science. While I never thought I was very good at math or physics, my master's includes nuclear and health physics.

AWIS: *Have you ever experienced gender discrimination as a woman in science?*

KANTOR: I think there are two pathways: one for men and one for women. It's subtle, but women don't get the salaries or the promotions.

With wisdom and experience, you learn to fight for certain things, let go of others, and not get discouraged. I think women have to work 10 times harder than men to get promoted.

Women and men have different ideas on how to approach the same problem. They also communicate ideas differently.

AWIS: *How important are mentors and role models?*

KANTOR: Women have to get into more positions of power. But I notice when women do, many of them keep other women out instead of being role models. If women started to serve as mentors to other women, I think we'd see policies start to change. We need more women mentoring women.

Students need someone to help them; and I've seen men help men but not women. As a postdoctoral student, you need a guardian angel to show you how to write grants, to acclimate yourself within a department, and to help you learn how to play politics.

AWIS: *What would be your advice to a young woman thinking of embarking on a scientific career?*

KANTOR: Get hands-on laboratory experience as soon as you can. If you know your way around the lab, you will succeed, because you will begin to understand cells, cell mechanisms, and cell regulation. Even if you just wash test tubes in the lab, you can talk with the people who are doing science, and you will learn.

When I did industrial science, I didn't like the restraints of having a product/dollar motivation. A lot of things get overlooked. But businesses do offer more money.

AWIS: *What are the most important characteristics for which to search in mentors or other advisors?*

KANTOR: Before you settle on who should be your mentor, ask other people in the lab what they think of the person you have in

47

mind. "Does this person help you along? Will they show me not just how to do experiments, but how to write a paper or how to present data?" Your mentor should teach you how to do these things, and not see you as competition.

If women's organizations can give advice in addition to that offered by a mentor, that's fine.

AWIS: Do you have any advice for women pursuing their doctorates?
KANTOR: Go down the road, and don't look back. Learn from the beatings you get along the way. You become a stronger person and more relaxed with yourself. You can and should convey that aura to other people. When we open a door that raises 10 new questions, we have to answer those 10 questions. When things work, it is wonderful!

AWIS: May women starting out in your field contact you for guidance?
KANTOR: Yes, they may write me at the National Institutes of Health, Building 10, Room 5B 46, Bethesda, MD 20892.

AWIS: What (or who) was the greatest help in turning you toward science?
KANTOR: My high school biology and chemistry teachers.

AWIS: What (or who) was the greatest help in keeping you in the field?
KANTOR: The subject itself. You never get bored. You do, however, also need a stiff upper lip.

AWIS: What (or who) was the worst hurdle in entering science? How did you overcome this barrier?
KANTOR: Organic chemistry. Then I realized that you didn't have to synthesize rubber every day; you could put those equations to more relevant use in terms of a cell.

Isabella L. Karle, Ph.D.
Chemist and Head of X-Ray Diffraction Section

B.S. in chemistry, University of Michigan	1941
M.S. in chemistry, University of Michigan	1942
Ph.D in physical chemistry, University of Michigan	1944

Karle, who received her doctorate at age 22, is the daughter of Polish immigrants who were "knowledgeable" but had no formal education. She grew up in Detroit, learning no English until she went to school, where the children spoke "all the languages of Europe. At that point," she laughed, "everybody had to learn English, since, without a shared language, nobody could communicate."

Science, said Karle, who would grow up to make significant contributions to the areas of crystallography, chemistry, and biophysics, was not a part of her family's tradition, and she did not discover her "fascination" *with*

chemistry until she chose it as her mandatory science course in high school. Mrs. Demming, Karle's chemistry teacher, must have done a good job: Karle decided to become a chemist, a decision that "confused" *her family somewhat.*

Graduating early from high school, Karle, along with two other women undergraduates, earned a baccalaureate in chemistry. Within three years, she had finished her Ph.D. and married future Nobel Prize winner Jerome Karle (chemistry, 1985). To support the war effort, the Karles joined the plutonium project at University of Chicago in 1942. She worked in compounds, fulfilling her assignment and becoming the first person to make pluto-nium chloride (replacing an impure oxide from the Oak Ridge [Tennessee] National Laboratory); meanwhile, her husband was successfully making plutonic metal.

Next, the Karles returned to the University of Michigan where Karle received an appointment as an instructor of chemistry. Although she was the first woman to have any faculty position in chemistry at Michigan, the rank carried no research possibilities, and, after the war, the Karles went looking for two research positions in chemistry in the same city. Universities almost universally enforced "nepotism" *rules against hus-bands and wives working in the same institution, so the Karles turned instead to the Naval Research Laboratory, the first and most esteemed such federal facility, which was in peacetime expanding its activities into basic research.* "It has supported us well," *Karle said.*

In 1963, while at the Laboratory, Karle developed the symbolic addition procedure for deriving molecular structures directly from X-ray diffraction experiments on crystals. This technique, which revolutionized structure analysis, is now used worldwide. Karle is the only woman member of the chemistry section of the National Academy of Sciences.

The Karles' research, she says, proceeds on "parallel tracks. We deal with the same sorts of topics, although my husband's interests are fundamentally theoretical, mine practical." *Her husband says he wishes he had been able to insist, as Pierre Curie did for Marie, that the Nobel be awarded jointly.*

The Karles have three daughters, born 1946, 1950, and 1955, who have all become scientists.

AWIS: What are the most important characteristics for which to search in mentors or other advisors?
KARLE: I'm not sure. There are some people who are not psychologically attuned to being mentors. I have been one for many people—both male and female—but now I'm stepping back from that role a bit. I try to help in other ways, such as, for example, giving lectures to women's groups.

AWIS: What would be your advice to a young woman thinking of embarking on a scientific career?
KARLE: This is a difficult time to be going into science. Opportunities for rewarding and significant work have shrunk with the economy and with reductions in funding. Industry is reducing its research staff, and it is not easy for a young person with a Ph.D. to get a permanent position. I'm torn, when I'm asked this question, between discussing my own happiness and noting the problem of making a reasonable living in my profession.

AWIS: How have you balanced your personal and professional commitments?
KARLE: My husband has always been helpful at home. When the children were small, I did not go to many meetings during the academic year. In the summer, the children came along when I traveled on business. Their travel experiences broadened their lives and their independence. We tended to choose social and recreational activities that included children.

AWIS: What are the prospects for increasing the numbers of women scientists?
KARLE: I don't know. My oldest daughter, 25 years behind me, also did her undergraduate work at Michigan, and—as when I was there—only two other women were classmates. My second daughter, in graduate school, similarly found very few women among her fellow students.

On the other hand, I see more women now when I go to scientific meetings or to lecture; however, my field of interest has turned more toward biological science, where there are more women than in chemistry.

AWIS: *What, so far, do you see as the most rewarding aspect of your career?*

KARLE: A number of things. I have been quite successful in research and have contributed to general science: It is always fascinating to solve problems. I have also enjoyed many opportunities to make friends and find colleagues worldwide.

AWIS: *Do you notice differences between the way men and women approach a task?*

KARLE: I think that's a very individual question. I can't make a generalization about *men* and *women*. Even when I talk of a man and a woman, the matter is complex: While my husband tends to be interested in theoretical matters and I in practical aspects, my oldest daughter also tends to the theoretical.

AWIS: *What would you like to see change about the science profession today?*

KARLE: I would like the public attitude toward science to change. I would like people to become more knowledgeable about what scientists do. The public tends to expect us to cure all problems, find all medicines, but if we are slow to do so, we're seen as ogres.

Science has contributed to the well-being of everyone. This fact is not appreciated in the media or by the general public. I'd like to see more in newspapers about the accomplishments of scientists and less about sports heroes' huge salaries or film stars' escapades.

AWIS: *May women starting out in your field contact you for guidance?*

KARLE: Women may write me for advice at Code 6030, Naval Research Laboratory, Washington, DC 20375.

AWIS: *What (or who) was the greatest help in turning you toward science?*

KARLE: My high school chemistry teacher.

AWIS: *What (or who) was the greatest help in keeping you in the field?*

KARLE: My own interest. Along the way, I've studied with faculty members who were extremely helpful; others, however, were discouraging.

AWIS: *What (or who) was the worst hurdle in entering science? How did you overcome this barrier?*

KARLE: Besides the good professors who encouraged me, there were some who didn't want me—as a female graduate student—to do research.

51

Naomi J. McAfee, B.S.

Engineer and Manager

B.S. in physics, Western Kentucky State College   1956

As a child McAfee was preoccupied with mechanics: "Sometimes my mother was irritated by my interest in machines, rather than dolls," she admitted.* But her parents encouraged her to pursue an education.

McAfee saw a science career as a promise of opportunity, and with her career in industry, she was able to attain her goals.

After earning her bachelor's degree in physics, McAfee accepted a job at Westinghouse Electric Corporation; she has worked there ever since, rising from assistant engineer to her current position as assistant to the vice president and general manager of the systems and technical development divisions. Her decision not to pursue an advanced degree has not hindered her career in industry. In 1966, she became the first woman in administrative management at Westinghouse. After mastering the new field of quality and reliability engineering in the early 1970s, McAfee was appointed director of corporate strategic resources in Westinghouse's headquarters in Pittsburgh, moving to an administrative post in Baltimore in 1977. In 1979, McAfee became deputy manager of the Westinghouse Defense Center; in that capacity she worked, often supervising as many as 800 employees, until 1988. In her present post as director of enterprises integration, she facilitates electronic communication among the Center's some 18,000 employees and between them and Westinghouse's total workforce of 100,000. She says that her ambition is, eventually, "to get rid of paper altogether."

McAfee has been married since 1958.

AWIS: *What made you decide to go into science? Into your particular field?*

McAFEE: I began to think about a career in science after a high school history teacher assigned me to write a paper on the development of the atomic bomb. While researching the paper, I read a great deal about Madame Curie and decided to become a chemist. During my sophomore year at college, an altercation between my-

---

*This interview follows up on an earlier discussion with McAfee appearing in the 1977, September/October *AWIS Newsletter*, 6(5), 8–12.

self and a chemistry professor got me kicked out of the chemistry department. I became a physics major and found that physics was more fun than chemistry.

Typically, people from my small Kentucky town went to college so that they could teach, but teaching was not my bag! I was one of the few in my graduating class who did not get a teaching certificate. I wanted a job where I could live reasonably well and not have to worry about survival all the time. Most teachers were poor: Industry seemed to be the only answer.

AWIS: Have you ever experienced gender discrimination as a woman in science?

McAFEE: I always intended to work, even if I married: I didn't like the thought of having to rely upon someone to supply all the basics. I wanted to be as independent as my brothers and father. No one ever told me until I was in college that women couldn't have a career, make their own decisions, or control their own lives. I was more intelligent and stubborn than my brothers, so I plowed ahead.

The major adverse factor became evident when I married. Everyone except my immediate supervisor assumed that I'd quit work and forget about a career. Once others realized that I was serious about my career and that my husband was supportive, things slowly changed. Even 10 years later, however, people worried about promoting me because I might get pregnant.

I coped with this problem by forcing a meeting with the manager . . . After discussing technical matters, I ended the issue forever. I said as I left his office, "I'll make a deal with you. In the future, I won't ask about your sex life if you don't ask about mine."

Today he tells the story with a touch of humor and adds that it was the most consciousness-raising experience of his life.

AWIS: What would be your advice to a young woman thinking of embarking on a scientific career?

McAFEE: Part of getting ahead is based upon performance. Doing an outstanding job helps, but success can also be attributed to being at the right place at the right time with the proper qualifications.

◆ Show initiative. Don't be afraid to take on responsibility. Nature abhors a vacuum. If you don't fill the job, someone else will.

◆ Be part of the team. One can disagree or compromise and still be a team member. Even when we fight with each other, I always realize that the team is more important than any one individual. It doesn't take long for others to recognize and respect you for it. With respect comes growing acceptance.

◆ Know your boss. Be able to communicate.

◆ Find a mentor. Someone higher in every department where I've worked has played that role for me. As I progressed, the people changed, but their role remained the same—they helped me develop my capabilities and assisted in avoiding pitfalls. Trying to master the political, technological and psychological aspects of a job is rough enough with help. Without help it is almost hopeless.

◆ Give credit when it is due and even sometimes when it isn't. If you are a leader, give credit to the group that performs the work— any failure is yours. After all, as their leader, they should be doing what you want them to do. If something goes wrong, there is only one person to blame: Yourself.

◆ Never fear to ask questions.

◆ If you disagree, then get your day in court. If you lose at that time, then shut up and get on with the show. If you haven't been able to convince people to change their minds, stubborn fighting doesn't help. If the issue is a real problem, you'll have another chance to fight it later. When you make mistakes, admit them. Be loyal. Criticism is okay, but make sure it stays within the organization, is justified, and is constructive.

◆ Be yourself. You have a certain style and mode of operation. The only real disaster I've had happen was when I was doing something with which I didn't feel comfortable.

◆ Always give the other person the benefit of the doubt and don't make needless enemies.

◆ Never ask more of your subordinates than you are willing to do yourself.

◆ Have a sense of humor. Laugh at yourself once in a while and it can really ease tensions.

AWIS: *May women starting out in your field contact you for guidance?*
McAFEE: Yes. They may call me at (410) 765-3400—voice mail kicks in after about 9 rings, and I return calls promptly. Or they may write to me at 13 Seminole Avenue, Catonsville, MD 21228.

AWIS: *What (or who) was the greatest help in turning you toward science?*
McAFEE: Marie Curie.

AWIS: *What (or who) was the greatest help in keeping you in the field?*
McAFEE: Once I was interested, no one. The challenge of the work, the fact that there's always something new to learn, was enough. On the other hand, it's reassuring that the laws of physics don't change. Even Einstein doesn't upend Newton—relativity just takes Newton's laws further.

AWIS: *What (or who) was the worst hurdle in entering science? How did you overcome this barrier?*
McAFEE: My father, who—when he found that I wanted to work— wanted me to go into home economics or teaching, where he figured there were always jobs available.

He finally came around when I landed the best-paying job in my class after college.

Caryn Navy, Ph.D.
Mathematician and Industrial Computer Scientist

B.S. in mathematics, Massachusetts Institute of Technology	1975
M.S. in mathematics, University of Wisconsin	1977
Ph.D. in mathematics, University of Wisconsin	1981

Mathematician and computer scientist Caryn Navy, partially sighted until just before her 11th birthday, has been completely blind since the

sixth grade. Her condition, retrolental fibroplasia, occurs when scar tissue forms on the retina and on sections of the eye.

Her father, a certified public accountant, encouraged her early preoccupation with mathematics, and loss of her sight did not prevent her from pursuing math after high school at the Massachusetts Institute of Technology. After graduation, continuing to overcome the isolation of being a blind woman scientist, she went to the Midwest to complete her graduate work. From there she went to Pennsylvania where she taught at Bucknell University before returning to Wisconsin to codirect with her husband Raised Dot Computing, a company that produces computer programs for the blind.

Navy and her husband David Holladay recently adopted a son (born in 1990).

AWIS: *What special difficulties arose for you because of your disability?*
NAVY: I think the most difficult thing was dealing with the attitudes of others.

I remember that in sixth grade and high school some of the teachers wanted to excuse me from math, but I had always liked it, so I just pushed ahead.

Later, teachers discouraged me from working in laboratories. In some classes, I was totally excused from lab work, and I really regret that now.

Usually at the beginning of a class I felt that I had to prove myself. One year I took a course in algebraic topology with a lot of diagrams. The professor had fairly low expectations for me. I usually made arrangements with each professor on how to turn in problem sets. This particular professor said I could give my answers orally. When I went in, he only asked for a couple of the answers, even though I had worked the whole set. Clearly he didn't expect me to do everything.

I took Braille notes in class, but if things went too fast, I had problems keeping up. So I brought a tape recorder, and I would go back and take Braille notes from my tapes: That was time-consuming. Some of the textbooks were available on tape from *Recording for the Blind*, but, as I advanced, the number decreased.

AWIS: *Did you like teaching? Why did you leave academia for industry?*
NAVY: I told the supervisor that I wanted to be a teaching assistant. He seemed surprised and unsure about how that would work out, but I taught a sample lesson, and then I taught for the next four years.

My position at Bucknell was not tenure track. I started with a two-year contract, which was renewed, but it still promised no future stability.

I still have some regrets about leaving mathematics teaching. I felt isolated at Bucknell, and I had a hard time doing research. I was so anxious about teaching that I spent all my time working on that, and I don't know if I could turn that pattern around.

AWIS: *What happened when you returned to Wisconsin with your husband?*
NAVY: Coming back to Madison was a difficult time for me because I didn't feel as if I were in a position to get a good academic job. I hadn't published. My husband urged me to work in the business; that's what I did, and I enjoy it.

At the company, I do design and software coding and provide technical support. As co-owner, I also share in management.

AWIS: What are the most important characteristics for which to search in mentors or other advisors?
NAVY: It's important to pick somebody who expects excellence from you and who will recognize special needs. I think the primary thing is finding an area that really suits you. The personality of the advisor might be secondary.

AWIS: May women starting out in your field contact you for guidance?
NAVY: Yes, they may phone me at (608) 241-2498 outside of business hours.

AWIS: What (or who) was the greatest help in turning you toward science and mathematics?
NAVY: My father, who loved math and helped to give me the confidence that I could do it. And Mary Ellen Rudin, my graduate school advisor, who helped me find a thesis topic, publicized my dissertation results, and generally helped to make me feel less isolated.

AWIS: What (or who) was the greatest help in keeping you in the field?
NAVY: That's a hard question because I sort of switched fields from mathematics to computer science. For example, I'm not using topology any more; however, many of the same strategies often apply.

AWIS: What (or who) was the worst hurdle in entering science and mathematics? How did you overcome this barrier?
NAVY: Professors who didn't verbalize what they were writing on the blackboard. I overcame this hurdle by asking them to explain, by having other students read me their notes, or by reading ahead in the textbook, so I could know in advance what was going on.

On the other hand, there are many people who look upon normal activities as extraordinary when performed by a blind person. They might be extremely impressed, for instance, when a blind person ties her shoe. This kind of response can make it hard for one to distinguish normal behavior from real accomplishments.

Constance Tom Noguchi, Ph.D.

Physical Biochemist

B.A. in math and physics, University of California, Berkeley   1970
Ph.D. in nuclear physics, George Washington University   1975

Noguchi originally intended to be a physician. When she found how much she enjoyed the physical sciences, however, she switched her major to physics and eventually earned her Ph.D. in theoretical physics. Upon acceptance of a grant from the National Institutes of Health, she entered the biomedical field and received on-the-job training in biology.

Noguchi examined substances from a biological perspective and learned protein chemistry and molecular biology. Noguchi's work concentrates on the study of sickle cell anemia.

Noguchi has been married to Philip Noguchi since 1969. They have two sons, now teenagers, born in 1977 and 1979.

AWIS: *What, so far, do you see as the most rewarding aspect of your career?*
NOGUCHI: One of the best jobs possible is to be able to do what you enjoy and get paid for it. In research, I have the opportunity to solve problems, to make scientific discoveries, and to share them with colleagues and students in the process. Some solutions can be found using tools ranging from sophisticated electronic equipment and high speed computers to string and wax or pencil and paper. The key is to be able to use your imagination and whatever else is available.

AWIS: *Why did you earn a Ph.D. rather than an M.D?*
NOGUCHI: I realized that I enjoyed the physical as well as the biological sciences, and the M.D. training focused on the life sciences and the application of that knowledge. Different degrees teach different skills. Graduate school showed me how to approach a problem. In the sciences you develop a method for going through the literature, pulling out the tools and resources you need, and talking to people to gain insight into your problem. Those techniques can be useful not only in scientific research but also in the social sciences and humanities. The M.D. gives you the credibility to

interact with patients and design clinical studies. There is no limitation on research with an M.D., but you develop a different set of skills than you gain through a Ph.D. program. With a Ph.D., you learn how to investigate a very specific area in depth.

AWIS: How have you balanced your personal and professional commitments?

NOGUCHI: There is *never* a convenient time to have kids. You just decide when to do it, and you do it.

Child-rearing does delay you professionally. I took some time off, but I decided that slowing down was worthwhile, and I don't think it damaged my career. One postdoc down the hall had her son and was back the next week working in the lab. It took me longer.

> **66**
> **There is *never* a convenient time to have kids. You just decide when to do it, and you do it.**
> **99**

If you do choose to have a career and a family, you have to feel comfortable with your situation. If you must worry the entire day about whether your children are in an appropriate child care situation, your productivity at work will suffer. If you're convinced that you're doing the best you can with day care—and that that best is good enough—then when at work, your primary focus can be work.

AWIS: Do you notice differences between the way men and women approach a task?

NOGUCHI: In the laboratory environments that I have experienced, the women are less vocal than the males. In general, the more vocal person gets noticed and is likely to be considered with higher regard. That's one of the disadvantages quiet and reserved women face.

AWIS: What are the most important characteristics for which to search in mentors or other advisors?

NOGUCHI: Students need to find someone, male or female, who has time for them. Some people mean well but are so busy that it's difficult for them to find time to help. Often the only people who have time are junior members of the group. This can be unfortunate if the mentor is too new, because s/he may lack the wisdom that experience brings, although this is not always the case.

You can do many things, but because time is limited, take advantage of the knowledge provided by the seasoned veterans, and seek out a number of them for advice and perspective.

AWIS: Is there a single pattern that a woman interested in a research career in science should best follow?

NOGUCHI: With the continuing changes in the job market and career opportunities, it is important to approach your education as would a wise consumer any product. Explore your options. If you stay focused in a particular area, you will have an easier job of establishing yourself in that one field. The exposure that you experience during your training can always be used to your advantage.

It's never too late to change direction, however, or to consider an unconventional career path. Ph.D. recipients who have returned to medical school can be found in research as well as private practice, and individuals who have had private medical practices can be found now doing basic research. Furthermore, some individuals with graduate degrees in the humanities or social sciences have found a home in scientific research.

AWIS: May women starting out in your field contact you for guidance?

NOGUCHI: Certainly. They may write me at the National Institutes of Health, Building 10, Room 9N 307, 9000 Rockville Pike, Bethesda, MD 20892.

AWIS: What (or who) was the greatest help in turning you toward science?

NOGUCHI: My family. My father was an engineer. As I was growing up, there was very little science education in elementary school. He made sure there were resources at home—mail-order science kits, books, and the like. My sisters joined in our various activities, and we did the projects together.

AWIS: What (or who) was the greatest help in keeping you in the field?

NOGUCHI: Again, my family. I originally intended to become a physician, and my only real discouragement occurred when I decided not to go to medical school. I have a number of relatives who are in science, and they helped me realize that medicine was not the only branch of science around, that with my interests, biophysics might be a field of study that I would enjoy. My husband and two sons continue to be very supportive, and we all appreciate our time constraints and try to adjust accordingly.

AWIS: What (or who) was the worst hurdle in entering science? How did you overcome this barrier?

NOGUCHI: I had trouble deciding which field of study to pursue. There were not a lot of people counselling students new to science about what field might be appropriate for them, particularly those students who liked all aspects of science. It took a while before I realized that a number of my professors were very approachable. In fact, I was looking for mentors.

Resha M. Putzrath, Ph.D.
Consultant in Toxicology, Risk Assessment, and Environmental Policy

A.B. in physics, Smith College 1971
M.S. in biophysics, University of Rochester 1974
Ph.D. in biophysics, University of Rochester 1978
Diplomate of the American Board of Toxicology 1986–1996

Putzrath says she was essentially born into science: both of her parents were trained in science, and family activities included fossil-hunting, watching the sky for eclipses and satellites, and other scientific adventures. Following graduation from a women's college, where she was one of

two majors in physics, Putzrath went on to graduate study. Her postdoctoral appointments were as a research fellow in physiology at Harvard Medical School and as a fellow in the Interdisciplinary Programs in Health at the Harvard School of Public Health. Between Harvard and her current position, Putzrath served as a consultant to the Hazardous Waste Enforcement Task Force at the U.S. Environmental Protection Agency; associate scientist at the National Research Council of the National Academy of Sciences; and Project Manager at ENVIRON Corporation, a consulting firm.

Putzrath now heads the Environmental Group (which she established) in the Washington, D.C. office of Organization Resources Counselors, Inc., a management consulting firm. Her duties include monitoring and analyzing environmental issues (health and ecological) under consideration by federal and state agencies with the goal of improving the use of science in risk assessments and regulatory decisions. She assists corporations with understanding and implementing environmental regulations and evaluates changes in environmental regulations for their implications for corporate strategy. In addition, Putzrath's research involves developing innovative procedures for incorporating qualitative and quantitative infor-

61

mation into risk assessment and risk management policies, including developing the use of meta-analysis for evaluating carcinogenicity bioassays and ancillary data.

Putzrath has been married since 1978 to Lawrence S. Olson.

AWIS: *Can you think of any instances of gender discrimination against women science students?*

PUTZRATH: Faculty members often hurry to set men students on their way, so they can start careers promptly. Women, however, are often encouraged to stay around to complete an area of research— an impossible task as each result generates more questions. This philosophy often continues in employment. Of men it is said, "Let's give him the job to let him grow, let him stretch." For women the refrain too frequently is, "Let's make her prove that she can do the job before we give her the title." That pattern is not always gender specific, but I've seen many people evaluated, and it happens more often to women than to men.

Such discrepancy in evaluations may only make a small difference at any given stage, but over time the delay accumulates: An extra six to twelve months to complete her thesis research, extended duration for each postdoc, and an additional year or two before each promotion in the job. Suddenly, a woman can find herself years behind where she might otherwise have been. Then she may not be viewed as a rising young superstar, but rather as an older scientist of whom it is said, "Well, if she's so good, why hasn't she achieved more by this age?"

AWIS: *Have you ever experienced gender discrimination as a woman in science?*

PUTZRATH: Of course. But instead of recounting experiences, I would like to broaden the question to discuss how to respond to such situations. For example, what do you do the first time you see a *Playboy* slide in a lecture? You behave differently than you do the fifth time such an image intrudes into a professional setting.

I would advise young scientists to talk with others to see how they have handled specific situations and think about what response is comfortable for them for each case. Being caught off-guard can produce regrettable responses. Sometimes, a meaningful glare is sufficient; other times, stronger action is appropriate. In some circumstances, it is best to change things quietly; other times, vocal support is needed. Find out what has worked for other people and then adapt those ideas for your own use. I try to focus on what result I am trying to achieve rather than why the action has upset me; this approach allows me to stay more objective.

AWIS: *What is the value of professional associations?*

PUTZRATH: One of the benefits of AWIS is meeting successful women in many areas of science who are examples of the fact that "woman scientist" is *not* an oxymoron.

AWIS: *How have you handled a two-career marriage, balancing your personal and professional commitments?*

PUTZRATH: I always joke that my husband has been following *me* around. The truth is, however, that we've worked together to achieve a successful, two-career marriage. It's not just luck; part is what you look for in a spouse. My husband is very supportive; I sometimes tease him about being more serious about my career than I am. We both, however, have tried to keep our careers flexible and mobile. When we have opportunities for change, we examine the issues in terms of both of our careers as well as our personal lives.

The balance between personal and professional life is always a challenge. While it is understood that the balance will be different for each person, it also can change during the stages of career or personal life. It's necessary to find a way to accomplish everything that's critically important to you—and to recognize that not everything you would like to do can be considered critically important.

AWIS: *What made you decide to go into science?*

PUTZRATH: I come from a family of scientists. My father is an electrical engineer. My mother trained as a chemist at a time when even fewer women entered the field than today. My sister (the *other* Dr. R. Putzrath) and I grew up in a household where science was as much a part of life as any other activity. Robin and I may be the only cooks who, when learning to make a cheese soufflé, were instructed to add the hot cheese slowly to the egg yolks so as not to denature the protein. Both of us became scientists.

When I give "career day" talks, I emphasize that there are many types of scientific careers. I start by saying that I'm not going to talk about familiar fields such as laboratory science, teaching, or medicine—everyone is familiar with those jobs. Instead I focus on less well known, more eclectic scientific careers, such as consulting or regulatory science, and how a scientific background is useful in numerous careers, such as market research or environmental law. When I was in school, I was unaware of these options. The result is that I've had four jobs that I didn't know *existed* before I was recruited into them.

I stress these options because many girls and women believe that if they become scientists, they will have to lock themselves away from the rest of the world. A lot of them say, "I like people, so I can't be a scientist, can I?" They also don't understand that you can be a scientist, get married and have kids, and be feminine. The notion that scientists—male and female alike—are all nerds is not yet dead.

AWIS: You began your career as a research scientist. Now your work is primarily managerial. What led you to change emphasis, and how do you feel about the decision now?
PUTZRATH: Becoming a manager is almost inevitable as people advance in their careers. Managing a laboratory has more similarities than differences from managing a consulting project.

Although I missed the lab initially, I don't regret the change. Outside the lab, you more frequently have an immediate effect on the manner in which science is used to solve problems. In some ways I feel I have the best of both worlds. As my current work involves a science that does not require a laboratory (i.e., risk assessment), it's possible to continue intellectually stimulating research while working to improve its application in a regulatory setting.

Besides, I enjoy being a manager. There's the challenge of solving a whole new set of problems, including my recent task of planning and developing a new practice area for my firm. Being a manager, however, also requires a new set of interpersonal skills. I used to think it would be enough to become a supervisor for whom I would like to work, but I learned that people want and need different things from a supervisor. In addition to on-the-job training and reading articles on management skills, I'm fortunate to have a network of colleagues who are also managers with whom I can discuss issues as they arise.

AWIS: May women starting out in your field contact you for guidance?
PUTZRATH: Yes. I would prefer that they initially write to me at 3223 N Street, NW, Washington, DC 20007, explaining their situation and what specific type of information they would like to obtain or discuss. Then, if I can't help them myself, I will try to direct them to someone who can.

AWIS: What (or who) was the greatest help in turning you toward science?
PUTZRATH: My parents encouraged my sister and me to explore ideas and how things worked. My mother especially emphasized that we could have any career we were capable of learning. Moreover, I've always enjoyed solving problems, and scientific research is a great arena for this skill.

AWIS: *What (or who) was the greatest help in keeping you in the field?*
PUTZRATH: A number of people, including my parents, my sister who is also a scientist, and about a dozen mentors, supported me. I also derived many benefits from attending a women's college. Coming from a public high school where I was usually the only or one of a few women in the honors science and math classes, I found having women scientists as colleagues refreshing. Now I find the same support in AWIS and the friends I've made through participation in the group's activities.

AWIS: *What (or who) was your worst hurdle in entering science? How did you overcome this barrier?*
PUTZRATH: The science itself, although often frustrating, was always exciting. Social situations, however, could be discouraging. People of various ilks—from boyfriends to teachers and supervisors—who didn't think women belong in science were disheartening. For example, at college dances, I often stated my major was "natural philosophy." Too many men excused themselves when they discovered I was a physics major. Similarly, in the lab, some supervisors assumed I wouldn't want to do messy jobs (who does?) or couldn't do tasks requiring strength (I increased the use of levers and jacks). In business, some supervisors have responded to a request for a raise by inquiring about my husband's income or have asked whether he would *allow* me to travel.

Judith A. Ramaley, Ph.D.
University President

B.A. in zoology, Swarthmore College   1963
Ph.D. in anatomy, University of California, Berkeley   1966

Ramaley has had a varied career since she earned her Ph.D.* Initially, she did research on the control of the onset of puberty, stress, and fertility and was a medical school faculty member. In 1976, however, she became an administrator. Several factors precipitated this transition, among them a year as a fellow of the American Council on Education, but most important was Ramaley's interest in and ability to see the big picture.

*This interview follows up on an earlier discussion with Ramaley appearing in the 1988, March/April *AWIS Newsletter, 17*(1), 8–11.

Following her fellowship year, Ramaley held high administrative posts at two branches of the University of Nebraska before going to the State University of New York at Albany as its chief academic officer. In 1988,

when she became executive vice chancellor of the University of Kansas at Lawrence, she was one of the few female top administrators of large university campuses. Now, as the President of Portland State University (Oregon), Ramaley continues her commitment to educational opportunities for women and minorities. She also continues her support of AWIS, which she has served as founding member, secretary, and president.

Ramaley has raised two sons (born in 1969 and 1971).

AWIS: *You began your career as a research scientist. Now your work is administrative. What led you to change emphasis, and how do you feel about the decision now?*

RAMALEY: You approach things differently in a laboratory/teaching setting than you do in an administrative setting. A basic scientist conducts a series of studies and tries to replicate them and do statistical analyses of various sorts. A clinician tries to draw conclusions about a patient and has to act because there's a sick patient. Administrators sometimes have to make decisions on the basis of degrees of certainty that would appall laboratory scientists.

I am not the kind of person who wants to know more and more about a smaller and smaller thing. In my area, neuroendocrinology, the field was splitting rather than lumping. I wasn't going to hang in there looking at very small pieces of a very large story. I'm much more interested in how things fit together. Science will have to turn itself around one of these days and move in the other direction, but it isn't doing it at the moment.

On the other hand, I use all same values and ways of thinking I learned as a scientist—science prepared me well for being an administrator.

AWIS: *How do others view you as a woman executive?*

RAMALEY: My actions are probably interpreted differently because I'm a woman. I have some difficulty dealing with older men who are leaders in the community and with people on executive committees and boards who are not accustomed to having women in positions of authority or leadership. Some men have no problem with that at all as far as I can tell, but others seem to feel awkward.

66

When the interactions do work, they really work because the differences of perspective and background can open up options that neither I nor my male colleagues would necessarily think of by ourselves. I believe in the importance of teams of men and women, majority and minority, working together, because if you fight your way past the misunderstandings to some mutual appreciation and respect, you can be a very powerful group.

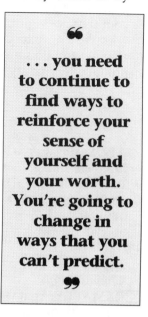

66

... you need to continue to find ways to reinforce your sense of yourself and your worth. You're going to change in ways that you can't predict.

99

It's important to learn your colleagues' styles when you take on a new role. Once in Albany during a particularly difficult budget year, I worked with a male associate whom I trusted and with whom I enjoyed working. He learned that sometimes I cry in exasperation as a way of releasing emotion, and I learned that he pounded the table for the same reason. After this, we did not misread each others' emotional cues. If you work with people different from yourself, you have to be willing to expose yourself, talk about those differences, and learn from them.

Since only a few women have headed campuses, I find that people often don't know how to respond to me. They wonder: Is she the way she is because she is a woman in that position?

AWIS: How have you balanced your personal and professional commitments?
RAMALEY: There were constraints with the ages of my two sons and how much disruption I was willing to create in their lives. The move from Albany to Kansas occurred after my older son finished high school, since I had made an agreement with him that I would not move once he started high school. I told my younger son that, after his freshman year, I wouldn't move until he finished high school, and I honored that commitment—I moved to Oregon after he graduated.

AWIS: What would be your advice to a young woman thinking of embarking on a scientific career?
RAMALEY: Keep talking to people who are a little further along whatever path you're on because they're very helpful in encouraging you. I think that many women in scientific careers are still being eroded by their daily interactions with their male colleagues, and

it's important that such women have ways to rebuild themselves. Also, the problems don't go away. You should not think there's a safe zone ahead. The problems don't end when you get your first position or tenure, so you need to continue to find ways to reinforce your sense of yourself and your worth.

You're going to change in ways that you can't predict. Expect change, and do something with it when it happens, because it can produce very satisfying and fulfilling career options.

This advice follows for administrative and managerial as well as science careers.

AWIS: May women changing from a specific academic or industrial field to administration contact you?
RAMALEY: Yes. They may write to me at the Office of the President, Portland State University, PO Box 751, Portland, OR 97207-0751.

AWIS: What (or who) was the greatest help in turning you toward administration?
RAMALEY: That would be the Administrative Graduate Council at University of Nebraska, which helped us learn how to work and to differ, how to talk productively and to handle various answers.

AWIS: What (or who) was the greatest help in keeping you in administration?
RAMALEY: Once I discovered what an excellent fit it was for me, nothing could have deterred me. It was, however, originally hard to pull out of research. My first major mentor was Stephen Sample, then at Nebraska, now president of the University of Southern California. Other friends and colleagues, too numerous to mention, were also essential. Also, I should mention the collegiality I enjoyed on the academic council of the National Association of State Universities and Land Grant Colleges between 1982–1987.

AWIS: What (or who) was the worst hurdle in changing from research to administration. How did you overcome this barrier?
RAMALEY: The really hard part was in learning to make an effective case for yourself as someone who could be responsible for people and budgets on a large scale. The single greatest help for me in this area was the American Council on Education's Forum Fellowship program.

Helen Rodríguez-Trías, M.D.
Pediatrician, Consultant, and Public Health Activist

B.S. in premedicine, University of Puerto Rico   1957
M.D., University of Puerto Rico, School of Medicine   1960

"I'm bilingual and bicultural because my childhood was spent in both New York and Puerto Rico," *said Rodríguez-Trías, who, after moving back and forth between the two places, graduated from high school in New York and then entered the University of Puerto Rico.*

Disturbed by student riots at the University, Rodríguez-Trías left school after her first year, moved to New York, and married at 19. After seven years of marriage and three children, however, she and her husband decided to return to Puerto Rico so that she could finish her degree. "There was an intellectual need to find something else," *Rodríguez-Trías recalls,* "but there was also a feeling of powerlessness as a young mother in a low-income family. Puerto Rico made it possible for me to return to school because it was easy for a good student to get scholarships."

After earning her undergraduate and advanced degrees, Rodríguez-Trías remained on the University of Puerto Rico's faculty for the next 10 years, doing research and teaching as well as directing services for newborns at the university hospital. A move back to New York in 1970 focused her career on social pediatrics, and her years (1970–1974) as director of pediatrics at Lincoln Hospital, a classic inner-city hospital, sensitized her to the need for changes in public policy. Rodríguez-Trías continued at Lincoln as a half-time attending physician while accepting appointments as associate professor of social medicine at the Sophie Davis Center, City College of New York, and at the Albert Einstein College of Medicine, Yeshiva University. She was also an associate professor of clinical pediatrics at the University of Medicine and Dentistry of New Jersey.

In addition to her practice and teaching, Rodríguez-Trías served on numerous city and national boards related to social pediatrics and public health. She became involved in AIDS work in 1985 and from 1988 to 1989 was medical director of the AIDS Institute, New York State Department of Health. Since moving to California in 1989, Rodríguez-Trías has been a consultant in developing and evaluating health programs, particularly those focusing on primary care and the human immunodifficiency virus. As president-elect and president of the American Public Health Association, Rodríguez-Trías became a frequent coast-to-coast commuter (1991–1992).

Rodríguez-Trías married Edward Gonzalez, Jr., in 1987. She has four adult children—two daughters, both scientists, and two sons from a previous marriage.

AWIS: *What are the most important characteristics for which to search in mentors or other advisors?*

RODRÍGUEZ-TRÍAS: A mentor should be someone who is herself accomplished but who is not threatened by others and therefore can be nurturing. This quality is extremely important, because the thrust in science has been so much on individual achievement, publications, and moving up the career ladder that it's easy to become competitive. Men or women who are excessively competitive cannot be good mentors because, consciously or unconsciously, they discourage younger people.

AWIS: *What would be your advice to a young woman thinking of embarking on a scientific career?*

RODRÍGUEZ-TRÍAS: Do it! Don't be deterred by the many discouraging voices you will hear. Also, don't be intimidated by the word "science." It's important for women to see that science is a body of knowledge and a set of tools. You can use science to probe reality and to expand the frontiers of knowledge in many areas, including those we have yet to define.

AWIS: *How have you balanced your personal and professional commitments?*

RODRÍGUEZ-TRÍAS: I wouldn't recommend it, but I had a baby during my internship. The balance between my personal and professional life has always been precarious. My advice to younger women is to choose well in your mate. Choose someone who is not going to be threatened by your growth and who is also growing. Also, be prepared to renegotiate at every stage. If you want children, be sure that your spouse is willing and able to be an active parent.

AWIS: *What made you decide to go into science? Into your particular field?*

RODRÍGUEZ-TRÍAS: I have liked science ever since I was a child. I can remember reading a comic strip that had an astronomy corner. When I was about eight years old, I told my aunt that I wanted to be an astronomer, thinking I was going to be looking up at the skies and discovering new planets. My aunt was crucial in my early years because she took care of me while my mother worked. When other relatives came over, she would tell them "Helen's going to be an astronomer!" She and my mother were both school teachers and very invested in learning. By the time I got into high school, even though I was good at physics, I decided I wanted to work more directly with people. Medicine seemed a natural choice.

AWIS: What, so far, do you see as the most rewarding aspect of your career?

RODRÍGUEZ-TRÍAS: One of the more rewarding aspects of my career has been the direct appreciation I've received. I don't mean just from patients but also from students and coworkers. The prestige and power that come from being respected in the later stages of your career mean that people will listen to you, that you can be persuasive.

AWIS: Do you notice differences between the way men and women approach a task?

RODRÍGUEZ-TRÍAS: Stereotypically, men tend to approach tasks in a more concrete, structured way, while women tend to see the totality of the task and do not necessarily choose to do step one first.

In this respect, my husband and I are opposites, but not in the way you might expect. He's far more intuitive, and, because of my training, I approach a problem in a much more structured way.

AWIS: How have your race and gender affected your career?

RODRÍGUEZ-TRÍAS: I think there has always been a wall of racism within the power structure in subtle and not so subtle ways, even though my colleagues are not necessarily guilty. People's ideology somehow makes them distort others' realities.

People see you not as you are but as worse (or better) than you are because of their prejudices about you. In my case, I can't say objectively that racism has kept me from getting promoted or other achievements. I have always felt, however, that I had a lot of explaining to do. I have had to tell administrators that these were *my* experiences in *this* community. I had to work to educate people.

AWIS: May women starting out in your field contact you for guidance?

RODRÍGUEZ-TRÍAS: Women may contact me by phone at (408) 338-2369 during business or evening hours, Pacific time.

AWIS: *What (or who) was the greatest help in turning you toward science?*
RODRÍGUEZ-TRÍAS: I was in a Catholic school and had very good science teachers in the first four grades. I knew I was interested in science from a young age.

AWIS: *What (or who) was the greatest help in keeping you in the field?*
RODRÍGUEZ-TRÍAS: My mother was very important. She was disheartened when I dropped out of school to get married. She told me, "Marriages may come and go. Get your degree. Be independent." It took me years to come around, but I'm glad she saw me back in school and doing well before she died.

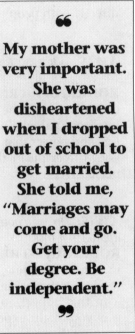

> **"**
> **My mother was very important. She was disheartened when I dropped out of school to get married. She told me, "Marriages may come and go. Get your degree. Be independent."**
> **"**

AWIS: *What (or who) was the worst hurdle in entering science? How did you overcome this barrier?*
RODRÍGUEZ-TRÍAS: We were a low-income family, but, with scholarships, the biggest hurdle wasn't money. Instead, it was the feeling that I had no right to go back to school with small children at home. It meant I was going to be doing my homework in the evenings rather than helping them with theirs. I remember asking a psychology professor why my little boy wasn't talking as early as his sisters had and being told, "Maybe it's because you're not in the home." That kind of pressure and the resulting guilt were very hard to take.

Nina Matheny Roscher, Ph.D.
Chemistry Professor and Chair

B.S. in chemistry, University of Delaware   1960
Ph.D. in chemistry, Purdue University   1964

Roscher originally hoped to study math, but, having been told early that girls don't do that, she opted for chemistry. Upon receiving her Ph.D. in the 1960s, she looked for employment, but she could find no one in industry or government interested in hiring a woman, "who was just going to get married and have kids," to work in any chemical field. On a temporary basis, she accepted a couple of dead-end jobs—one running  *labs at a university, another in quality control at a soft drink company.*

Finally, in 1968, Roscher found a job teaching at Douglass College, the women's college of Rutgers University. She later took on a deanship at Douglass, serving from 1971 to 1974, when she joined the staff of American University in Washington, D.C.

There she has remained, as professor in and, since 1990, chair of the chemistry department, with the exception of the two years she spent on leave at the National Science Foundation working to improve undergraduate science education.

Roscher has been active in mentoring women in science and has worked in special programs geared to helping people who want to return to school after years of work.

She has been married to David M. Roscher since 1964.

AWIS: *Can you think of any instances of gender discrimination against women science students?*

ROSCHER: There were about 9 women and 450 men teaching in the chemistry department at Purdue—and all students there took chemistry. The women chemistry graduate students taught the women undergraduates—mostly home economics majors—organic or quantitative labs especially tailored for them.

The male graduate students taught everyone else.

This was in the early 1960s; things have admittedly changed a lot. But that kind of treatment was everywhere then, and no one thought it was wrong.

AWIS: *How have you balanced your personal and professional commitments?*

ROSCHER: One aspect has changed a lot: There is more sharing of domestic work by couples where both the men and women work. Several of my graduate students have children, and generally their husbands are supportive. One person takes the child to day care, and the other picks her up. It's not totally the woman's responsibility.

My husband has always been very supportive of what I do: He listens to me expound when I'm upset and recognizes that I may not always be home for dinner. That has been important in my success as an administrator and a faculty member because it's an irregular lifestyle. I initially made moves in support of his career, and he later made moves in support of mine. He's my best friend.

If a woman has a "significant other" who is not supportive, it can be difficult and stressful for both of them: They either get divorced, or she gives up her career.

AWIS: What, so far, do you see as the most rewarding aspect of your career?
ROSCHER: I do science because I think it's fun. I enjoy working in the laboratory. I like teaching, working with people, and solving problems. It's important to like science if you're going to go into it, because science requires a big time commitment.

AWIS: May women starting out in your field contact you for guidance?
ROSCHER: Sure. They may call at (202) 885-1750 or write me at the Department of Chemistry, American University, Washington, DC 20016-8014.

AWIS: What (or who) was the greatest help in turning you toward science?
ROSCHER: My high school chemistry teacher.

AWIS: What (or who) was the greatest help in keeping you in the field?
ROSCHER: Although my family always told me I could succeed at whatever I wanted, and I am grateful for their support, my own stubbornness is the real answer.

AWIS: What (or who) was the worst hurdle in entering science? How did you overcome this barrier?
ROSCHER: Probably not being able to find a job after I finished my Ph.D. Any job is better than no job—I overcame this state by taking an interim job in industry and, then, going to New Jersey, which my husband and I chose because there were *hundreds* of chemical companies located there. *One* of them should want me.

Instead, Douglass heard of me, an *organic chemist,* and hired me to replace a woman who was not getting tenure. My assignment was to teach large classes in *quantitative analysis.* That, in itself, was no small hurdle, but I got over it.

Vera C. Rubin, Ph.D.
Astronomer and Staff Scientist

B.A. in astronomy, Vassar College 1948
M.A. in astronomy, Cornell University 1951
Ph.D. in astronomy, Georgetown University 1954

Rubin has maintained her enthusiasm for and preoccupation with astronomy since she first looked at the night sky.* As she was growing up, her father encouraged her interest in many ways.

After receiving her doctorate, Rubin spent another 10 years at Georgetown before accepting a position in 1965 at the Carnegie Institution where she

is now a staff scientist in the astronomy section of the Department of Terrestrial Magnetism. Rubin's work, focusing on the motion of stars in galaxies, was recently highlighted in a Public Broadcasting System documentary, The Astronomers.

Rubin, with only 69 other women, numbers among the 1634 elected members of the National Academy of Sciences. She has received several honorary degrees.

Her commitment to women's issues is illustrated by her efforts to help women scientists cope with discrimination. She spends "an enormous amount of my time running, on the side, a business called 'trying to help young women.' "

Rubin married Robert J. Rubin in 1948. Their four children, born in 1950, 1952, 1956, and 1960, all went into science—two are astronomers, one a geologist, and one a mathematician.

AWIS: *Have you ever experienced gender discrimination as a woman in science?*
RUBIN: You show up at a meeting, and you're the only woman there. Every word you utter is remembered in a way that a young man's isn't. I survived. The real tragedy is the hundreds of women who would have made outstanding astronomers but never made it because they were discouraged all along.

---

*This interview follows up on an earlier discussion with Rubin and her daughter, astronomer Judy Young, appearing in the 1986, September/October *AWIS Newsletter*, 15(5), 8–12.

Academic and professional circles are still male dominated. You will go through three or four days of meetings and never once hear the word "her" used. Every scientist is "he." Maybe this is just language, but after a few days, it becomes very annoying. I write a letter every year to the National Academy of Sciences objecting to something they have just sent me in which all the personal pronouns are masculine. I think we're kidding ourselves if we don't realize that science is still a male-dominated profession, and some of the males enjoy this dominance.

AWIS: *Can you think of any instances of gender discrimination against women science students?*
RUBIN: I meet an enormous number of young women who tell me that when they entered college they intended to study science, which probably means they took high school math and physics. They are already unusual women because they've taken the high school courses. But when they entered college, they were not nurtured and became convinced that they weren't meant to do science. I don't think they were meant to do something else; they lacked a nurturing atmosphere.

AWIS: *What are your beliefs on affirmative action?*
RUBIN: I believe in affirmative action, but it is almost a dirty word right now: Young male postdocs are scared of not getting jobs. All affirmative action means is that women should have equal treatment. When you have a department that is virtually all male, with an all-male committee choosing the next faculty member, they don't even know who the young women are. All-male search committees shouldn't be allowed to look for new faculty. They try, but they just can't do the job that would be done if half the committee were women. I think academia is failing in that aspect.

AWIS: *How have you balanced your personal and professional commitments?*
RUBIN: I had two children before receiving my Ph.D. and two afterwards. I had no help except my husband and my parents. I did my thesis work and my research at home from about 7:00 at night to 2:00 in the morning. I put the children down to nap at the same time, regardless of their age. I didn't do anything but take care of the children, work, and study. It was very hard, but I wanted to do it, and it was do-able. My husband was very supportive.

When I went to Carnegie, I told them I wanted to go home at 3:00 every day. They offered me a job and a salary that was less than two-thirds of my salary as an assistant professor at Georgetown. I took the job and went home at 3:00 every day until our last child was in high school. I worked at home: I probably worked 18 hours many days and on weekends, but I was paid two-thirds salary. We got a new director in the early 1970s. He came to me shortly after he took over and said, "Every time we review the salary structure, your low salary is an embarrassment to us. When you want to become a full-time employee, tell us."

I was writing the Andromeda work then, and by Monday afternoon I realized I had worked 60 hours since we had spoken. I told him I was ready to be called a full-time employee, but I was still going home at 3:00 PM. My salary really jumped.

AWIS: What would you like to see change about preparation for the science profession today?
RUBIN: It seems to me that the real changes have to take place at the high school level. Until you have a larger number of women taking physics and calculus courses in high school, you won't find them in science further on. There's undoubtedly a lot of peer pressure at the high school level against girls achieving in math and science.

AWIS: What would be your advice to a young woman thinking of embarking on a scientific career?
RUBIN: Tell young women (and men) that they can do it, that they are no different now than people who made important contributions were in their youth. Few at age 18 think they are going to make an important contribution to science. If you persist, get a good education, learn what you have to know, and get a meaningful degree, then it's pretty much up to you.

Don't let anyone discourage you. There will be all sorts of episodes that could be very discouraging. Hang in there.

AWIS: May women starting out in your field contact you for guidance?
RUBIN: Yes, they may call at (202) 686-4370 or write me at the Carnegie Institution, 5241 Broad Branch Road, NW, Washington, DC 20015.

AWIS: What (or who) was the greatest help in turning you toward science?
RUBIN: The sky. Watching the sky.

AWIS: What (or who) was the greatest help in keeping you in the field?
RUBIN: Geoffrey and Margaret Burbridge who, early in my career, when I had four young children and when I had not begun to move in astronomical circles, treated me as a real astronomer. Their support and encouragement gave me essential confidence.

AWIS: What (or who) was the worst hurdle in entering science? How did you overcome this barrier?

RUBIN: Being a student and a mother at the same time and finding adequate care for the children. It was harder to do so then than now, but it was a constant worry and kept me being paid and treated as a part-timer for many, many years.

M. Antoinette Schiesler, Ph.D.
Academic Dean, Chemist, and Science Educator

B.A. in chemistry, College of Notre Dame of Maryland	1967
M.S. in science and science education, University of Tennessee at Knoxville and Oak Ridge Associated Universities	1968
Ph.D. in science education and chemistry, University of Maryland	1977

Schiesler traveled a long, difficult road to arrive at her present position as dean of academic affairs at Cabrini College (Pennsylvania). She has

weathered discrimination not only as a woman but also as an African American and as a nun. Raised by a single mother who instilled in her a reverence for education, Schiesler persevered to achieve her goals. She began her collegiate education in 1957, while teaching elementary school, by taking classes nights and Saturdays. After 10 years, she received her bachelor's degree in chemistry, a subject she taught at the convent's college. There, she also taught calculus—despite her earlier math anxiety.

During the course of her career, Schiesler has designed programs to aid minority students in academic trouble, worked as a program manager at the National Science Foundation, and held various teaching posts.

In 1972, before receiving her doctorate, she left the convent. She married Robert A. Schiesler in 1973.

AWIS: What are the most important characteristics for which to search in mentors or other advisors?

SCHIESLER: Ask yourself: Am I getting the same treatment from my advisor as are other people, and am I able to meet with him/her when I need to? Find out about that person's status in the institution: Is s/he well respected? Does s/he publish a lot?

AWIS: *What are the differences between undergraduate and graduate advisors?*

SCHIESLER: We try to get undergraduates through four years of college and into the "real" world. We assist them with the transition from high school to college, prepare them for graduation, and help them determine what they want to do.

At the graduate level, students should have some idea of what they want to do. At this point, they need help getting through the dissertation or thesis research and writing. If you come to graduate school not writing very well, you have a big problem that must be dealt with immediately.

AWIS: *What are your observations about the reactions of white women and women of color to racial issues?*

SCHIESLER: In the summertime, I'm a visiting faculty member at Bryn Mawr College for the Higher Education Resources Services (HERS) Institute, which every year schedules a session on diversity. This meeting is difficult for both the black women *and* the white women. In 1986, for instance, one black became extremely angry about the film we were showing and lashed out, upsetting the whites.

"We are *not* racist. Why is she *calling* us racist?" they asked.

When black women get angry, white women react with fear.

I began examining myself: Why am I not angry? I've acknowledged: Yes, there is racism. It's in the university, the college, and the church, and it is not going to go away anytime soon. If you're angry, fine, but you've got to work through that anger and get on with the rest of your life. Getting bogged down with the anger, saying, "Look what's been done to me," won't get you anywhere. Take that anger and use it to better yourself.

If a job is intolerable, and you're so angry that you can't work, then leave. There's no sense staying and being a martyr. But white women have to accept that black women can be angry.

AWIS: *What would be your advice to a young woman thinking of embarking on a scientific career?*

SCHIESLER: First of all, be good in math. Get over math anxiety. When I saw how math solved chemistry problems, and how important it was to chemistry, I began to understand the beauty of it.

People can learn a lot on their own. I want to see more of that intellectual confidence in women. I had to learn trigonometry and calculus on my own because I didn't have them in high school. I overcame my math anxiety and learned both subjects—so can others.

AWIS: How do you like your current administrative position?
SCHIESLER: On some days, I like my job very much; on others, I find myself faced with so many decisions that I feel none of them has received the appropriate time. I think to excel as a dean, you have to be well-organized, thick-skinned, a skilled manager, and a leader. You need good communication skills and flexibility. Most important: you have to have a sense of humor.

AWIS: How have your race and gender affected your career?
SCHIESLER: I constantly feel the pressure of having to be better because of my race and gender, so I push.

In Tennessee, the discrimination was overt. . . I was a black sister in full habit, and people had never seen anything like me before. Children walked into poles because they were so busy looking at me.

AWIS: May women starting out in your field contact you for guidance?
SCHIESLER: Yes. Have them write me at Cabrini College, Office of Academic Affairs, 610 King of Prussia Road, Radnor, PA 19087.

AWIS: What (or who) was the greatest help in turning you toward science and mathematics?
SCHIESLER: My high school chemistry teacher, Sr. Frances, in Baltimore.

AWIS: What (or who) was the greatest help in keeping you in the field?
SCHIESLER: Dr. Marjorie Gardner, who died about two years ago. She was the first woman professor in the chemistry department at Maryland and my advisor. A magnificent woman. She finished her career at the Lawrence Hall of Science in Berkeley.

AWIS: What (or who) was the worst hurdle in entering science and math? How did you overcome this barrier?
SCHIESLER: My religious community. When I wanted to go into science, the community was opposed, and the community usually chose our majors. Chemistry was not the kind of field sisters should go into. In addition, the community wanted me to teach in elementary school (the order had only one high school). I said "chemistry," and I said "high school." I was very docile, then, but somehow I won.

Faith Spotted Eagle, M.A.

Consultant

B.A. in sociology, University of South Dakota	1973
M.A. in counseling, University of South Dakota	1974

Spotted Eagle, a Native American of the Yankton Dakota tribe, owns her own Spokane, Washington-based consulting firm for human services and environmental organizational leadership.

Spotted Eagle's father raised her not only to be reverent toward her tribe's beliefs and culture but also to understand the importance of learning how to succeed and work within the majority culture. While in high school, she decided on a career as a medical technologist; however, her precollege teachers, unable to recognize that she did not learn in most students' linear manner, channelled her into general math classes. When faced with science courses at Black Hills State College, Spotted Eagle was hampered by her inadequate math training, and, as a result, performed poorly in science and left after two-and-a-half years.

She returned to the reservation. There, her father encouraged her to attend the University of South Dakota, where she enrolled and graduated with a baccalaureate and a master's. She was fortunate to discover a special services program at the university that encouraged Native Americans to pursue advanced degrees. She attributes the confidence necessary to her success to the work of a wise and supportive counselor, who encouraged her to pursue graduate work.

Spotted Eagle's work involves training Native Americans in organizational leadership. Often, her counseling involves issues of environmental ethics—Native-American lands are still being threatened with development. Spotted Eagle is a board member of First Nation, an organization that facilitates indigenous small businesses and economic development.

Spotted Eagle married Brian Collins in 1975. They have two children (born in 1976 and 1981).

AWIS: *What are the most important characteristics for which to search in mentors or other advisors?*
SPOTTED EAGLE: I think that the most important thing is an ability to listen. When I went to the University of South Dakota, the

counselors listened. Second, a sense of humor is important. I remember that the counselors at the university teased me. Even though I had failed at Black Hill State, it felt good to laugh about the experience, and I realized that it wasn't so painful after all. Last, a counselor should not be judgmental.

AWIS: What would be your advice to a young woman thinking of embarking on a scientific career?
SPOTTED EAGLE: I would encourage her and let her know what a fine choice she had made. Then I'd have her tell me about how she arrived at that choice and what she was thinking about, rather than immediately launching into a counseling or mentoring session. Listening first makes you able to see a person's existing strengths and to encourage, support, and mentor her.

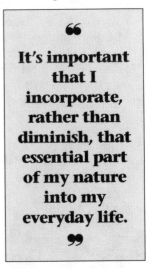

> **It's important that I incorporate, rather than diminish, that essential part of my nature into my everyday life.**

AWIS: Are both urban and rural environments comfortable for you?
SPOTTED EAGLE: I live in Spokane, which is an urban area, but I spend a vast amount of time on the reservation, and when I go back, I feel revived, empowered, and refocused. The surroundings are the structure for my value system. Going back to the reservation validates who I am, and it reminds me of how I formed my world view. It's important that I continue to incorporate that essential part of my nature rather than diminish it into what I am doing in my everyday life. The other thing that I do to keep myself in touch is spend time outdoors; I do a lot of walking and hiking.

In years past, some people said that Indians couldn't cope with the outer world. That wasn't the point. If a scientist went onto our reservation, s/he probably couldn't cope either.

AWIS: Do you notice differences between the way men and women approach a task?
SPOTTED EAGLE: Yes. I think that women verbalize more and make many statements such as "I feel." Men don't spend a lot of time talking about their emotions, unless the arena is appropriate.

I was raised by my father, and a lot of times in problem-solving situations in everyday life, my father would go ahead and act without discussion. There was a time to talk, however, and, for me and my father, that time was when we were hunting together.

AWIS: How have your race and gender affected your career?

SPOTTED EAGLE: When I was growing up, probably one of the most powerful influences on my life was my father. He clung very strongly to his native value system, but he translated it for me for use in today's age as much as he could. One of the things that he told me was that, as an Indian, I have to try harder than average. I would be in a world whose rules are nearly all dictated by white people. Under this hardship and adversity, one can gain understanding, strength, and insight about oneself that might not have been available otherwise. I certainly have experienced gender discrimination, but my upbringing has helped me to understand and deal with it.

My father was a man who wasn't afraid to cry and talk, and he also showed me when it was time to be strong.

AWIS: What would you like to see change about preparation for the science profession today?

SPOTTED EAGLE: Number one, identify role models who can come into the classroom. Also, universities and institutions should invest financially in leadership programs like the one that I benefited from at the University of South Dakota.

AWIS: May women starting out in your field contact you for guidance?

SPOTTED EAGLE: Of course. They may write to me at East 4328 Seventeenth Avenue, Spokane, WA, 99223.

AWIS: What (or who) was the greatest help in turning you toward science?

SPOTTED EAGLE: Definitely my father.

AWIS: What (or who) was the greatest help in keeping you in the field?

SPOTTED EAGLE: My college counselor, who worked closely with me and encouraged me to go for my master's.

AWIS: What (or who) was the worst hurdle in entering science? How did you overcome this barrier?

SPOTTED EAGLE: The worst hurdle was the linear thinking I was expected to do in high school and at my first college. It would have taken a real mind shift for me to think that way.

I thought I knew what science meant, but when I got into actually teaching some of it, I learned to my relief that it actually meant something very different.

Judith S. Sunley, Ph.D.
Mathematician and Executive Officer

B.S. in mathematics, University of Michigan   1967
M.S. in mathematics, University of Michigan   1968
Ph.D. in mathematics, University of Maryland   1971

As a girl in school, Sunley enjoyed and was adept at both math and the physical sciences. When she enrolled in the University of Michigan's

unified science honors program, however, she discovered that she enjoyed manipulating numbers and ideas more than doing laboratory work. After completing her graduate work in mathematics, Sunley joined the faculty at American University, where she divided her time between teaching and research.

Advancing in a field heavily dominated by men, Sunley came to the National Science Foundation in 1980. She is presently executive officer of the Mathematical and Physical Sciences Directorate, where her administrative duties call for close contact with mathematics and its community.

She is married to Emil Sunley. They have two daughters and one son (born in 1972, 1974, and 1975).

AWIS: *What career opportunities has your background afforded you?*
SUNLEY: The career path of mathematicians seldom includes the kind of postdoctoral experience you find in physics, chemistry, or other areas. It is more traditional to move into some form of faculty position. Those with degrees from the best schools sometimes go into the equivalent of postdoctoral positions, but they're called "research instructorships" or "research faculty" posts. They comprise half-time teaching and half-time research positions.

AWIS: *How would you describe your work as a government administrator?*
SUNLEY: I started my work at the National Science Foundation as a program officer—I was deputy division director for three years and division director until June, 1992. In these positions, I handled grant proposals, first in the area of algebra and number theory and then across the mathematical sciences.

The individual program officers make recommendations on grant proposals. As division director, my responsibility was two- or threefold: First, I conferred with colleagues about their recommendations on the disposition of the grant proposals. Second, I worked with the mathematics community to develop plans for the future. Third, I took those plans and argued for them in terms of budget preparation.

In my current position as executive officer, I balance the budget and deal with the planning arguments of the five divisions comprising the mathematical and physical sciences.

Expanding my knowledge to learn about other disciplines has been very exciting.

AWIS: *How have you balanced your personal and professional commitments?*

SUNLEY: I had my children early in my years as a faculty member. The first year or two, I had a variety of different arrangements, but from the time the youngest was a year old until two years ago I had the same housekeeper. I was very lucky, but many of my friends were not so fortunate.

Once your kids reach the age of three, many public school systems provide some form of day care that you can hook on to. The most difficult part is the couple of years when the children are not able to care for themselves.

When you have two or three children, if you can afford to put them in day care then you can probably afford to have a single person come into your home, and that usually works best.

I deliberately waited to have a family until I finished my Ph.D. because I thought I was unlikely to finish the Ph.D. if I had children first, mostly because of the time demands.

I would encourage women, however, not to drop out if they have children during graduate school. If graduate students expect to complete their degrees sometime in the near future, they're better off taking a few courses, attending seminars, and keeping in touch.

AWIS: *What are the most important characteristics for which to search in mentors or other advisors?*

SUNLEY: Ideally, you should be associated with the best person in your area in the department. Watch out, however: In any field of science, some people are doing research that is off on narrow tracks. If such a person becomes your dissertation advisor, you'll find it much more difficult to branch out and move in new directions.

In terms of a mentor, you want to look for someone with whom you're comfortable talking. That person can be difficult to find.

AWIS: Has the process of networking with others in your field proved valuable to you?

SUNLEY: Once you are working on a dissertation you should make an effort to go to scientific meetings and make presentations. Talk to your advisor and find out what local or regional meetings you could attend where you could meet people who are interested in the same kinds of issues.

AWIS: What is the value of professional associations?

SUNLEY: Professional organizations like AWIS provide points of contact and help an individual become recognized in ways not often possible through large national professional societies.

AWIS: Is there a single pattern that a woman interested in a research career in science should best follow?

SUNLEY: The Department of Education has done a study: Once factors such as gender, ethnic background, and level of education are discounted, salary differences are explained by the number of undergraduate math courses taken.

AWIS: May women starting out in your field contact you for guidance?

SUNLEY: Sure. Have them write to the Mathematical and Physical Sciences Directorate, National Science Foundation, 1800 G Street, NW, Washington, DC 20550.

AWIS: What (or who) was the greatest help in turning you toward mathematics?

SUNLEY: My freshman calculus instructor, D. J. Lewis, who took time to talk to me and other female students to encourage us to keep on with our studies in math.

AWIS: What (or who) was the greatest help in keeping you in the field?

SUNLEY: Lewis helped there too, but it was fundamentally my own stubbornness.

AWIS: What (or who) was the worst hurdle in entering mathematics? How did you overcome this barrier?

SUNLEY: There were a couple of instances in graduate school where the thrust, spoken or unspoken, was that in spite of the grades I had earned, I didn't have "what it takes" to complete a dissertation in the field. As before, my own stubbornness got me through that problem.

Marsha P. Trevilian, B.S.
Engineer

B.S. in mathematics, Longwood College   1975

In elementary and high school Trevilian loved mathematics and, despite a lack of encouragement from teachers and guidance counselors, took every math course open to her, both at the precollege level and later during

her undergraduate years.* Uncertain about the future she wanted to pursue, she followed her friends' example by enrolling in a women's college in Virginia and declaring a major in elementary education. Her dissatisfaction with her choice of field mounted, however, and, by the end of her sophomore year, she changed to mathematics. It proved to be the right move.

Following graduation, she took a position at Union Carbide performing statistical analyses and writing computer programs. Since that time, she has done some graduate work in management science at the University of Tennessee. At present, she works at Martin Marietta Energy Systems in Oak Ridge as an engineer. Trevilian is especially interested in the education of girls in the fields of science and math.

She married Richard C. Trevilian in 1975.

AWIS: *Are you glad to have studied at a women's college?*
TREVILIAN: Attending a small, rural women's college had both pros and cons. Seeing women in student leadership roles became natural; they served as government and class presidents, as team captains, and so forth. The small school environment provided opportunities for individuals to shine both academically and socially and allowed more one-on-one contact than is usual at a large university. There were typically no more than 20 to 30 people in a class. The science labs were limited to a small number of students.

There are also negatives, however. Longwood modeled an ideal, not a real world. When I entered business, I was shocked to find so few women in mathematics and engineering. I was in an environment where men held most leadership positions—just the opposite

---

*This interview follows up on an earlier discussion with Trevilian appearing in the 1988, November/December *AWIS Newsletter, 17*(6), 8–10.

of what I was accustomed to. It took me a while to adapt to working in a male-dominated business world.

AWIS: What is the scientific component of "management science"?

TREVILIAN: Management science or operations research is characterized by a scientific approach to managerial decision making. Useful courses include math, statistics, computer programming, linear programming, queuing theory, and simulation. These quantitative techniques are adapted and applied to decision making—identification, formulation, solution, validation, implementation, and control. Management scientists develop mathematical models and apply the capabilities of computers to the difficult and often unstructured problems confronting managers.

Management science techniques help solve a wide variety of business, industrial, military, and public sector problems. For example, such techniques are useful in transportation systems, such as scheduling airplanes and trains; in managing computer time-sharing systems efficiently, and in selecting a business portfolio. Industrial engineers use management science techniques to study and evaluate production processes and make recommendations that promote efficiency, improve productivity, and reduce costs, primarily in manufacturing.

AWIS: How have you balanced your personal and professional commitments?

TREVILIAN: My husband has always given me a lot of support and encouragement in my career. The biggest problem we've had has been making a decision when one of us has had a job opportunity that would require relocation. When I finished college and we were both looking for jobs, we decided we would take the best first offer. Richard was offered a job in this geographic area, and then I found a position with Union Carbide. Another time, he turned down an offer that involved a move.

Since we have decided not to have children, we are spared the problems encountered by working parents. I never viewed the decision about having children as a choice between motherhood and my career: My husband and I simply do not want to be parents.

AWIS: May women starting out in your field contact you for guidance?

TREVILIAN: They may write me at 209 Nutwood Circle, Knoxville, TN 37922.

AWIS: What (or who) was the greatest help in turning you toward mathematics?

TREVILIAN: My seventh grade math teacher Mrs. Pauline Harris who built upon my interest by bolstering my confidence. When she formed a special math group, she selected me to be among the students who should be part of it.

There have been many others along the way.

AWIS: *What (or who) was the greatest help in keeping you in the field?*
TREVILIAN: The support from my parents—particularly my mother, who encouraged me in my studies, although she had not attended college herself.

AWIS: *What (or who) was the worst hurdle in entering math? How did you overcome this barrier?*
TREVILIAN: A major barrier was that, during the time when I was in college, there just were not many women in math, the field in which I did my degree. When I graduated, I faced cultural barriers— both those in my own mind and those placed by society's attitudes. It was acceptable, on the one hand, to be a *teacher* of math, but, on the other, I was often asked questions like this: *"What* are you going to *do* with math by itself?"

In the workplace, when I started in 1976, there were the usual barriers—again, there were no women.

It's definitely better now. Not only are there more women engineers—it's almost rare to be the only woman in a group of engineers—but also male colleagues are starting to appreciate us now. Before, women had almost to act like men to succeed; now both women's and men's approaches are valued.

Carolyn Ruth Armstrong Williams, Ph.D.
Science Educator

B.S. Tennessee State University, in history	1966
M.A. Northwestern University, in history of science	1972
M.A., Ph.D. Cornell University, in science education, in education	1978

Born in Birmingham, Alabama, Williams attended an all girl high school in Elizabeth, New Jersey, where her mother (a nurse), her father (a teacher and social worker), and her teachers supported her interest in science. Williams and her brothers and sisters all showed talent in the sciences. Two high school science teachers were "wonderful mentors," and she credits them with encouraging her to follow her interests and excel, in contrast to another teacher, who discouraged her.

While working on her doctorate, Williams served as the associate director of the Cornell University Career Center and developed an interest in

helping students with their career planning. After graduation, she was a postdoctoral fellow at Harvard and worked for Paul Tsongas, then U.S. Senator from Massachusetts, for a year. Later, she had a Woodrow Wilson fellowship to study in England.

She next served as assistant vice chancellor for university relations and coordinator of biomedical programs at North Carolina Central University. Since 1987, Williams has been associate professor for the practice of engineering education and assistant dean for minority affairs at Vanderbilt University. As the first woman dean in Vanderbilt's School of Engineering, Williams has been instrumental in greatly increasing the number of minority faculty and students in the school. Williams is in charge of the award-winning minority student summer research program that introduces students to college and to various engineering fields before they begin their freshman year.

Her public service career has been varied and full. Among other activities, she has served on the AWIS executive board and is a member of the National Institutes of Health Minority Biomedical Research Support Advisory Committee.

A committed science educator, Williams enjoys school herself and attends conferences worldwide. Her achievements and awards echo her feeling that "you don't have to be paid to do something to help somebody. Many of my experiences have been supportive," *Williams explains.* "That's why I want to help others."

Williams married James Alvin Williams, Jr., in 1968.

AWIS: *What are the most important characteristics for which to search in mentors or other advisors?*
WILLIAMS: It is most important that a mentor be knowledgeable about your discipline and be someone who's personable and sensitive to your concerns. It also helps immensely if that person is in a position to be of active help, someone whose own career will not be jeopardized if s/he supports you. Personal contact outside of class is important—being invited to that person's home, for instance—be-

cause it gives you a chance to get to know each other personally and not just professionally.

AWIS: How have you balanced your personal and professional commitments?

WILLIAMS: I've been married for 25 years to an unusual person. He has his own career as a metallurgical and mechanical engineer, and he has supported me in my schooling and career. He has been willing to relocate with me in the past, and we have had to have a commuter marriage at times. But we always talk on the phone at least once a day, even when we can see each other only a few times a month.

AWIS: Has the process of networking with others in your field proved valuable to you?

WILLIAMS: Networking is very important, to share information on employment, professional contacts, and other matters.

AWIS: What, so far, do you see as the most rewarding aspect of your career?

WILLIAMS: The most rewarding aspect of my career is seeing students go on and do something with their lives in science. Students need to know that their career possibilities can be virtually endless, and that's how I can help. At Vanderbilt and other engineering schools, there are few women and minorities, and it can therefore be difficult for students to find role models and mentors. The battles will get easier as more women pursue science and engineering careers, but we need to help students while they are fighting their battles.

AWIS: Do you notice differences between the way men and women approach a task?

WILLIAMS: Yes, women and men have different ways of doing things. I think that men may look at things with more tunnel-vision than women. They are not as receptive to newer ways of doing things, especially if suggested by a woman.

AWIS: How have your race and gender affected your career?

WILLIAMS: Race and gender have been a factor for me. Going to a high school where I was the only black was difficult in some respects. In college, I began study as a premed major, but there were major obstacles because of ethnicity, and I changed majors after that. In my position now, however, I feel that the faculty and administration are very supportive.

AWIS: *May women starting out in your field contact you for guidance?*
WILLIAMS: Yes, definitely. They may call at (615) 322-2724 or write me at Vanderbilt University, School of Engineering, Box 1826, Station B, Nashville, TN 37235. I have written articles in *Women in Engineering* and *Minorities in Engineering*, and I always include a statement that students are welcome to contact me if they have problems or questions.

AWIS: *What (or who) was the greatest help in turning you toward science?*
WILLIAMS: Both Hazel Price (a white woman) and Paul Cotroneo (a white male), my high school science teachers, were the greatest help to me when I was not sure of my abilities. As an aside, some of my high school teachers in music and science, including Dr. Price, had doctorates, and that may have influenced my interest in school and helped me to see myself as a college student and then a graduate student.

AWIS: *What (or who) was the greatest help in keeping you in the field?*
WILLIAMS: My Ph.D. faculty advisor and the dean at Cornell were both very influential in helping me to keep working with students in science education.

AWIS: *What (or who) was the worst hurdle in entering science? How did you overcome this barrier?*
WILLIAMS: The high school teacher who did not believe in me was the worst hurdle. It is especially unfortunate that this person was a black female. I was lucky, however, to have other high school teachers who were able to convince me that I could do science.

Students

LaVerne Bitsie, B.A.
Graduate Student in Mathematics

B.A. in mathematics, Fort Lewis College   1992

A graduate student in mathematics at Oklahoma State University, LaVerne Bitsie introduces herself as a Navajo from Tohatchi, New Mexico, of the Towering House People Clan and the Bitter Water Clan. Born and

raised on a Navajo Indian Reservation in New Mexico, Bitsie recalls that, "Someone told me I was good at math when I was in the eighth grade." *She cites a female math teacher in her middle school as her first motivator.*

Bitsie enjoys math because, depending on the numbers plugged into it, one equation can describe different things. In this, math is somewhat like words in Navajo with more than one meaning. "It's another way of communicating," *says Bitsie.*

Bitsie joined the American Indian Science and Engineering Society as an undergraduate and received a lot of encouragement from the native Americans she met through the organization. She also had a woman professor of engineering who encouraged her to pursue her doctorate, and, "who never stopped asking me, 'Where are you going to go to graduate school?' "

At Oklahoma State University, Bitsie hopes to get her master's degree, to teach high school for a few years, and then return to school to get her doctorate. Eventually she would like to teach at a college or university in her native New Mexico.

AWIS: *What are the most important characteristics for which to search in mentors or other advisors?*
BITSIE: Look for someone who is really consistent—who encourages you but doesn't lie to you.

93

AWIS: What would be your advice to a young woman thinking of embarking on a scientific career?
BITSIE: Always find a support group that shares your interests. Surround yourself with success, and seek out people with common goals.

AWIS: How have you balanced your personal and professional commitments?
BITSIE: By combining my personal and professional life and making each a part of the other, I maximize my strengths. Through the American Indian Science and Engineering Society, I met a lot of people in industry and teaching who shared their experiences with me. It helps to hear how they handled being away from home for the first time, and how they use the strengths of the Navajo traditions to their advantage in the regular world.

I encourage my younger sister, who matriculated as a freshman at Oklahoma State University this year, as I entered graduate school.

AWIS: How have your race and gender affected your career?
BITSIE: Being a woman and being a Navajo, I stand out a bit. I have to be a role model and think of the implications for those coming after me. You have something to show other students.

I am one of the first Navajo women to study for a Ph.D. in pure mathematics.

It's a little bit of weight.

AWIS: What would you like to see change about preparation for the science profession today?
BITSIE: I would like to see schools encourage kids to use math earlier. I think elementary school students should be exposed to math. Math is the basis for many technologies that can help people.

In the Indian communities, there is often no water or electricity in homes, and there are sometimes even threats from nuclear waste dumps. Science can inform people both about the nature of such dangers, and, often, how to correct and avoid such problems. Native Americans are encouraged to go to college, and that's good, but they need to see what they can give back to their communities.

AWIS: May women starting out in your field contact you for guidance?
BITSIE: People can contact me by mail at 1815 North Boomer Road, A-22, Stillwater, OK, 74075, and I will answer their questions in depth.

AWIS: *What (or who) was the greatest help in turning you toward mathematics?*

BITSIE: My eighth grade teacher motivated me to enter the field, and my family always assumed that I would go to college. There's a lot to be said for expectations.

AWIS: *What (or who) was the greatest help in keeping you in the field?*

BITSIE: I was back home from school for Christmas break my senior year when I ran into my high school physics professor. When I told him that I was a senior math major, he commented that I probably knew more math than he did. That surprised me and made me realize that, with persistence, you can do anything.

AWIS: *What (or who) was the worst hurdle in entering math? How did you overcome this barrier?*

BITSIE: Being one of the few women in the field. There were only two or three women in most of my classes. I always found it difficult to ask for help. After grudgingly asking several times, however, I realized that people usually would explain.

Jo Ann Eder, Ph.D.

Research Associate in Astronomy

B.A. in mathematics, New York University	1967
M.A. in Indian Education, University of New Mexico	1970
M.S. in astronomy, San Diego State University	1982
Ph.D in astronomy from Yale University	1990

Eder's enthusiasm and love for learning led her to return to science after a hiatus of many years. When she was a child, a great uncle took her out stargazing and gave her books on astronomy to encourage her curiosity about the universe. She began her undergraduate studies in astronomy but completed them with a bachelor's degree in math and a teaching certificate. Then, through the Volunteers in Service to America program, Eder taught high school in Montana on a Native-American reservation for two years.

After earning a master's degree in education, she married Bert P. Eder in 1969 and spent most of the next 10 years raising nine of his children from a previous marriage, born between 1952 and 1963, and a tenth of their own, born in 1971.

95

Her interest in astronomy persisted, and, with only four children remaining at home, she returned to school, first locally for a master's, then to the

East coast for her doctorate. She next did postdoctoral work at the Carnegie Institution in Washington, where she studied galaxies.

Since 1992, Eder has worked as a radio astronomer in the National Astronomy and Ionospheric Center at the Arecibo Observatory in Puerto Rico.

With her youngest child now 21, Eder's child care responsibilities might seem to be lessened. And they are. She notes, however, with a laugh, that the next generation is already an important part of her life.

AWIS: *Why did you decide to go to graduate school?*

EDER: When our youngest child started school in 1976, I went back to school myself. I decided that time was passing and, if I wanted to be an astronomer, I'd better get on with it.

I wasn't really sure I could do it because I'd been out of school for about 15 years; obviously, science changed a lot during that time. So I experimented by going to a local college and taking a year of courses there. I did fine.

AWIS: *Do you have any advice for women pursuing their doctorates?*

EDER: You have to give up *something.* I gave up *everything* except my family and work on my degree. It was three years before I read a book for fun. When everyone else went to bed, I stayed up for at least three more hours.

AWIS: *How have you balanced your personal and professional commitments?*

EDER: With a two-career family, you shuffle and manage and enjoy your kids and hang onto your career. It takes a lot of effort. You just trim your life down to the bare essentials. When I started applying to graduate schools, they laughed at me.

It was discouraging but it didn't stop me. I decided, if I can't do it one way I'll do it another. I went to San Diego State for a terminal master's, a degree geared towards people who want to teach at the junior college level, work for a planetarium, or return to the field after an absence. There, I took the equivalent of a physics major, an undergraduate astronomy major plus a graduate degree in astronomy.

96

Almost everyone assumed that I couldn't complete a degree in astronomy, everyone except the wonderful people at San Diego State. They took in everybody; they gave everybody a chance. There is a real need for more places like that.

AWIS: Why did you decide to go on for your Ph.D.?
EDER: There wasn't much you could do with a master's degree if you didn't want to teach, and I really wanted to do research. I fell in love with the research that went into my master's thesis and I wanted to keep pursuing it.

AWIS: Have you ever experienced gender discrimination as a woman in science?
EDER: It's people's expectations that do damage. During the interviews for graduate school, I answered questions such as, "How do we know that you're not just going to drop out after two or three years? We've had other women with family priorities do that."

College staff would tell you until they were blue in the face that it wasn't discrimination, but they operated with the expectation that a woman couldn't balance all the different roles she had and be successful.

AWIS: What would be your advice to a young woman thinking of embarking on a scientific career?
EDER: Making it in science is 75 percent drive, and 25 percent ability. The greatest thing I learned when I decided to do science is that I could do it if I worked hard.

I know I'm not brilliant. My mind is slow and steady, but I know that if I bang my head against a problem, I'm going to solve it. Just let your brain integrate the information and finally come up with the solution.

AWIS: May women starting out in your field contact you for guidance?
EDER: Yes. We women in astronomy are beginning to network more. Calling is fine—use the telephone ([809] 878-2612) or use E-mail (eder@naic.edu on the Internet system). Or women may write me at the Arecibo Observatory, PO Box 995, Arecibo, PR 00613.

AWIS: What (or who) was the greatest help in turning you toward science?
EDER: I've always been turned on to science. But I had special help and opportunities given me by my uncle, my father, and my high school science teacher James Powers.

AWIS: What (or who) was the greatest help in keeping you in the field?
EDER: My own stubbornness. I had a lot of help, but I also survived a lot of discouragement. My mother was particularly supportive.

AWIS: What (or who) was the worst hurdle in entering science? How did you overcome this barrier?
EDER: For me it was coming back after being out of school for so long. San Diego State was the critical factor in overcoming that hurdle—if they hadn't accepted me and brought me up to snuff, I probably wouldn't even be in science. And my husband and children helped—sometimes. Sometimes they were part of the hurdle.

Theresa R. Gamble, B.S.

Doctoral Candidate in Biophysics

B.S. in electrical engineering, Massachusetts Institute
   of Technology   1988

Gamble's mother, a biochemist, influenced her daughter's taste for math and science from the beginning. Her family's support, seconded by that of a high school counsellor, encouraged Gamble to study at the Massachusetts Institute of Technology, from which she graduated in electrical engineering with a minor in German.

She spent the following year at the Max Planck Institute in Heidelberg, Germany, where, in addition to her job as a systems manager for its minisuper computer, she was introduced to biophysics and learned X-ray diffraction techniques and crystallography. Now a graduate student in biophysics at the University of California, San Francisco, she is studying to become a protein crystallographer, using both X-rays and neutrons.

AWIS: Was your path into science smooth?
GAMBLE: My drive to become a scientist has always been strong, but the types of science I have chosen to pursue have varied. My experience with freshman physics directed me towards electrical engineering. Gaining hands-on experience in X-ray diffraction techniques was one of the deciding factors in my making the transition from engineering to biophysics.

AWIS: *Has the process of networking with others in your field proved valuable to you?*

GAMBLE: Forming and maintaining a network of peers and mentors is absolutely essential. Women graduate students should make sure that they attend scientific meetings and frequently talk to members of their departments. Along with two other women (see also Christine A. Settineri's interview, pages 112–114), I helped to found a support group for women in the life sciences here at the University. Through this group, I've been exposed to women in many scientific fields, both at my level and above. Forming and participating in this group has helped me to build a network from which to seek advice and has helped fight the isolation that many experience in graduate school.

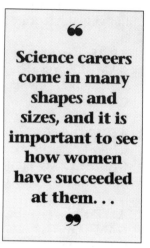

66

Science careers come in many shapes and sizes, and it is important to see how women have succeeded at them. . .

99

AWIS: *Have you ever experienced gender discrimination as a woman in science?*

GAMBLE: There are still professors who tell jokes about their secretary's legs, but those jokes fall flat when more than half the students in the class are women.

Harassment hampers a woman's career and can have hidden consequences down the road. I worked for someone eight or nine years ago who made blatant sexual advances towards me, which I rebuffed. The incident upset me, but I put it out of my mind, because it happened at the end of my research for him, and, more importantly, he held no power over me—for example, he wasn't grading my papers or paying my salary.

However, last year one of my mentors, a woman, suggested that I become acquainted with this person—he now holds a powerful position, she said, and could be helpful in my career. I told her of my reluctance and the reasons for it, and she suggested someone else.

I felt angry and cheated, though, that an avenue had been shut off. For all I know, he may have forgotten the incident, but, if he remembers, interactions with him could be quite awkward, or worse, hazardous to my career, especially if he felt threatened by me in any way. If the harassment had not occurred, I might have been able to make use of him as a positive contact.

AWIS: *How important are mentors and role models?*

GAMBLE: At the Max Planck Institute I was able to use the X-ray crystallography equipment that Rosalind Franklin had owned. It inspired me to think about her using the same equipment to make exciting scientific discoveries. Still more important, however, is meeting women currently doing successful science and seeking out their advice. Science careers come in many shapes and sizes, and it is important to see how women have succeeded at them in light of individual scientific and lifestyle choices.

AWIS: *May women starting out in your field contact you for guidance?*
GAMBLE: Yes. They may either call (415) 225-1172 or write me at Mail Stop 27, 460 Point San Bruno Boulevard, South San Francisco, CA 94080.

AWIS: *What (or who) was the greatest help in turning you toward science?*
GAMBLE: My family. Education was its top priority, and my siblings and I were encouraged to excel in whatever field we chose.

AWIS: *What (or who) was the greatest help in keeping you in the field?*
GAMBLE: The support group I helped found (see above), and the very encouraging head of my department—who is, incidentally, a man.

AWIS: *What (or who) was the worst hurdle in entering science? How did you overcome this barrier?*
GAMBLE: *Entering* wasn't the problem, *staying* is. The field is completely male dominated, and I run into the consequences of that daily.

Professors' *expectations* that women do not intend serious careers but will marry, have children, and disappear from the field are among the worst hurdles. If the people in charge don't expect you to succeed, they may (albeit unconsciously) stop providing opportunities equitably.

The only way I know to overcome this barrier presently is to be aware of it, point it out to others, and to set very high standards for yourself.

Lisa Lucio
Undergraduate Biology Major

Lucio, born in Orange, California, was the youngest of six children in a Mexican-American family. Her father died when she was 11. Because her brothers and sisters were substantially older than she was, Lucio and her

mother spent a great deal of time alone together. "My mother finished high school but never went to college because she was very shy, and none of her friends were going," *Lucio said.* "But my older brothers and sisters were really good examples for me. They all went to college, and two of them are in the sciences. One of my brothers went back East to graduate school, and now he's a geologist."

Lucio went to parochial schools through high school. She knew she wanted to go into science from an early age, but she wasn't sure into which area. When she got to California State University, Fullerton, and looked over the programs, biology seemed to her to encompass most of the other sciences. There, Lucio joined the Minority Biomedical Research Support program. This National Institutes of Health-supported program funds minority undergraduates to work with faculty members on their research projects. Lucio worked two years with Barbara Findlayson-Pitts on the thermal decomposition of compounds. This year, Lucio is working with Christina Goode on the purification and characterization of proteins.

Lucio is currently applying to Ph.D. programs in several graduate schools on the east and west coasts.

AWIS: *What are the most important characteristics for which to search in mentors or other advisors?*
LUCIO: For me, the most important thing is to choose someone who is approachable. It's important for me to be able to go in and ask questions. The person should be easy to talk to, patient, and willing to take time with me. I don't like the idea of working in someone's lab if s/he is not willing to show me what's going on. The person should also have a good sense of humor. I know in research, a lot of times, things don't work out. The advisor should be able to take failures in stride and not get upset. I also want someone who values my input instead of someone who just tells me what to do.

AWIS: *What would be your advice to a young woman thinking of embarking on a scientific career?*

LUCIO: If I were talking to a high school girl, I would say, "Stick with your plan to be a scientist, and try to do the best you possibly can." I had a hard time with chemistry, but I stayed with it. If you don't let a subject intimidate you, it's rewarding to know that you did well on that test or in that course. Don't get discouraged when you don't understand. Get to know your professors, and ask them questions about classwork, jobs, or whatever. I've found my teachers have always been willing to help me.

AWIS: *How have you balanced your personal and professional commitments?*

LUCIO: I'm going to be married soon, and this problem has already come up in choosing a graduate school. My fiancé is giving up a lot so that we can move away, and I can go to graduate school for five years. It's important to take both our needs into consideration when we make the final decision. In choosing a school, we have to decide not only what's good for me but also what would be best for his career.

You give up a lot when you're in science because of the time you have to put into school, but my sense of accomplishment seems worth my sacrifice.

AWIS: *What made you decide to go into science? Into your particular field?*

LUCIO: In high school, I didn't take a lot of science; however, I even enjoyed general science. In fact, I can remember my first science book in elementary school. I wanted to know how things worked or why they were happening.

AWIS: *Has the process of networking with others in your field proved valuable to you?*

LUCIO: Through the university's Minority Biomedical Research Support program, I have had the opportunity to present posters at scientific meetings at several local universities. I also attended the program's national meeting in Washington last year. This conference helped me to present my own data and to see how other people presented theirs. It gave me insight into aspects of a science career involving activities other than sitting in a classroom or doing lab work.

AWIS: *What are the prospects for increasing the numbers of women scientists?*

LUCIO: I think it's important to start in elementary school interesting girls in science and reinforcing the fact that they can do well. When I wasn't very good at math, it seemed as if all the guys raised their hands and did all the hard stuff. If women in science went into the schools, then girls could see that it's possible for *them* to be scientists.

AWIS: *How have your race and gender affected your career?*

LUCIO: Up to this point, my race and gender have worked *for* me. Being able to participate in the minority research program has been very helpful. In applying for graduate school, I have had a number of responses from well-known graduate schools, in part because I am a member of a minority group, but also because my grade point average is high.

I don't know how those factors apply outside of school.

AWIS: *May women starting out in your field contact you for guidance?*

LUCIO: High school students are welcome to contact me at 1307 North Eastwood, Santa Ana, CA 92701.

AWIS: *What (or who) was the greatest help in turning you toward science?*

LUCIO: My older sister and brother were probably the most important influences. By the time I was old enough to remember anything, my older sister was already working as a scientist. I saw my older brother apply to and attend graduate school, so I've already seen the process.

AWIS: *What (or who) was the greatest help in keeping you in the field?*

LUCIO: Getting to know the professors at school and having them encourage me has been very important. Outside of school, my mom and my fiancé have also been very supportive. They always told me that I can do it, that I'm smart.

AWIS: *What (or who) was the worst hurdle in entering science? How did you overcome this barrier?*

LUCIO: Although I went to a private school, I didn't do well in mathematics, so I didn't take many science classes. I can remember going to see a counselor with my mom after I failed geometry. The counselor told us that I could become a secretary or a buyer in a store. Even then, I knew had so much more potential than that. Instead of discouraging me, that conversation motivated me to prove to the school that I could do better. I retook the geometry class and did much better. When I got to the university, I took math classes at a junior college, starting with algebra review and going through calculus. I got *A*s. I guess it was just my age. The analytical parts of math didn't make sense to me the first time.

Leigh Anne Rettinger, B.S.

Engineer, Computer Scientist, and Master's Candidate in Computer Engineering

B.S. in electrical engineering, North Carolina State University
   at Raleigh   1991

Engineering concerns were familiar to Rettinger at an early age: her father was an electrical engineer. She remembers the day he brought an oscilloscope home. "When I saw the patterns on the screen, I decided to

become an engineer," *she summarized. After graduating in her father's field, she took a year-long position with Westinghouse, where she analyzed radar data using computer software while teaching an evening programming class.*

Rettinger is currently pursuing a master's in computer engineering at North Carolina State and working part-time at a computer-aided design company.

AWIS: *Was your path into science smooth?*
RETTINGER: I had a hard time learning fractions in fourth grade, but my father sat down with me and helped me learn them. I needed extra help with math, but I always got through it.

AWIS: *What made you decide to go into science? Into your particular field?*
RETTINGER: As a teenager, I went to a week-long summer camp that exposed me to different types of engineering. We spent a day on aerospace engineering and a day in an electrical engineering laboratory, and I liked them both.

AWIS: *What is the relationship between academic and industrial sciences?*
RETTINGER: I was accepted to graduate school at North Carolina State, but I also got a job offer from Westinghouse to participate in

a graduate development program for engineers straight out of college. The program fell through, so I returned to graduate school. I still could have had certain higher education options through Westinghouse, which encouraged and helped their employees to earn masters' degrees. Most of the younger people took classes at Johns Hopkins, for example.

I may go on to get my Ph.D., so I can work at a university and do some private consulting work. This would give me more flexibility if I have a family: I'll have more power over the hours I work and the time I take off.

There are two women at Westinghouse who had children and shared a job, including salary and benefits, but they arranged it themselves. If industry had a lot of flexibility in terms of maternity leave and day care, I might return to it.

AWIS: How important are mentors and role models?
RETTINGER: The classes I had were large. Unless you made an effort to meet a professor, they didn't get to know you. With 80 students in a class, a single professor couldn't be a mentor for everyone.

AWIS: Has the process of networking with others in your field proved valuable to you?
RETTINGER: It's one of the best ways to get the inside track on a position. You get to know people in the field, and they can give you recommendations, since they know how you work.

AWIS: Can you think of any instances of gender discrimination against women science students?
RETTINGER: About 20 percent of the students in my sophomore classes in science were women, but by my senior year the number had dropped to less than 10 percent.

To become an engineer, you have to be willing to take the harder road. But if you become involved in women's organizations, you can see that you're not alone, you're not the only one going through this.

AWIS: May women starting out in your field contact you for guidance?
RETTINGER: Yes. They may telephone me at (919) 846-1004 or write to me at 11009 Farmwood Drive, Raleigh, NC 27613-6822.

105

AWIS: What (or who) was the greatest help in turning you toward science?

RETTINGER: The support I received from my father at a young age. I have friends who are really smart but who were turned off by math and science early on.

AWIS: What (or who) was the greatest help in keeping you in the field?

RETTINGER: Several undergraduate faculty members reached out and encouraged me to go to graduate school.

AWIS: What (or who) was the worst hurdle in entering science? How did you overcome this barrier?

RETTINGER: The lack of feminine companionship in my college engineering classes made me feel lonely at times. I'd look around, and there were only boys in the classes. While that was frustrating, it also had its pluses—it made me want to excel, to prove myself, to really do well. And I found female friends by joining a sorority.

Nicole Samuels
Undergraduate Biochemistry Major

Born in Los Angeles, Samuels moved to Orange County, California, with her parents and younger brother when she was 11. An unmotivated and indifferent student until sixth grade, she explains that she doesn't blame

"bad people" for her poor record, but "After I moved, it seemed more important to do my best. I tried to excel, and I got better grades. I think it also helped that my parents didn't push me. A lot of kids rebel because their parents push."

When Samuels entered California State University, Fullerton, in 1989, she intended to be a chemistry major because she had liked the subject so much in high school. Her freshman chemistry instructor suggested she apply to the Minority Biomedical Research Support program. After starting to work in biochemistry research as a sophomore, she switched her major to biochemistry. She says of her advisor, biochemistry professor Bruce Weber, "He converts everybody."

Samuels thinks being able to help others will be the most rewarding aspect of her career: "If younger people see a black woman scientist, they'll think," she says, " 'Wow, I can do that!' " Her dream is do research to find less toxic chemotherapeutic drugs for treating cancer. Now a senior, Lucio currently does research involving purifying and labeling enzymes. She is applying to doctoral programs in biochemistry.

AWIS: *What are the most important characteristics for which to search in mentors or other advisors?*

SAMUELS: I look up to two of my male professors here at the university because they seem so wise. But in high school and junior high, all my science teachers were women. *Their* example is really what helped me make the decision to go into science.

AWIS: *What would be your advice to a young woman thinking of embarking on a scientific career?*

SAMUELS: My advice to a high school girl thinking about going into science is this: Don't be scared by certain classes that may seem hard. Those classes are only as hard as you let them be. My motto is you can do anything you want to on this earth, as long as you work hard. You can pass any class as long as you do your work.

AWIS: *How have you balanced your personal and professional commitments?*

SAMUELS: That's the problem. It isn't balanced right now. It's been leaning more towards school. I live at home with my parents, and they think I'm not spending enough time with my family. It's tough. If you want to graduate in a reasonable amount of time, some things get sacrificed. In my case, it's my family. And I'm just an undergraduate! What am I going to do when I go to graduate school?

AWIS: *What are the prospects for increasing the numbers of women scientists?*

SAMUELS: You have to start early. The major thing that determines whether a girl will go into science is her math training. If you don't get through at least second year algebra in high school, you can't go on to calculus. People are scared by math and science because they think they're hard, but if students can do the math, the rest is easy.

AWIS: *How have your race and gender affected your career?*

SAMUELS: People tell me that I won't have any problem getting into graduate school and achieving the career I want because being a black woman is a "double whammy." But I think it will be easier to get *in* than to move *up*. I personally haven't been confronted with any open racism.

AWIS: May women starting out in your field contact you for guidance?
SAMUELS: If a girl who is thinking about science wants to call me, I would be happy to talk to her through the chemistry department at (714) 773-3621. (When I leave for graduate school, the department will know how to reach me.)

AWIS: What (or who) was the greatest help in turning you toward science?
SAMUELS: Mrs. Siefert, my high school chemistry teacher, was one tough lady, and I barely made it out of her class with a *B*. I had never worked so hard in a high school class. That was the first time I really worked. And I liked it!

AWIS: What (or who) was the greatest help in keeping you in the field?
SAMUELS: Participation in the minority biomedical program really cemented everything and gave me direction. Our department is small, compared to the one at a place like California at Los Angeles, but it's close-knit, and you get to know all your professors. Getting to know the other students in the program—10 full members who are paid to do research, unpaid associates, and freshmen affiliates— has also been important. As a freshman, I didn't know anyone and wasn't comfortable asking upperclass students questions. Now, I'm a senior, and I have a freshman "mentee." I've been able to give her useful information about classes and professors that she can't get from her official advisors.

AWIS: What (or who) was the worst hurdle in entering science? How did you overcome this barrier?
SAMUELS: Physics! It wasn't so bad in high school, but when I got to the university, that second semester of physics was awful. I think I had a mental roadblock that made it worse than it actually was. "Why are the guys excelling in this and not the girls?" I wondered. Now I think that the problem was that the terminology was just so new.

I took physics in summer school the first time and got a *C*, but I hadn't learned anything, so I took it over and did better.

Marsha Segerberg, Ph.D.
Postdoctoral Fellow in Neuroscience

B.S. in chemistry, University of Cincinnati — 1972
Ph.D in neuroscience, University of Wisconsin—Madison — 1989

Segerberg began her undergraduate work in chemistry at the University of North Carolina, because she liked the subject, despite advice from a high school teacher that girls shouldn't major in a "man's field."* In college,

she was concerned because her grades weren't as good as she wanted them to be. When she asked a professor for advice, he responded that girls shouldn't go into chemistry. This time, she became discouraged and dropped out in 1966 just shy of graduation, all of her last semester's grades translating into Fs.

Segerberg worked for a while in industry without a baccalaureate but, after losing a dead-end job because of discrimination, depression, and frustration, she abandoned science and sought a career in another area. While working testing blood samples in a doctors' office, she enrolled in an extension program at Julliard to study music composition. Although she loved studying music, she realized that it probably could not offer her a living and decided not to pursue it professionally. She enjoyed a subsequent job in sleep research, but she realized that a baccalaureate was essential for job security and finished her interrupted undergraduate studies.

Through the help of a reentry program at George Mason University and the encouragement of two established women scientists, Segerberg resumed her work in science, earning a doctorate more than 25 years after she started her undergraduate degree. She then did postdoctoral work at Cornell University and is currently working in a second postdoctoral position at the University of Arizona.

AWIS: *Can you think of any instances of gender discrimination against women in science?*
SEGERBERG: In college we were the targets of negative comments. I remember a professor defining a nanosecond as the time it takes for a woman to change her mind. Silly things like that hit us

---

*This interview follows up on an earlier discussion with Segerberg appearing in the 1990, September/October *AWIS Magazine*, 19(5), 6–8.

all the time, but I didn't realize how badly they affected me. Eventually I couldn't bear to go to class anymore, and I didn't understand why I felt that way. I gradually fell into depression.

Many years later, when my women mentors had helped me apply to graduate school, two University of Wisconsin faculty members interviewed me and informed me that I was "too old" to enter. They were overruled, and other professors there later were most generous and supportive—apologizing for their colleagues' statement—but it wasn't fun at the time.

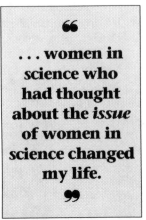

... **women in science who had thought about the** *issue* **of women in science changed my life.** *""*

AWIS: *How should women scientists cope with gender discrimination?*
SEGERBERG: It really upsets me when women deny or minimize the effects of sex discrimination on their lives. This kind of discrimination almost ruined my life, and it's why I'm "old" with a new Ph.D. It took me 13 years to figure out what happened to me, and it cut that much time from my years of scientific productivity and enjoyment.

Things were not a whole lot better in industry. When I asked my boss if I should finish my baccalaureate and go on for an advanced degree, he said, "It really isn't worth the $20,000 capital investment for a female Ph.D. because she would probably just get married and quit her job."

AWIS: *How have you balanced your personal and professional commitments?*
SEGERBERG: Like many of the women in science whom I know and who are important to me, I have neither chosen to be part of a patriarchal marriage, nor have I decided to have children. It makes me angry when questions about satisfying the demands of career and private life focus only on the needs of married women needing child care.

There are other stresses and other choices.

AWIS: *Was your experience in the women's reentry program you entered helpful?*
SEGERBERG: Yes. George Mason's was a year-long, physics-oriented program. I had a blast, and I got straight As. I felt good because I understood the material, and I also received emotional support. We students encouraged each other; I enjoyed the material. It didn't feel like work. It was fun—the way I felt about science when I was young. The positive self-image I regained helped overcome the

bad experiences I'd had with male scientists, businessmen, and professors.

AWIS: *Has the process of networking with others in your field proved valuable to you?*

SEGERBERG: During the year of the physics program, I went to an American Association for the Advancement of Science meeting, where one of the symposia was about feminist science. Ruth Bleier (now deceased) was one of the speakers I met there. After the meeting, I decided to do anything I could to get back into science. I wrote her a letter describing myself and asking for her advice.

She called me about three days after I mailed the letter. I was overwhelmed that she thought my predicament important enough to respond that quickly. She told me that I should try to get into the neuroscience program at the University of Wisconsin because, in her opinion, the field needed women, and she thought I'd enjoy it.

I got in in spite of my early string of bad grades because of my good Graduate Record Examination scores and recommendations from Ruth and from George Mason's Natasha Meshkov, who traveled from Virginia to Wisconsin to persuade the program head to admit me.

AWIS: *Do you have any advice for women pursuing their doctorates?*

SEGERBERG: I don't believe that it takes brilliance to get a Ph.D.: It takes work and opportunity. The important thing is how excited you are about something, how hard you are willing to work for it, and what kind of chance you're given to perform.

AWIS: *What would be your advice to a young woman thinking of embarking on a scientific career?*

SEGERBERG: Don't become isolated. Don't rely upon yourself to figure everything out—use the external resources you have available. If you find yourself getting depressed or demoralized, but you still like science and you don't know what's wrong, talk to an AWIS member. Or find a woman or man whom you feel comfortable with and talk to that person. If that doesn't work the first time, try again. Keep trying until you hear what you want to hear.

AWIS: *May women starting out in your field contact you for guidance?*

SEGERBERG: Yes. They may call (602) 762-5987 outside of working hours or write to me at 10510 East Observatory Drive, Tucson, AZ 85747.

AWIS: What (or who) was the greatest help in turning you toward science?

SEGERBERG: Probably *Mr. Wizard.* The other science programs I watched as a child on television were also important.

AWIS: What (or who) was the greatest help in keeping you in the field?

SEGERBERG: Certainly no one in the field until *I* actively started back in. Then, Ruth, and, now, Natasha with her fine and essential program for women returning to science. Natasha made me *feel* as if I were intelligent.

In short, women in science who had thought about the *issue* of women in science changed my life.

AWIS: What (or who) was the worst hurdle in entering science? How did you overcome this barrier?

SEGERBERG: Sexism was the hurdle. Spending 10 years in the women's movement helped me to understand and transcend it.

Christine (Tina) A. Settineri, B.S.

Doctoral Candidate in Pharmaceutical Chemistry

B.S. in forensic chemistry, Ohio State University   1987

Both Settineri's parents held bachelors' degrees in chemistry: Her father worked in industry, and her mother raised seven children. Elementary and junior high school science had been Settineri's favorite subject, and she knew early that she would go to college to study some scientific field.

She began graduate study in chemistry at Purdue University, where she worked with a peptide chemist and a mass spectronomist. Purdue offered limited opportunities in biological mass spectroscopy, however, the field which interested her most, and she transferred to the University of California, San Francisco. Now, as a graduate student in its pharmaceutical chemistry department, she uses mass spectroscopy to study the structural biology of various glycoprotein drugs.

112

Settineri opted for graduate school when she discovered that most of the jobs available to baccalaureate-level forensic chemists were in crime labs. Not wanting to be a technician analyzing blood samples, she embarked on an advanced degree to prepare her to explore medicinal chemistry.

Settineri married David H. Lloyd in 1988.

AWIS: *How have you balanced your personal and professional commitments?*

SETTINERI: While in graduate school at Purdue, I was dating a postdoctoral fellow who got a job in San Francisco, so I applied to the University of California, where I entered the doctoral program in pharmaceutical chemistry. Because my husband is also a scientist, he understands the kinds of demands I must meet as a graduate student, and we both know how the field can affect our entire lifestyle. This helps a lot, when one or the other has to spend long hours or weekends in the lab.

AWIS: *Do you have any advice for women pursuing their doctorates?*

SETTINERI: Don't let anyone tell you that you can't do what you want to do. Try to find female mentors and peers for support. A supportive partner can help a lot as well.

AWIS: *How are you financing your graduate work?*

SETTINERI: We are paid stipends. In my case, my advisor's grants pay for my research assistantship of close to $15,000 per year. Before orals, I had to pay fees—about $2,000 per year. After I passed my orals, the cost went down to about $300. Having a husband with a well-paid job helps a lot!

AWIS: *Have you ever experienced gender discrimination as a woman in science?*

SETTINERI: Yes. It is usually very subtle, but it is definitely always there, especially when I first went to graduate school. I suddenly realized that, although there were some other women graduate students in my program, there was not a single female professor in pharmaceutical chemistry who could be a role model. I felt as if I had to prove myself, simply because I was female. Women, particularly younger women, need to talk amongst themselves. Constant subtle messages that women don't really belong in science (or only as second-class citizens) as well as overt harassment create a feeling of isolation, as if you are the only one affected. Women need to constantly educate themselves and remember that they are no alone.

AWIS: *May women starting out in your field contact you for guidance?*
SETTINERI: Sure. They may write to me at 850 Point Pacific Drive, #1, Daly City, CA 94014.

AWIS: *What (or who) was the greatest help in turning you toward science?*
SETTINERI: My whole family influenced me the most because we were all science oriented. Both my parents trained as chemists (my mother taught for two years), and they produced me, two engineers, one physician, one beginning biochemist, in addition to one automobile expert and one band director. We were all encouraged to do well, especially in math and science.

AWIS: *What (or who) was the greatest help in keeping you in the field?*
SETTINERI: My own personal interest in the field—I couldn't see myself doing anything else. I always knew science was the right thing for me to pursue.

Also, with two other women graduate students, I began a support group to help women graduate students and postdocs in science with various decisions—for example, balancing having children and maintaining one's career and what to do about discrimination. Our core group now numbers about 50 people. (See also Theresa R. Gamble's interview, pages 98–100.)

In addition, I have had lots of encouragement from my husband.

AWIS: *What (or who) was the worst hurdle in entering science? How did you overcome this barrier?*
SETTINERI: Being female *looked* as if it were the worst hurdle. I got over this barrier when I gained confidence in myself as a scientist, in spite of the fact that there aren't very many like me out there.

Terryl Stacy, Ph.D.

Postdoctoral Fellow in Biochemistry

B.S. in biochemistry, University of Vermont   1980
Ph.D in biochemistry, Dartmouth College   1990

Stacy, a nontraditional student, started her undergraduate work in the 1960s majoring in biology.* She was told, however, that she could not pursue this major because she hadn't taken a chemistry laboratory course in high school. Not understanding her right to choose, Stacy switched her major to political science and then dropped out of college.

Her desire to learn about physical science, however, did not change, and she worked briefly as a laboratory technician. After marriage to Dodd Stacy in 1966 and the birth of two sons in 1967 and 1969, Stacy returned to school in 1976 as an undergraduate.

This time, she excelled in science. Expertly dividing her time among her responsibilities as commuting student, mother, and wife, she earned her bachelor's and then her doctorate.

She now works in a laboratory that is part of Tufts University's medical school.

AWIS: *When did you decide to finish your baccalaureate? How did you fit your studies into your family commitments?*
STACY: I always intended to stay home with my children when they were young, but I always thought I'd go back to school. In the mid-1970s, when we moved from California to New England, I was 20 miles from the closest four-year college—Dartmouth—and 80, from the University of Vermont at Burlington. At that time, Dartmouth was still an all male school, but even when it became coed, it wouldn't accept transfer students.

I took a few community college courses, and then, in desperation, started commuting to the University of Vermont. With Vermont winters, that can be an exciting commute.

---

*This interview follows up on an earlier discussion with Stacy appearing in the 1989, January/February *AWIS Magazine*, *19*(5), 10–12.

AWIS: How do you feel about the work you did as a technician in comparison to your academic research?

STACY: You're much more emotionally tied to your work when it's *your* thesis than when you're an employee. I cared a lot about the experiments I did as a technician, but I didn't lose much sleep over them. Now, I lie in bed and think, "Why didn't this experiment work?" or I wake up out of a sound sleep thinking, "Oh my God you didn't do this, and you should have." The night before my qualifying exams, I didn't sleep at all. I worked much longer hours as a graduate student than I did as a technician, and I was paid a lot less, but the experience was invaluable.

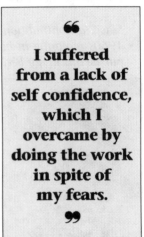

> 66
>
> **I suffered from a lack of self confidence, which I overcame by doing the work in spite of my fears.**
>
> 99

AWIS: Describe your experiences as a mature student in comparison to those of younger students.

STACY: I probably didn't work as many hours as typical graduate students. I probably put in 60 hours a week as opposed to their 80, and I came home at a reasonable hour in the evenings. I think I got as much done with shorter hours because I brought more focus to the work. That might have stemmed both from my being older and from having family responsibilities less demanding than when the boys were little.

I think I had more perspective than some graduate students on where science fit into my life then and now. When my work is not going well, I can go home and say, "I still have another life." Although I get depressed now and then, I know the world isn't over when my experiments don't work. I have seen graduate students get really beaten down when their work doesn't go well, which is bound to happen in any graduate student's career.

AWIS: May women starting out in your field contact you for guidance?

STACY: Yes. They may write to me at the Department of Microbiology, Tufts University Medical School, 136 Harrison Avenue, Boston, MA 02111.

AWIS: What (or who) was the greatest help in turning you toward science?

STACY: There was really no one—my own interest.

AWIS: *What (or who) was the greatest help in keeping you in the field?*
STACY: I had to rely on myself for that too.

AWIS: *What (or who) was the worst hurdle in entering science? How did you overcome this barrier?*
STACY: I suffered from a lack self confidence, which I overcame by doing the work in spite of my fears.

Part II
The Consensus

The Consensus
Deborah C. Fort

The preceding section of *A Hand Up: Women Mentoring Women in Science* comprises interviews with 28 women scientists, engineers, administrators, and mathematicians and 9 postdoctoral fellows and students. Although AWIS has tried to pick a broadly representative group of practitioners and scholars, this section in no way aims to present a cross section of women's views of the profession's joys and sorrows, problems and solutions, strengths and weaknesses. That would be the purview of a widely distributed survey, and such an approach is neither within the intention nor the scope of this volume. But even though the interviews do not provide much usefully countable data, certain themes occur and reoccur. This piece will note a few of them.

Before turning to these concerns, however, a few statistics about our respondents seem in order. Among the students are three postdoctoral candidates, four graduate students, and two undergraduates. Student respondents, mostly from the western United States, come from four racial/ethnic groups.* Like women in the profession as a whole, they cluster in the life sciences, although a number are in combining fields (biochemistry and biophysics, for example), two are in mathematics and/or computer science, and one is an astronomer.

The scientists are an even more diverse group professionally, ethnically, and in terms of seniority. Although respondents often defy single classifications, partially because of the rich complexity of science as practice and profession, the women interviewed fall into these broad groups: About nine devote themselves primarily to research, nine, to administration—from a grants officer to a university president, six are academic scientists, two are mathematicians or engineers, and two, mental health professionals. The categories, however, are misleading; they inevitably require generalization and simplification. For example, should Esther Arvilla Harrison Hopkins be classified as a chemist, a patent attorney, an environmentalist, or an administrator? She is, of course, all of these things and more.

---

*Ethnic and racial designations, always a sensitive matter, are also complex. Is a woman black, an African American, or of Afro-American extraction? Is another Hispanic, Latina, or Chicana? Arguments can and are advanced for—and against—all such descriptions. In *A Hand Up*, AWIS has used the designations most often chosen by the respondents themselves. This implies no endorsement of one term over another. In fact, AWIS plans a publication soon that will help girls to examine the impact of connotations of various labels and views of science.

Classification according to field is similarly slippery; however, broadly, the 28 respondents' focuses are as follows:

◆ 14 in the life sciences (half in medical fields; half in biology or combining fields such as biotechnology)

◆ 4 in chemistry

◆ 4 in mathematics, engineering, and/or computer science

◆ 2 each in physics/astronomy, environmental science, and science education

As each woman explains her perceptions about what factors encouraged her—and what discouraged her—some themes reoccur, but much is uniquely individual. The impetus to move into fields often empty and intolerant of women and the courage to remain in them has three touchstones: Madame Curie, mentors, and stubbornness. A handful of respondents* see in the life and work of Marie Curie a model and a confirmation of the possibilities open to them as women and as scientists. While the great French scientist stands in some ways as a distant mentor as well as a model, many women who chose science mention specific guidance from family members and teachers—the mentors in the flesh that historic figures and paper guides like this book can but help to support. Finally, those interviewed cited their own stubbornness—or "determination" or "inner-directedness" or persistence—as essential factors in their professional choice and continuation. To quote one of the scientists, those who wish to enter science should "stay the course, putting up with whatever is necessary to get through first the degree and then into the first job." In a slightly different vein, a research associate in astronomy explains, "I know I'm not brilliant. My mind is slow and steady, but I know that if I bang my head against a problem, I'm going to solve it. Just let your brain integrate the information and finally come up with the solution."

Briefly and impressionistically, some of the patterns in the fabric of the interviews follow.

Starting Out: Education and the Job

Most respondents view the mentoring relationship as one often vital link in the whole process of education, which occurs—or can occur—at any time and in any place. Although formal education is important and was discussed by many respondents, most learning takes place outside classroom walls. A child's first teachers are,

---

*One of their spouses, himself a Nobel Prize winner, also cites her precedent.

usually, her parents, and many respondents cited the support of family members as being crucial in leading them toward science and mathematics. Others spoke of teachers and other mentors; a few, of networks. (On the last, see pages 132–134.)

Informal Education

A number of respondents, however, found their early environments strewn with roadblocks to science. Parents and relatives often believed that scientific activities, much less an eventual scientific career, weren't appropriate pastimes for girls. One scientist reports that the opposition from her mother "who could not understand that I did not want to be the *wife* of a vice president—I wanted to *be* the vice president" caused lifelong damage to their relationship. Another, who remembered being preoccupied with mechanics as a child, mused that "Sometimes my mother was irritated by my interest in machines, rather than dolls." Almost without exception, future scientists growing up in home environments hostile or indifferent to science had their interest awakened by gifted teachers.

In contrast, many girls discovered their passion for science through the enthusiasm and guidance of parents and other relatives—grandparents, aunts, siblings, and the like. One respondent came from a "family of scientists," and she suspects that she and her sister, also a scientist, "may be the only cooks who, when learning to make a cheese soufflé, were instructed to add the hot cheese slowly to the egg yolks so as not to denature the protein." An aunt encouraged a third girl by characterizing her to relatives as a future astronomer (actually, she became a pediatrician), while another woman, acknowledging her father's guidance, says quietly that she chose her path into astronomy simply because she "watched the sky."

Early interest in nature, on occasion sharpened by growing up on a farm, often led to a permanent commitment to science. Betty P. Preece also notes the importance of guidance and support from home, school, and community.

Formal Education—Precollege

In a book on mentoring, it is fitting that so many respondents, particularly those coming from science shy backgrounds, cite their schoolteachers as among the important reasons they went into science. Nearly all mention a teacher at some level—from kindergarten to graduate school—with the large majority remembering positive experiences. And, among the women who received discouraging treatment from some of their science instructors, a couple simultaneously praise the work of others.

High school teachers receive the most acclamation. One woman, who became one of America's preeminent chemists, attributes the birth of her career entirely to the work of a high school chemistry teacher. At the same time, she recalls with distaste certain professors who did not want a young woman, no matter how talented, in their laboratories. Much of the current recent reform in science education has focused on the elementary school and middle school years, and a number of the women interviewed discuss the vital need that it continue—that, for example, minority and female exemplars come into classrooms and that children learn more math earlier. Nonetheless, the appreciation that nearly half the respondents show to their dedicated and talented secondary teachers indicates the vital importance of high school education in encouraging fledgling scientists.

In spite of their gratitude, none of our respondents became precollege teachers, although about a third had in the past and/or were currently teaching in institutions of higher education. In fact, a number of the scientists resented being pushed, by family or other teachers, toward the high school or elementary school teaching, which, in their youth, was an "acceptable" profession for a woman. The reasons for this gap are various, one certainly being chance, but perhaps the lack of teachers among the respondents is in some ways indicative of an American anomaly to which Lynn Margulis makes reference. Although we as a nation pay lip service to the importance of precollege teaching, particularly to science and math teaching, the profession lacks prestige and, of course, funds. One science educator cautions,

> When scientists who have "made it" in their scientific disciplines decide to make pronouncements about science education, the science community listens to them. If scholars get Ph.D.s in science and go straight into education, they should have their eyes open. There's not as much prestige in education as there is in being a research scientist.

Although she is speaking of university-level science educators and not precollege teachers, her generalization, unfortunately, applies to both.

Formal Education—Undergraduate

Says another respondent, tartly, "Women are usually good teachers. Chairmen say 'You're so wonderful with the students, I want you to continue.' The trick is not to be good at it: The person who wins the teacher-of-the-year award never gets tenure at the more prestigious schools." Whether this scientist is literally right or not, she expresses a not unusual opinion.

Nonetheless, while few respondents called their relationships with their mentors and teachers at the postsecondary level *formative* in helping them choose science—by their undergraduate years, most had already found their vocation—many report warm and important relationships with professors. One woman, for example, after having dropped out of a science major so that she could take more liberal arts courses, had her first disheartening experience in a chemistry class of 1,000—probably an example of the "weed-out" introductory science courses Sheila Tobias criticizes—corrected by a galvanizing woman bacteriology teacher. The former dropout is now a preeminent marine biologist.

A small percentage of the scientists attended women's colleges; three of those four found their experiences supportive and important in their decision for science. The fourth was less positive, noting both "pros and cons." She enjoyed the small classes her women's college offered and one-on-one contact with many of her teachers. And she liked seeing women faculty and students in leadership positions. But the experience, she said ruefully, had its drawbacks. Her college "modelled an ideal, not a real world," she explained. When she entered business, it was a shock to find so few women in mathematics and engineering. She had moved to an environment where men were mostly in charge—just the opposite of what she was accustomed to. Barbara Furin Sloat suggests ways that coeducational colleges and universities could better encourage women in science.

The two California undergraduates interviewed both advised high school girls interested in science to persist, even if the work at first seems difficult, and to tackle their math anxiety and take as many math classes as possible.

Presumably, they will follow up on their own suggestion. And the results, according to a government mathematician, could be anything but "academic." Once factors such as gender, ethnic background, and level of education are discounted, she said, salary differences are explained by the number of undergraduate math courses taken.

Summarized one student, "You give up a lot when you're in science because of the time you have to put into school, but my sense of accomplishment seems worth my sacrifice." As undergraduates, the two were already facing the problems of balancing commitments to family and to school with which the adult scientists would also wrestle at length. Both members of minority groups, the students extolled the value of the support group for undergraduates in biomedical fields at their institution. For the undergraduate view of science study, see interviews with Lucio and Samuels.

Formal Education—Graduate

Respondents remembered and discussed their graduate education in greater detail than they did their undergraduate years. Their perceptions were buttressed by Virginia Walbot's suggestions elsewhere. Among other issues, they talked about the value of teaching assistantships and research fellowships and the importance of laboratory experience. They also analyzed the need to choose the right institution, the right courses, the right undergraduate and graduate degrees, and the right advisors and mentors. See also pages 137–143. In graduate school, as all throughout the educational process, both students and scientists emphasized the importance of support networks for women in science. Among her many achievements, one black biophysicist and university administrator was proudest of the postbaccalaureate program she developed for premed minority students. For a year, it supported financially and brought up-to-date academically minority students with demonstrated undergraduate learning skills who decided late in their college careers that they wanted to go to medical, dental, or veterinary school.

A number of the scientists had held teaching and research assistantships themselves during their student days, and some of them commented on the worth of such experiences not only because of what is learned but also because of the contacts formed. The students also generally found assistantships valuable. Said one scientist on the subject of teaching fellowships,

> Teaching or tutoring is a good way to get a clearer understanding of subject matter, to understand thoroughly things you may have glossed over before. Many students who get graduate degrees in chemistry don't want teaching assistantships: They want to get right to the bench. That is unfortunate in terms of their own understanding of science.

Academic assistantships for science students often involve teaching or work in the laboratory, a process the majority of those interviewed heartily approved. An academic scientist advised that students who do not get their hands dirty, analyze the results, and make deductions, can't be scientists. "The sooner you get into the lab the better," she concluded. A federal scientist echoed her advice:

> Get hands-on laboratory experience as soon as you can. If you know your way around the lab, you will succeed, because you will begin to understand cells, cell mechanisms, and cell regulation. Even if you just wash test tubes in the lab, you can talk with the people who are doing science, and you will learn.

Graduate students must make many important choices. First, they must decide where to apply and what institution to attend. According to an academic researcher, women can use the underenrollment of students in graduate programs to their advantage. A number of respondents emphasized what they see as the importance for future career success of doing graduate work at a prestigious research university. Others advised students heading for a cross-field degree (for example, environmental science or biochemistry) to do their undergraduate preparation in a rigorous single field, and, according to one scientist, their master's-level study as well. While several scientists recommended that students take as much math as possible, the three women discussing kinds of advanced degrees to take reached no clear consensus on whether an M.D., a Ph.D, or both is a candidate's best course. Both degrees have their merits, they agreed. Which to take depends on one's professional and personal purpose: Explained a Ph.D.,

> The M.D. gives you the credibility to interact with patients and design clinical studies. There is no limitation on research with an M.D., but you develop a different set of skills than you gain through a Ph.D. program. With a Ph.D., you learn how to investigate a very specific area in depth.

"For unorganized people like me," quipped a holder of two degrees, "both were the answer."

For more advice on graduate education, see the following interviews: Anders, Haseltine, Sunley, Colwell, Noguchi, Schiesler, Douglass, and Cox.

The three doctoral and one master's candidates interviewed found their interest in science through paths similar to that of the established scientists: In three cases, encouragement from family buttressed by gifted formal education struck the spark; in the fourth, a talented middle-school teacher's guidance and praise plus a resonance between mathematics and the Navajo culture was the impetus.

The four agreed about the importance of support groups—formal, as in the networks for women students in science at the University of California, San Francisco and the American Indian Science and Engineering Society at Oklahoma State—but personal as well. Said a Ph.D. candidate in chemistry, "Don't let anyone tell you that you can't do what you want to do. Try to find female mentors and peers for support. A supportive partner can help a lot as well."

Like the scientists, the graduate students emphasized the importance of math in entering and surviving in science; however, said one, for her "*Entering* wasn't the problem, *staying* is. The field is completely male dominated," she continued, "and I run into the consequences of that daily."

Both students and practicing scientists also face the hard reality of funding—where to get enough of it as salary or as grants. In this volume, Barbara Filner provides detailed advice on applying for fellowships and grants. Joked one student holding a research assistantship from her advisor's grants, however, "Having a husband with a well-paid job helps a lot!" Failing that, Lisa A. Zuccarelli describes other paths to financial self-sufficiency in graduate school. Teaching—particularly as a part-time adjunct—is not always the best answer.

See the following interviews to understand the students' view of the graduate school experience: Bitsie, Gamble, Rettinger, and Settineri.

Postdoctoral Work

For many new Ph.Ds and M.D.s, the next career step after graduation is to embark on a postdoctoral program. Both the scientists and the students had thoughts to share on this experience, which, said one fellow, puts one in a kind of limbo—not necessarily an unpleasant one—between studenthood and full-fledged membership in the profession. Recalled one of the scientists of a former colleague,

> She had been in the department as a postdoc and was well-respected there as a scientist. But once she was an assistant professor, a peer, all of that changed. It seemed to me that as long as a man was validating you, things were fine, but academic science couldn't quite cope with an independent woman.

A number of the scientists provided advice on postdoctoral positions—how to win them, how long to stay in them, the status of the fellows, whether such positions are always an essential part of the professional path into science. Postdoctoral fellowships are more usual than not in the laboratory sciences and are almost always undertaken by students bound for academia, but are not so essential for those planning clinical, industrial, or mathematical careers. Explained an executive officer at the National Science Foundation,

> The career path of mathematicians seldom includes the kind of postdoctoral experience you find in physics, chemistry, or other areas. It is more traditional to move into some form of faculty position. Those with degrees from the best schools sometimes go into the equivalent of postdoctoral positions, but they're called "research instructorships" or "research faculty" posts. They comprise half-time teaching and half-time research positions.

Jobs are often awarded through professional networks; here is another place where such contacts can be of significant value. For example, reports another federal scientist, her office awards several postdoctoral fellowships, and

> since I've been here, only one person has been appointed whose major professor did not have connections here. The professors call up and say they have a student coming out who is looking for a postdoc and who is interested in this, this, and this. And somebody says, "that sounds great," and then the student has a job here.
>
> If your professor never makes that call, you don't have much of a chance to do a postdoc here.

While there are other avenues into good postdoctoral positions—for example, one candidate wrote a letter to virtually everyone in the scientist's branch and succeeded—the government scientist warned that "You have to work a lot harder, however, if you're not connected." Agrees another respondent, "As a postdoctoral student, you need a guardian angel to show you how to write grants, to acclimate yourself within a department, and to help you learn how to play politics."

A couple of the scientists warned upcoming women in science not to stay too long in postdoctoral positions. Expanding her advice to the career schedule as a whole, an environmental consultant noted the importance of keeping to a timetable:

> An extra six-to-twelve months to complete her thesis research, extended duration for each postdoc, and an additional year or two before each promotion in the job. Suddenly, a woman can find herself years behind where she might otherwise have been. Then she may not be viewed as a rising young superstar, but rather as an older scientist of whom it is said, "Well, if she's so good, why hasn't she achieved more by this age?"

Among the women interviewed were three postdoctoral fellows, all three nontraditional students. Two had taken years off between their bachelors' degrees and their doctorates in order to raise children (see below, pages 134–137); the third had turned in despair from the sexism she found in many scientific settings and tried another field—music, which she loved but which could not support her. Two of the three cited the importance of different kinds of networks in their successful negotiation of graduate and postdoctoral study; however, the third overcame what she called her lack of self-confidence, "by doing the work in spite of my fears."

One student went back to her interrupted studies in astronomy at a nurturing college of the sort Shirley M. Malcom praises. Says the new astronomer it helped to produce: "They took in everybody; they gave everybody a chance. There is a real need for more places like that." One of the others, now doing postdoctoral work in neuroscience, cites the generous and active encouragement of two senior women scientists as formative in her return to school after a 25-year hiatus.

For a focus on the participants' view of postdoctoral programs, see interviews with Eder, Segerberg, and Stacy.

Thoughts on Mentors

In a book committed to the value of mentors, the fact that all 37 respondents, many of them extremely busy, offered themselves as mentors to women entering science seems both generous and appropriate. In addition, an overview of the scientists and the students' views of what effective and helpful mentors and advisors are like brings to fitting closure to this education section of *A Hand Up*.

Most of the respondents commented on what they thought were the most important characteristics for which to search in mentors or other advisors. With few exceptions, their thoughts dovetail with the ideas and advice tendered by Bernice Resnick Sandler and Betty M. Vetter. A few, however, particularly women who for some reason find themselves out of the mainstream, make useful and original additions.

Several women of color and a deaf scientist noted the importance of students seeing that a female out of the mainstream has made it in science. The latter noted that her biology sections produce more deaf majors than those taught by the hearing, presumably because the students see that she has made it as a deaf female scientist and conclude that they can too. A black science educator explains, "Students need to know that their career possibilities can be virtually endless, and that's how I can help. At . . . engineering schools, there are few women and minorities, and it can therefore be difficult for students to find role models and mentors." On the other hand, another black scientist found a mentor in a white woman doctor. According to a Native American counselor, who came to her vocation partially through expert help from a counselor who helped her with difficulties in college, a very important characteristic of a mentor or an advisor is a sense of humor.

A couple of scientists provided cautions. The role of mentor is not for everyone. A Hispanic pediatrician noted that competitive people make ineffective mentors, and a chemist explained that, although she had served as a mentor for many men and women in the past, at this point in a long and distinguished career she was needing to pull back.

See the following interviews for more information about advisors and mentors: Ramaley, Dillehay, Haseltine, Sunley, Noguchi, Hardy, Anikeeff, Scheisler, Kantor, Douglass, Navy, and Rettinger.

Professional Opportunities

One of the most persistent themes running through the interviews of *A Hand Up* is—difficult though the profession may still be in some ways for women—that science offers a stunning range of job opportunities. Evelyn Fox Keller's path is one example of this versatility. A respondent trained in physics and biophysics and working as a consultant in toxicology, risk assessment, and environmental policy sums up the breadth of the possibilities as follows:

> When I give "career day" talks, I emphasize that there are many types of scientific careers. I start by saying that I'm not going to talk about familiar fields such as laboratory science, teaching, or medicine— everyone is familiar with those jobs. Instead I focus on less well known, more eclectic scientific careers, such as consulting or regulatory science, and how a scientific background is useful in numerous careers, such as market research or environmental law. When I was in school, I was unaware of these options. The result is that I've had four jobs that I didn't know *existed* before I was recruited into them.

Another respondent has used her training in chemistry to work in industry, in the patent office (after she had added a law degree to her Ph.D), and as an administrator charged to protect the environment. She sees an intimate relationship among the fields in spite of their apparently different emphases, explaining that she is currently using all her past experience to answer one central question: How can we give our children a clean world?

An Asian-American biophysicist working for the federal government also emphasizes the freedom to change science offers. She points out that, because of the rapidly changing job market, it is important to approach education as a wise consumer. Focusing on a particular area, she continues, will help to establish a place in a specific field. Nonetheless, you are never trapped:

> It's never too late to change direction, however, or to consider an unconventional career path. Ph.D. recipients who have returned to medical school can be found in research as well as private practice, and individuals who have had private medical practices can be found now doing basic research.

Agreed an industrial biotechnologist who had returned to academia,

> One of the important consequences of my work in industry was that I discovered a whole new range of interests. I was amazed to find that there were so many new careers that I could enjoy. We should be careful not to limit ourselves because we haven't looked at career

alternatives. It is important to take risks occasionally to continue to learn and to be challenged.

Asked what she saw as the most rewarding aspect of her career, a federal scientist laughed. "To do what you enjoy and get paid for it." Said another, "It's seeing students go on and do something with their lives in science." Though both spokeswomen are members of minority groups, they expressed a majority consensus.

About a third of the respondents went from laboratory and/or academic science into administrative posts of various kinds. None expressed regrets, although several found the choice hard. Two offered particular insights on the similarities and differences between the two professions. According to a consultant working in several fields, who "enjoys being a manager" and who believes that more management responsibility is a virtually inevitable part of career advancement,

> Outside the lab, you more frequently have an immediate effect on the manner in which science is used to solve problems. In some ways I feel I have the best of both worlds. As my current work involves a science that does not require a laboratory, it's possible to continue intellectually stimulating research while working to improve its application in a regulatory setting.

Another administrator, once a member of a medical school faculty and now a university president, believes that science prepared her well for her managerial future, in which she uses "all the same values and ways of thinking." The main difference between the two approaches, she says, is between focus on the part and on the whole: She is

> not the kind of person who wants to know more and more about a smaller and smaller thing. In my area,... the field was splitting rather than lumping.... I'm much more interested in how things fit together. Science will have to turn itself around one of these days and move in the other direction, but it isn't doing it at the moment.

See the following interviews for more advice on job opportunities: Cobb, Putzrath, Hardy, Douglass, Settineri, and Rettinger.

Connecting

The scientific network as a whole and within its parts is a valuable resource for the exchange of ideas and information on new breakthroughs and technology. It operates within academic departments, across fields, within industry and government, and throughout the profession as a whole. Women need to break into existing networks, respondents agreed, as well as to form their own.

A number of respondents reported their feelings of exclusion from certain male rituals. But said one, things are changing. She explained that the rapport with male students that she had been unable to develop in graduate school—"I had a few close friends, but I didn't go to study groups or stay up late doing problems and drinking beer"—she has now achieved with her colleagues. As her field expands, she said, "there are not many of us women, but there is very little evidence of discrimination. I think that bright new-comers are welcome."

Some of the students interviewed appropriately linked the process of participating in networks and support groups to the need for mentors. Many of the scientists discussed the value of the connections made through individual contacts with colleagues, associations like AWIS, other women's groups, and professional meetings. The umbrella network, according to several women interviewed and activists Tobias and Anne M. Briscoe, is feminism itself.

Respondent after respondent spoke not only of her isolation as a female but also of her pleasure in seeing other women at conferences and other gatherings. (Some also spoke of the necessity of increasing the numbers of women in science, but, except in the life sciences, saw little hope of redressing the underrepresentation anytime soon.)

If women's numbers in science rise, according to a science educator, it will be when women's networks come to rival those of the "good old boys" currently in place and working so well for men. One chemist, the mother of three daughters who have become scientists, noted sadly that the numbers of women in her daughters' college and graduate classes haven't risen at all since her own schooldays 25–30 years earlier.

There was general agreement about the importance of attending professional meetings to make face-to-face contact with others in the field. When an opportunity arises to present a paper or a poster session, scientists agreed, it should be seized. And if the invitation doesn't happen, it should be created. Heidi B. Hammel offers helpful advice on how to make a presentation effective. And Marian G. Glenn, Dorie Monroe, and Judith Lamont note another important network that will help to insure that women speakers make their way to the podium as invited speakers—the more women organizing the conference, the more women speaking and presenting.

Most significant jobs are filled through personal contacts rather than through official notices. And, note several scientists and students, a strong network of colleagues both within and without organized groups, is a strong force for women to not only enter but also stay in the profession. Women, who are often excluded from this network, must find their way in and/or form networks of their own. Now, for whatever reason, women's names frequently don't circulate widely. Though not many respondents addressed the job search directly, the Association for Women in Cell Biology offers some broadly applicable advice on how to find a position in academia or industry. Florence P. Haseltine also makes useful and frank suggestions on how to find a good position, while Stephanie J. Bird notes the responsibilities that go along with it.

See the following interviews for advice on networking: Cobb, Brenchley, Anders, Sunley, Douglass, and Rettinger.

Leaping the Barriers

All women interviewed were asked what (or who) was the worst hurdle for them in entering science and how they overcame this barrier.

Besides the opposition from family members and from some teachers discussed above, a few women described their own lack of self-esteem as a hurdle to be crossed. Other hurdles were external: Some cited gender discrimination and sexism from both men and women; others, economic difficulties—debts, expenses, no jobs. Some felt they had received little or no useful guidance; some, once out of the system for family or other reasons, had difficulty reentering. Others needed child care, while three respondents had to overcome disabilities: One, her deafness; another, her blindness; a third, her dyslexia. A Native American targeted as her biggest hurdle the "linear thinking" expected of her in high school and at her first college, which would have taken "a real mind shift" to achieve.

"Introductory science courses," said one. "My religious community" said another, explaining that the order to which she formerly belonged did not welcome the idea of sisters as chemists. "Organic chemistry," laughed a third. "Then I realized that you didn't have to synthesize rubber every day; you could put those equations to more relevant use in terms of a cell."

A few overcame the barriers by avoidance—leaving the person or situation that was the problem—but the majority relied on their own sheer stubbornness to triumph over conditions adverse to their career in science.

Balancing

All respondents were asked about their family situation, whether they were married and whether they had or planned to have children. While these questions might not appear in a book of interviews with male scientists, they probably *should.* AWIS finds the balancing act between personal and professional commitments

134

of the first order of importance for women going into science. Neither having a career, nor being a responsible parent, nor participating in a meaningful spousal relationship is easy. The thought of doing all three successfully is at best daunting; at worst discouraging. But, although the vote was by no means unanimous, most respondents—disagreeing with Margulis—believed that women who planned carefully could, if they wished, succeed in all three roles simultaneously. But to do so, they agreed, certain hard choices were necessary.

Some put off having children until their careers were well underway. Others, agreeing implicitly with Tobias' point that the importance of getting started professionally early may be overrated, chose to bear children when they wished, regardless of where they found themselves professionally. Some downplayed their careers during the time when their children needed them most. As one of the postdoctoral fellows, who returned to school after she had helped to rear 10 children, puts it, "You have to give up *something*. I gave up *everything* except my family and work on my degree. It was three years before I read a book for fun. When everyone else went to bed, I stayed up for at least three more hours." An Asian American expresses what may be a majority view:

> There is *never* a convenient time to have kids. You just decide when to do it, and you do it.
>
> Child-rearing does delay you professionally. I took some time off, but I decided that slowing down was worthwhile, and I don't think it damaged my career. One postdoc down the hall had her son and was back the next week working in the lab. It took me longer.
>
> If you do choose to have a career and a family, you have to feel comfortable with your situation. If you must worry the entire day about whether your children are in an appropriate child care situation, your productivity at work will suffer. If you're convinced that you're doing the best you can with day care—and that that best is good enough—then when at work, your primary focus can be work.

Said an astrophysicist and the mother of five, were she to start over, she'd be more relaxed about the opportunities that would still be available when the children were grown up. "Sometimes I got depressed," she admitted, "when other people were presenting my work, and I felt as if that were going to go on forever. As soon as I was ready, everybody was glad I was on my own."

Whatever the decision about the if and when of childbearing, scientists and students agreed on the need for excellent child care arrangements, one woman postponing having children until she could afford the latter. A government medical researcher, the mother of two daughters and a partner in a commuter marriage, argues persuasively that "Part of every job package should be day care. Our nation needs children, but day care is often unavailable for people who need to work. Day care should be part of the working environment, like having safe water to drink."

Along with children, usually, go spouses. About three quarters of the respondents were or had been married, and the majority of that group had chosen to have children. Virtually all these respondents praised their husbands' support and help with childrearing, and with household tasks, and (see below) with their professional needs and aspirations. One offered this tribute, as she named her husband as the greatest help in keeping her in science: "He is a man who helps people see what they can do and then sees how he can help them do it." Sharing domestic responsibilities seems to most respondents necessary and natural. Commented an academic scientist and administrator,

> There is more sharing of domestic work in couples where both the men and women work. Several of my graduate students have children, and generally their husbands are supportive. One person takes the child to day care and the other picks her up. It's not totally the woman's responsibility.
>
> My husband has always been very supportive of what I do: He listens to me expound when I'm upset and recognizes that I may not always be home for dinner. That has been important in my success as an administrator and a faculty member because it's an irregular lifestyle. I initially made moves in support of his career, and he later made moves in support of mine. He's my best friend.
>
> If a woman has a "significant other" who is not supportive, it can be difficult and stressful for both of them: They either get divorced, or she gives up her career.

See the following interviews for advice on balancing career and family: Champagne, Hopkins, Ramaley, Dillehay, Haseltine, Rubin, Eder, Sunley, Colwell, Noguchi, Douglass, and Rettinger.

The spouses of virtually all married respondents were also employed. The demands put upon a dual-career marriage are—perhaps—even greater than those in the now rare (6 percent) *Leave it to Beaver* family whose stay-at-home mother takes care of her children while her husband works. Even that unrealistic paradigm by no means stays out of divorce courts. Compromise in all relationships seems essential, and various couples found various solutions to the peculiar demands of a two-career marriage. One, embraced by several respondents at one point or another, is the commuting marriage, which no one defended as ideal but which sometimes seemed a necessary solution. Says an environmental scientist who had for a time to live in a different city from her husband, "We had big telephone bills, but we were both very involved in our research at the time, and the arrangement worked out." Says a black college administrator, on occasion also forced into a commuter marriage, "My husband has been willing to relocate with me in the past, and we have had to have a commuter marriage at times." Her phone bills also soared during those periods. Laughs an environmental consultant,

> I always joke that my husband has been following *me* around. The truth is, however, that we've worked together to achieve a successful, two-career marriage. It's not just luck; part is what you look for in a spouse. My husband is very supportive; I sometimes tease him about being more serious about my career than I am. We both, however, have tried to keep our careers flexible and mobile. When we have opportunities for change, we examine the issues in terms of both of our careers as well as our personal lives.

To avoid the commuter marriage, compromises are sometimes but not always necessary. For example, a Hispanic scientist gave up a tenured university post to follow her husband but then found an equally good job in the new city. Several couples embarked together on the two-job search, choosing a location only if it could employ them both. If an institution really wants to hire one person, often it will use its network to find employment for his/her spouse. Although the end of the nepotism rules of the past now sometimes makes it possible for a couple to work at the same institution, finding positions for two professionals in one place is often far from easy.

Still, the search to achieve symbiosis between family and other personal relationships and job responsibilities is well worth making. If it is successful, as that of an American Indian respondent has been, the synthesis is sustaining and valuable. She says,

> By combining my personal and professional life and making each a part of the other, I maximize my strengths. Through the American Indian Science and Engineering Society, I met a lot of people in industry and teaching who shared their experiences with me. It helps to hear how they handled being away from home for the first time, and how they use the strengths of the Navajo traditions to their advantage in the regular world.

See the following interviews for more advice on dual-career couples: Filner, Trevilian, Putzrath, Roscher, Hardy, Cox, and Settineri.

Gender Issues

Women scientists, operating in a feminist age and in a male-dominated profession that they have had to brave terrific odds to enter, tend to be sensitive in the extreme to a broad range of gender issues. Scientists and students alike were articulate and, often, angry about the many forms of sexual politics at play in scientific fields. When gender issues arise, women are nearly always at risk in some way—Affirmative Action, which Briscoe says has been curtailed in recent years, being a major exception. One respondent jokes that she may have been one of the only people for whom the program worked.

Gender issues run a long gamut. On the negative side, behaviors range from the differential treatment often meted out to men and women students or professionals to active sexual harassment of women by their superiors. Also a minus is the isolation many women feel as one of the few. Equally upsetting to many are those situations in which women collude with their detractors, either by encouraging flirtatious behavior in the workplace or by denying their own femininity through what has been called the Queen Bee syndrome. When racial or ethnic prejudice join sexism, the result is even more damaging.

Some apparent gender differences carry a less negative impact. Allowing for the difficulty and danger of generalizing, a number of respondents thought they noted certain divergences in the way men and women typically assert themselves, compete, approach a task, relate. At times, these apparent differences work against women and are therefore unfortunate. At others, feminists would assert, the female approach is better than the male's and should be adopted. At still others, the two could be complementary rather than oppositional.

Negatives

Echoing the advice of the anonymous contributor to the next section, who warned women to beware of belittlement masked as chivalry, a practicing psychologist defined one typical kind of gender discrimination. She explains,

> If you are being discriminated against by male administrators because of your competence in a world that is unfriendly to strong women, if you are being unequally paid for equal work, for example, you are facing one kind of injustice that many women face.
>
> What are some signs of this kind of discrimination? One clue is if you are given mysterious deadlines that don't seem necessary or real. Or deadlines may be suddenly moved forward. Or there may be comments such as, "Don't apply; it's not time yet." Or "Maybe this grant shouldn't be yours but should go through someone else." Or "Maybe it's not time for you to be independent yet."

This kind of differential treatment of men and women takes place in the laboratory/workplace, in academic settings, at scientific conferences, in any professional area. And it can happen to women of any rank—from students to top-level researchers and administrators.

According to an academic marine biologist, this kind of prejudice, which has long been a factor, has a continued presence in the academy:

It's just underground. There is kind of a "snicker-snicker" pretense that administrators practice—they have to act as if they were open and giving women opportunities. This is a generalization, and perhaps it's unfair, but some male researchers use women graduate students as technicians, no matter what the detriment to the women's careers.

That's changing, but what I often see is women getting stuck at low academic levels. There is a glass ceiling, and it needs to be smashed. It's going to take a lot of persistence, because women are recognized as good assistant professors and laboratory technicians, but they don't get promoted as readily as their male counterparts. There aren't very many women senior professors.

There aren't many women in most science departments in most universities, and that is the result of sheer prejudice. Jobs are scarce now; therefore, any excuse is used to cut someone out, and a "different" person is the one they cut.

And, according to an academic chemist, this approach is neither new nor confined to faculty. She remembers her graduate school days in the 1960s when the handful of women chemistry graduate students taught the women undergraduates—mostly home economics majors—especially tailored labs, and "the male graduate students taught everyone else." While she admitted a better climate now, she remembers that "that kind of treatment was everywhere then, and no one thought it was wrong."

A postdoctoral fellow, a Ph.D. and the mother of 10, says the situation has improved, perhaps, but that it still has a way to go. She remembers,

It's people's expectations that do damage. During the interviews for graduate school, I answered questions such as, "How do we know that you're not just going to drop out after two or three years? We've had other women with family priorities do that."

College staff would tell you until they were blue in the face that it wasn't discrimination, but they operated with the expectation that a woman couldn't balance all the different roles she had and be successful.

Another returning student remembers being told she was "too old" to enter graduate school. Though her interrogators were overruled and other faculty were "generous and supportive, it wasn't fun at the time." It was especially discouraging for this woman, who had left a job "where things were not much better" to pursue her Ph.D.

A government scientist sees "two pathways: one for men and one for women. It's subtle, but women don't get the salaries or the promotions." She continues, striking a familiar coping note, "With wisdom and experience, you learn to fight for certain things, let go of others, and not get discouraged," concluding, "I think women have to work 10 times harder than men to get promoted."

A number of women brought up their anger at the sexist jokes they were expected to endure cheerfully. A federal grants officer remembers during graduate school in the 1960s that it was considered "cute, indeed complimentary, to sexually harass a woman student. This was something a professor would boast about, and the department would make jokes about." At least now, reports a doctoral candidate, although there are still professors who tell jokes about their secretary's legs, "those jokes fall flat when more than half the students in the class are women."

One woman engineer turned the joke back on her boss. She said she found her first real experience of gender discrimination when she married:

> Everyone except my immediate supervisor assumed that I'd quit work and forget about a career. Once others realized that I was serious about my career and that my husband was supportive, things slowly changed. Even 10 years later, however, people worried about promoting me because I might get pregnant.
>
> I coped with this problem by forcing a meeting with the manager . . . After discussing technical matters, I ended the issue forever. I said as I left his office, "I'll make a deal with you. In the future, I won't ask about your sex life if you don't ask about mine."
>
> Today, he tells the story with a touch of humor and adds that it was the most consciousness-raising experience of his life.

Not everyone, unfortunately, can laugh off and turn away their tormenters so easily. And the result of being treated as a token or a joke or an outsider can lead to the profound isolation reported by a number of respondents. One woman notes, that although she is often one of but a few women at meetings, the situation is improving. "The problems, however, remain," she points out. "Many difficulties formerly overt are now merely buried." Another remembers meeting conveners trying to register her as a spouse rather than a participant. And a third respondent, a woman astronomer, expresses what amounts to a consensus statement on the feelings of exclusion suffered by many, perhaps most, women in science:

> You show up at a meeting, and you're the only woman there. Every word you utter is remembered in a way that a young man's isn't. I

survived. The real tragedy is the hundreds of women who would have made outstanding astronomers but never made it because they were discouraged all along.

Academic and professional circles are still male dominated. You will go through three or four days of meetings and never once hear the word "her" used. Every scientist is "he." Maybe this is just language, but after a few days, it becomes very annoying. I write a letter every year to the National Academy of Sciences objecting to something they have just sent me in which all the personal pronouns are masculine. I think we're kidding ourselves if we don't realize that science is still a male-dominated profession, and some of the males enjoy this dominance.

Isolation is bad enough, but even worse is the active sexual harassment respondents at all levels of the academy, business, and the federal government report. One of the doctoral candidates had to fend off "blatant sexual advances" from a man who would later turn out to be important in her field. Another woman, speaking for a number of mature women scientists, said, "Of course," she had experienced gender discrimination. But, she went on,

instead of recounting experiences, I would like to broaden the question to discuss how to respond to such situations. For example, what do you do the first time you see a *Playboy* slide in a lecture? You behave differently than you do the fifth time such an image intrudes into a professional setting.

I would advise young scientists to talk with others to see how they have handled specific situations and think about what response is comfortable for them for each case. Being caught off-guard can produce regrettable responses. Sometimes, a meaningful glare is sufficient; other times, stronger action is appropriate. In some circumstances, it is best to change things quietly; other times, vocal support is needed. Find out what has worked for other people and then adapt those ideas for your own use. I try to focus on what result I am trying to achieve rather than why the action has upset me; this approach allows me to stay more objective.

She offers a number of useful responses, as do Briscoe and Linda S. Wilson. At times, however, the situation becomes such that legal action becomes the only solution. In a case when sexism took a particularly ugly turn, the harassers were not men but other women colluding with lascivious superiors, a government psychologist decided that she had "had enough," and she sued on the grounds that she should not have to work in a "hostile sexual environment." Though her action was absolutely necessary, a lawsuit is a draining procedure, and she had some other advice:

I encourage speaking out against harassment, but you must be aware of the possible ramifications. You may be unpopular with your col-

141

leagues, and road blocks may be placed in your way. Before you accept a position, make sure that it is part of a cultural environment where you feel comfortable and where you think that your views and research would be encouraged and rewarded.

In any case, it is good to talk to someone who has seen discrimination before and can make suggestions.

That someone might be AWIS Affirmative Action counselor Briscoe, whose piece in this volume also provides useful advice on harassment situations.

Several other respondents discussed certain kinds of female anti-feminism. Some women, notes a biology professor, infight among each other. "This sets us back," she said, "because the pie is so small. We are all fighting for a bit of it instead of trying to make the pie bigger." Sheella Mierson and Francie Chew discuss the dangers of internalized sexism.

Also to be avoided is the Queen Bee syndrome, whose participants advance by being like men. Such women, points out a science educator, are not particularly nurturing to women. Concurred another:

> Many years ago, I listened to women who were supposedly successes and felt that many had paid a dreadful personal price for their professional achievements, a price that men need not pay. Women should be able to choose whether or not to buy into the male game.

A black and a Hispanic scientist concurred on the particularly poisonous mixture of sexism and racism. One fights it as follows:

> I have never been able to separate the effects of being black from the effects of being a woman. I was aware of racism, of the feeling you can't afford to fail because others will have a problem because of your failure. I also knew that there were boys who resented girls who did better than boys. Each individual must make her place in the world. It helps to know that paths have been made. People have survived, and you can also. There are people who are supportive. I wish there were better ways that women could support one another, so each woman could do what was right for her.

Also aware of what she called "a wave of racism within the power structure," adding that her colleagues are "not necessarily guilty" of it, the Hispanic pediatrician explained that "People's ideology somehow makes them distort others' realities, and people see you not as you are but as worse (or better) than you are because of their prejudices about you."

Differences

Several respondents tendered opinions on areas where men's and women's approaches appeared often to differ, only sometimes to the detriment of women. There are, as Lorraine J. Daston eloquently puts it, many ways of knowing. The two sexes tend to approach the same problem in different ways and communicate their ideas differently, according to one scientist. Women are more open and expressive, according to another. "I think that men may look at things with more tunnel-vision than women," said a third. While it is important that women not be so retiring that they are ignored, a pattern about which several respondents worried, they should not become like certain aggressive men or like Queen Bees either.

Instead, noted one scientist,

> There's another factor we're only beginning to recognize: Women work differently than men do. I'm not sure that the cultures of industry or academe are hospitable to a woman's perspective. Women tend to run very open shops. Information is accessible—everybody knows what's going on. Men see information as power, and they share it only grudgingly. These factors must be better understood, for they are critical in getting women into positions of power.

But there is no clear consensus on gender differences. To conclude with the opinions of two respected women scientists on the matter:

♦ "Stereotypically, men tend to approach tasks in a more concrete, structured way, while women tend to see the totality of the task and do not necessarily choose to do step one first. In this respect, my husband and I are opposites, but not in the way you might expect. He's far more intuitive, and, because of my training, I approach a problem in a much more structured way."

♦ "I can't make a generalization about *men* and *women*. Even when I talk of a man and a woman, the matter is complex: While my husband tends to be interested in theoretical matters and I in practical aspects, my oldest daughter also tends to the theoretical."

For further advice on gender issues, see interviews with Anikeeff, Brenchley, Cox, Filner, Hopkins, Kantor, Putzrath, Rodríguez-Trías, Rubin, Spotted Eagle, Bitsie, Gamble, Lucio, and Samuels. A number of these respondents also touch on matters of race and ethnicity.

Staying Put

During the course of the interviews, women have proffered advice on many professional and personal subjects. They have suggested ways to smooth one's educational path and to move into a job. The next problem is how, if she wishes, the new employee can become a veteran. Respondents share their advice in terms of what was most helpful in keeping them in science or mathematics once they had entered the field. Scientists and students usually credited several sustainers, but far and away the greatest gratitude went to their mentors and teachers at all postelementary levels. They also cited their own determination and interest in their work and their family's support. For further advice on retention, see the interviews with Filner, McAfee, Hardy, Douglass, and Cox.

Advice

A majority of respondents offered "advice to a young woman thinking of embarking on a scientific career." Like the women themselves, the responses are richly individual, useful, quirky, and virtually uncategorizable. For example—

◆ "Gravitate toward people who have bad attitudes. That means they are *thinking*—Darwin, Freud, the Curies, and Pasteur all were asking disturbing questions."

◆ "There's no use saying that you should have done something sooner, or that it's too late now."

Nearly a third of the scientists and students counseled persistence in the face of discouragement. "Stay the course," said one, speaking for many. "Don't take no for an answer," agrees another, "and remember: If somebody else can do it, so can you."

AWIS invites you to follow their suggestions.

Deborah C. Fort, Ph.D., is a Washington, D.C., writer and editor who writes for science and education programs in the private and public sectors. Along with her work for AWIS, she recently served as association editor for the National Science Teachers Association's Gifted Young in Science *and is currently working on a book about women in transition.*

Part III
Advice From the Field

Philosophic Questions

Ways of Being Rational*
Lorraine J. Daston

I must preface this personal account of my experiences as student and later teacher of the history of science with a *caveat lector*. In no field are the trajectories of entry so zigzag and divergent as those

that lead to careers in the history of science. Because almost nothing human—or natural—is foreign to the history of science, and because colleges and universities rarely offer an undergraduate concentration in the subject, historians of science come from backgrounds in the sciences, history, philosophy, sociology, and even literature. Therefore, no one's experience counts as typical, least of all my own. Nor can the pedagogical generalizations based on that experience be safely generalized without canvassing a larger sample. With that caution, I offer my experiences and observations as that notoriously untrustworthy statistical device, the sample of one.

Like the vast majority of high school students (and for that matter, college students), I was taught only a few paragraphs' worth of the history of science in the many hours I spent in chemistry, biology, physics, and mathematics classes. These were the sentences of praise and blame that were the stuff of textbook introductions. They were riveting, these condensed narratives of Galileo and Darwin, of Gauss and Mendel, for they were full of the heroism of the mind—a hopeful alternative for those of us who did better at algebra than at field hockey. But for just that reason, these brief tales of truth triumphant and error vanquished would hardly have inspired the best students to careers in the history of science, even if we had known that there was such a thing: We burned with the ambition

---

to become the subjects of these legends, not their chroniclers; to become Holmes, not Watson.

My first intimation of a different, richer history came in an entirely different context: Learning Euclidean geometry. The ideology of progress ran strong in the textbook paragraphs, and with it the unspoken but unmistakable implication that if newer was better, old was bad and older was worse. Yet here were arguments and conclusions—the most pellucid arguments and compelling conclusions I had ever seen—that were purportedly over two thousand years old. I looked up "Euclid" in the *World Book Encyclopedia* and read and reread the article until the pages were dog-eared and smudged. I spent the greater part of ninth grade trying to trisect an angle with ruler and compass. I drove my parents to distraction by insisting on demonstrations for statements like, "You must make your bed in the morning." Years later, I learned how many figures in the history of science and philosophy, both major and minor, had been bewitched by the arrow-straight, crystal-clear deductions of Euclid. For many of these thinkers, the clarity and certainty of geometry had stood in opposition to the vagaries and obscurity of history. But for me, the discovery of Euclidean geometry was the rehabilitation, if not the discovery, of history: It taught me that the present and future had no monopoly on rationality.

What a genuine history of that kind of rationality (better, rationalities) we call scientific might look like was the discovery of my first few years in college. I had the great good fortune to attend one of the few institutions where history of science had been cultivated in its own right, with a small but lively department dedicated to its study, and where it had been integrated with rigor and imagination into many introductory science courses. As a freshman at Harvard, I had never heard of the discipline of the history of science, so it was simply blind luck that led me to Professor Owen Gingerich's introductory astronomy course. In Natural Sciences 9, as it was then called, we learned not only how to find latitude from the pole star and how to read stellar spectra; we also learned Aristotle's arguments for the quintessence, the admirable complexity of Ptolemy's devices, how Kepler had triangulated the orbit of Mars, the observations that had driven Planck to quantize energy, and the observations that had *not* driven Einstein to the theory of relativity. Professor Gingerich's lectures were studded with vivid anecdotes and with elegant laboratory demonstrations that always worked (not until I began teaching did I realize that this was a feat bordering on the miraculous: The laws of nature cannot be depended upon to hold in the classroom), but what most impressed me then and now were his explanations of past scientific theories, clear and convincing once certain plausible assumptions and unavoidable constraints were conceded. These explanations were fortified with exercises: We not only learned about equants and eccentrics, we applied them to the inequality of the seasons; we not only studied Kepler's triangulations, we repeated them; we not only listened to Professor Gingerich's proof that Newton's laws of force and Leibniz's conservation principles were technically equivalent, we solved problems using both. The explanations persuaded us of the reasonableness of past scientific theories, even if they hinged upon assumptions (for example, the unity and harmony of the cosmos) that we could no longer embrace. But it was the exercises that allowed us to see the world as the framers of these theories had seen it, for the exercises allowed us to categorize and manipulate that world as the framers had. The pedagogical lesson of Natural Sciences 9 was a behaviorist one: to think in a certain way, one must act in a certain way. Or to put it in different terms, world views begin with in-the-fingers knowledge.

Natural Sciences 9 won me over to the history and philosophy of science. In the course of my undergraduate and graduate studies, my fine teachers, including I. Bernard Cohen, Erwin Hiebert, Gerald Holton, and Dirk Struik, taught me the importance of situating scientific thought in its cultural and philosophical context and of a sort of anthropological sympathy with conceptions of nature other than our own. Without ever abandoning the precept that scientific theories must be reasoned accounts of nature, they showed their students how broad and deep the realm of reason could be and had been. In my own subsequent teaching, it is this catholic approach to the rational understanding of nature that has kindled the interest of the most thoughtful students, be they trained in the sciences or the humanities. Once the history of science ceases to be a history of error, it becomes a source of unsuspected insights into the role of methods and metaphysics for the scientists; once it ceases to be the history of inexorable, headlong progress, it becomes an example of the contingencies and complexities that fascinate the humanists.

Lorraine J. Daston received a Ph.D. in the history of science from Harvard University in 1979 and has taught at Harvard, Princeton, Brandeis, Gottingen, and the University of Chicago. Her research interests include the history of probability and statistics, the place of the marvelous in early modern science, and, most recently, of the ideals and practices of scientific objectivity since 1600.

The "Problem" of Women in Science: Why Is It So Difficult to Convince People There Is One?

Sheila Tobias

In this volume, Betty M. Vetter (pages 267–270) and Shirley M. Malcom (pages 181–193) present some of the discouraging statistics

about women in science. There are various interpretations of what those statistics mean—but it is still surprisingly difficult to convince working scientists that there *is* a problem or that it is *their* problem and not the fault of women scientists themselves.

I have spent the past 20 years as a feminist analyst and activist—in that order—because analysis must precede activism if policy recommendations are to be effective. During the last eight of those years, I have been studying the ideology of science and science achievement. That study has led me to link the ideology of patriarchy to the mythologies that dominate the search for new scientific talent.

Patriarchy

From a feminist point of view, patriarchy is the domination of a society by males whose primary purpose is to construct and to maintain a certain power over women. In such a society (and we feminists believe that we live in one), much of what we take to be traditional or even "true" is really an extended political maneuver to maintain the unequal power relationship between males and females.

This does not necessarily imply a conspiracy, in which every man colludes with every other man to keep women out of power. Rather, in their enjoyment of privilege and individual advantage, most men accede to the system that is in place and have no particular interest in making change.

This theory was first sketched out in modern times by theoretician Kate Millett (1970), who observed that there were three dimensions on which males and females are differentiated: Temperament, role, and status. The man on the street and the traditional psychologist will both typically assert that women are temperamentally, that is, psychologically, different from men. Women, they believe, are more passive and men are more active; women are more dependent, and men, more independent. If such theories are true, this means that women are less comfortable with and less likely to seek a life of their own. In terms of rationality, these theories contend, women are intuitive and rely on their feelings for truth, while men are more concerned with what is demonstrably true and are more systematic in their thinking.

Consider what such "sex differences" mean for women in science.

As to the second dimension—adult roles—patriarchs want people to believe that adult role differentiation is as "natural" as (and, indeed, grows out of) temperamental differences. The mothering desire to marry and to make a home is as natural for females as the male's need to make his mark in the outside world. Woman is a private entity; man a public one.

Finally, as an equally inevitable consequence of role differentiation, men enjoy higher status than women, because what men like and do is socially more important than what women like and do.

Virginia Woolf, one of our inspirators, once observed that Leo Tolstoy was considered a greater writer than Jane Austen because he wrote about war and peace, while Austen limited herself to dramas of interpersonal relationships. But who decides, Woolf asked, that war is more important than interpersonal relations? Someone else— the society in which the novelists wrote and are read. Since men derive status from what they do, the argument is cyclic: *What* men do is more important *because* men do it.

In the popular view, to sum up, the causal chain of temperament-role-status begins with temperament and ends with status. Temperamental differences, which supposedly coincide with birth, lead inevitably, logically, and naturally to role and status differentiations. Since the key years of professional advancement (in our era) are between 25 and 40, the years when "normal" women are fulfilling their mother-home yearnings, men end up in higher status positions than women.

Upending Traditions

Thus, Millett explained how patriarchy works. But her more important contribution was simply to *reverse* that causal chain, much in the way that we tell our political theory students that Marx stood Hegel on his head. *Status,* argued Millett, *comes first.* For patriarchy, the essential task is to maintain the superiority of males over females. And to do so, to keep women out of power, women are assigned roles that busy them in caretaking in isolation from other adults.

How are these different roles assigned? And what causes women to accept them? With brilliant insight, Millett defined the people-professionals (social and behavioral scientists, therapists, and educators) as being a new "priesthood" exercising social control by redefining what is "normal" and what is not. Let a woman declare the mother role constricting, and she is found unnatural, abnormal, and in need of professional help. And that, Millett helped us see, is the modern-day punishment for inappropriate role behavior.

Because it sheds new light on so many previously accepted traditions, and because it made us angry, Millett's analysis was a powerful motivator for the new feminism of the 1970s. Her assertion had an impact like that of the Copernican revolution. It evicted from centrality conventional assumptions about women's temperament, roles, and status, as Copernicus did the earth when he set the sun at the center of the solar system. Millett influenced many women in the early 1970s to look at the arrangements they had made with life, their relationship to men and other women, and the result was often the "click!" experience: When women suddenly saw their circumstances in these political terms, something went "click!" and life was never the same thereafter.

Implications for Women in Science

I think that the temperament required for dedicated, original work—the staying-up-all-night kind of work, the I-can't-think-about-anything-else-darling-not-even-you-tonight, because I've-got-those-things-growing-in-the-petri-dish kind of intensity—is antithetical to what is considered normal behavior for a female. Insofar as she experiences the feelings of the scientist, she is not feminine, and insofar as she accedes to the needs of her feminine nature, she won't be taken seriously as a scientist. Those childbearing years, when a woman is healthiest and has the most energy for child rearing, coincide with the peak opportunity years in any profession. And, to the extent that she is tempted to take a break, the cost to a woman's career, given the dominance of the male model in science, is high. Indeed, many of the reasons women give for leaving science and the reasons men give for not encouraging them to stay involve this double bind.

Where Millett's analysis particularly applies to women in science is in her consideration of the double bind. There are only three appropriate roles for women in our society: One is the mother role, the second is the wife-like role (in science, the research associate), the third is the decorative role (only possible, incidentally, when you are young). If you don't fit naturally into any of those, you've bought a fourth option, the *witch-bitch trough*.

Careers considered appropriate for women are extensions of these three roles. Working with children or old people in some nurturing capacity is, of course, an extension of the mother role. Women who are research associates all their lives, or secretaries, or assistants-to are playing out a wife-like role for those they serve. And women who entertain, in every variety of that function, are decorative objects.

Youth and Genius

Within the ideology of science one additional bias is at work that we don't see in other professions: This is the powerful idea that any really good work must be done when the scientist is young. If a woman returns to a university to do science at 35, even if she intends to spend the next 30 years at it full time, her colleagues tend to believe she's unlikely to make a major contribution. Science as a young person's game is a myth that originates in data culled from 18th- and 19th-century science when men (and women) didn't live very long. Most likely, according to a number of historians of science including Thomas S. Kuhn (1970) and C. Stewart Gillmor (1984, May 15, and 1972), another variable is at work besides the number of brain cells in youth: Newness to the field. See also Paula E. Stephan and Sharon G. Levin (1992), Jonathan R. Cole (1987), and Harriet Zuckerman, Cole, and John T. Bruer (1991).

In the end, of course, knowledge is power, and so it is not surprising that any dominant group will try very hard to keep subordinate groups away from knowledge. We know that during slavery and beyond, African Americans were forbidden to learn to read, the first tool of knowledge. In the same spirit, every colonial power has kept its "natives" to a limited educational avenue. As women seek the very highest achievements in their knowledge gains, it will bring them not only status but power, and that is exactly what the entire patriarchal structure is designed to prevent.

The Third Gender

There have always been women scientists. How did they deal with such traditions and proscriptions? Mostly, as Margaret W. Rossiter (1982), Evelyn Fox Keller (1985), and Vivian Gornick (1990) have amply documented, by accepting the restrictions and accommodating their ambitions to men's needs for domination. Until the new wave of feminism about a quarter of a century ago, the survival

153

strategy of the typical American woman scientist was to persuade the men who taught her, funded her, and with whom she worked, that there were (as Betty Friedan puts it baldly in her oft-delivered talk) three sexes—men, women, and me. "What must be true of women *in general* is not true of *me*," such women asserted.

> To prove that to you, I will make myself as much like you, the dominant sex, as I can. I will deny my sisterhood with other women if that is the price I have to pay, deprive myself of family, if that is necessary. I'll have no spouse, pretend to have no social life, and certainly not display my sexuality. You may safely conclude I am not like other women, and therefore I don't deserve a female's status.

There is documentation for this pattern of accommodation, which Sheella Mierson and Francie Chew call *internalized sexism* (pages 261–266) and others the *Queen Bee Syndrome*. Rossiter, the historian of American women in science, tells us that women scientists were thankful for the tradition of using initials, not first names, on research papers, so they could appear as much like men (that is, to disappear as women) as they could. Rossiter reports that many such achievers were reluctant to answer questionnaires about being women in a man's world. Those who were married followed their husbands as research associates, happy to be able to do science at all.

When Gornick interviewed 100 women scientists in the 1970s, some of them by then in their 60s and 70s, most of them had had, they reported to her, "good lives." It did not occur to them that they might have had better lives, might have done science at a much higher level, had they been willing to fight for what they deserved. They had not organized; they had not made waves; they had not complained. Such women might do science, even good science, but—and this is my interpretation—being "in denial" of how their own lives and work had been affected by their gender, they could not have been good mentors for young women. They had internalized the values of their oppressors, feminists would say.

Like men, such female scientists would most likely concur that, on average, women were probably not as good scientists as men—they, of course, being the exception. Such women would probably have had as little time and tolerance for gender-specific role conflict as the men with whom they worked. So a younger woman coming to talk about her need to schedule a pregnancy might find in older women scientists as deaf an ear as she would find in men. Of course, there were exceptions, but denial, historians say, was the norm.

When Keller's much heralded biography of the late Barbara McClintock came out (see Bill Moyers' interview with Keller on pages 164–175), arguing that McClintock's insights into corn genetics were "feminine" in their challenge to the dominant command-and-control paradigm in mainstream cell biology, and that her isolation as a scientist was gender related, McClintock's response was, "Hogwash." She insisted that there was nothing in her work that had anything to do with maleness or femaleness. Despite neglect and bad treatment from the scientific establishment, she continued to internalize the values of the dominant class to the end of her life.

Feminism has been in the air for twenty years. Instead of denying her womanhood, today's woman is willing to associate with other women and she knows that the *men-women-me* strategy must fail. But, as she pursues her scientific career, she runs into unregenerate views of what science is and what makes a good scientist that are held by most of her male mentors and colleagues—views virtually unchanged from the 1960s.

Many well-intentioned graduate professors, lab directors, and deans can and do point with pride to their fairness in handling their women students and to the absence of sexism, chauvinism, and sexual harassment in their domains. Individually, they attend to such issues because, *superficially*, they are liberated. But when a woman scientist fails, or quits, or doesn't achieve her predicted potential, they still blame her entirely. They are still unwilling to examine their behavior or her failure in terms of the prevailing norms (in politics we call these "belief systems") in science.

In Pursuit of "Excellence"

Why improve perfection? Those seeking to open science, to feminize it, will face serious opposition. Tens of thousands of scientists don't think science could be any better than it is. When Radcliffe College president Linda S. Wilson (see pages 255–260) herself a chemist, in a talk at the National Academy of Sciences criticized the competitiveness and "fierce rivalries" in today's science, scientist-respondents to the report of her talk in *The Scientist* (1992, January 20) wrote, at times in an angry tone, that they were merely defending "excellence." Such entrenched scientists think the quality of American science, at least at the graduate level, is the best in the world— educationally, the best it can be. Their approach, which is unashamedly elitist, means that only a very few can do science; hence, the educational process must be selective, must weed out all but the very fit in first-year college courses, graded on a curve. (For further analysis, see Tobias 1990, 1992.)

Predestinarianism—a term I borrow from seventeenth century Protestant theology—also stands in the way of reform. Many scientists believe that people who are going to do science are born, not made, and will be discovered early, if at all. That's the reason why, when scientists get interested in education, they tend to tinker with the schooling of the very young. The Education Directorate of the National Science Foundation, to take but one example, spends over $500 million per year on precollege science, a mere $70 million on undergraduate science. Why this skew? Because, many scientists believe, only educational investment in children is likely to pay off.

The third component of the dominant ideology that resists change in the practice of science is the idea that science, unlike most other professions, is a calling. As a result, issues of mobility and family needs are necessarily secondary to the work itself. This tradition not only inhibits women; it also weighs heavily on many men. A recent Ph.D. in chemistry told his chairman he didn't want to leave town right away because his wife was moving ahead in a banking job. His professor's response was to cease to help the young man find a postdoctoral position, stating: "If you're not going to take your career seriously, I don't have to." This professor spoke entirely from ideology. He had no data that men who are married to dependent wives lead more productive lives in science than men who are not. His unreflective view was that a scientist must focus—whatever the personal cost—continuously on his career.

Linked to all these barriers to change in the practice of science is solipsism, the tendency to find truth and inevitability in one's own experience. The men in science—the professors and the mentors—are going to extrapolate from their own experience in helping women design theirs. With the best of intentions, they'll say, "When I was 28, I . . ." or "After my postdoc, I . . . ," all of which may or may not be relevant for a woman. In the best circumstance, the woman can educate them, and explain to them why this particular career line isn't appropriate for her. In the worst possible case, as with the young chemist just described, they may think less of the student who is not moving in familiar tracks.

None of these conservative forces—elitism, predestinarianism, science as a calling, or solipsism—is particularly directed against women. But all four philosophies have a disproportionately negative effect on anybody whose lifestyle or values or expectancies doesn't mirror theirs.

The Purpose: To Change Scientific Dogma

It is as difficult to argue someone out of a set of beliefs that have worked very well for their colleagues and themselves as to persuade someone to change religions. The feminist strategy of the 1990s has, therefore, shifted from an argument about *means* to a focus on *outcomes*.

In the first stage of our drive for equity, feminists attempted to achieve equality of opportunity or fairness, which we assumed to be synonymous with impartiality. We thought that if we could just remove structural barriers—male privilege, segregation, and gender bias—we would achieve educational equity. Later, it became clear that, even without barriers, women and men have different experiences in school. Minority students, all the more. Teachers are influenced by stereotyping, latent status, gender, skin color, and ethnic origin.

Feminist activists and researchers soon learned that removing barriers would not suffice. It would be necessary somehow to achieve *equality of experience.* How? Some approaches include all-girls' math classes, Summermath, compensatory training, career awareness, consciousness raising, and an extra dollop of math/science self-esteem. The test of whether there had been equality of experience would be whether there were *equality of outcomes.*

Today, the feminist educator's position is this: It doesn't matter to us how an institution gets there, what rules it adopts, or what rules it changes. We want to see women equally represented among the math/science majors and in the math/science professions. (For more specifics, see Elizabeth Fennema, 1990.) If, as some longitudinal studies of gifted children show, 8 percent of the top 1 percent of math-achieving boys attain the Ph.D. in math, science, or engineering (as, according to David Lubinski and Camilla Persson Benbow [1992, April] they do), then we want to see 8 percent of the top 1 percent of math-achieving girls do the same. Whatever the individual behavior, we're looking for aggregate outcomes. So for every female who drops out, there has to be some female who's attracted in.

The Benefits—For Humankind

Whatever we do to enhance the attainment of women in science is most probably going to benefit men as well. We've already seen evidence that those changes that make women feel more comfortable in math and science—personal attention in a more collaborative atmosphere—help men as well. In response, many feminists are shifting focus from individual differences to a more organizational perspective. See Mary Frank Fox (1993, January/February) for a similar view.

We are no longer asking women to adapt themselves to existing structures, but to negotiate from strength for changes in established institutions and places of work. This means feminist scientists ought not look for palliatives but for more radical action. To make a lasting impact, young women in science must embrace feminism and acknowledge both their debt to the feminists awakened in the 1970s and their obligation to serve similarly the needs of the next generation of young women. There is no question in my mind that this country would not have moved off the male-dominant model had we not forced open doors during the past two decades. Whether a woman in science sees herself as "political" or not, out of a sense of obligation, or a wish to change history, all have a stake in the struggle.

There's a terrible staple of tradition in American feminism (recently documented in Susan Faludi, 1992): Every 75 years or so, we have to start over from scratch. Our movement disappears from the history books and from our consciousness. For our sake, for the sake of our younger sisters, make sure this does not happen again.

References

Cole, Jonathan R. (1987). *Fair science: Women in the scientific community*. New York: Columbia University Press.

Faludi, Susan. (1992). *Backlash: The undeclared war against American women*. New York: Crown.

Fennema, Elizabeth. (1990). Justice, equity, and mathematics education. In Gilah C. Leder and Elizabeth Fennema (Eds.), *Mathematics and gender* (pp. 1–9). New York: Teachers College Press.

Fox, Mary Frank. (1993, January/February). Women, men, and the social organization of science. *AWIS Magazine, 22*(1), 17.

Friedan, Betty. Remark made frequently in public addresses.

Gillmor, C. Stewart. (1972). Personal communication to the author.

Gillmor, C. Stewart. (1984, May 15). Aging of geophysicists. *Eos, 65*(20), 353–354.

Gornick, Vivian. (1990). *Women in science*. New York: Simon and Schuster.

Keller, Evelyn Fox. (1985). *Gender and science*. New Haven: Yale University Press.

Kuhn, Thomas S. (1970). *The structure of scientific revolutions* (2nd ed., rev.). Chicago: University of Chicago Press.

Lubinski, David, and Benbow, Camilla Persson. (1992, April). Gender differences in abilities and preferences among the gifted: Implications for the math/science pipeline. *Current Directions in Psychological Science, 1*(2), 61–66.

Millett, Kate. (1970). *Sexual politics*. New York: Doubleday.

Radcliffe president lambastes competitiveness in research. (1992, January 20). *The Scientist, 6*(2), 3, 7.

Rossiter, Margaret W. (1982). *Women scientists of America* (Vols. 1–2). Baltimore: Johns Hopkins University Press.

Stephan, Paula E., and Levin, Sharon G. (1992). *Striking the mother lode in science: The important age, place, and time*. New York: Oxford University Press.

Tobias, Sheila. (1990). *They're not dumb, they're different: Stalking the second tier.* Tucson, AZ: Research Corporation.

Tobias, Sheila. (1992). *Revitalizing undergraduate science: Why some things work and most won't.* Tucson, AZ: Research Corporation.

Zuckerman, Harriet, Cole, Jonathan R., and Bruer, John T. (1991). *The outer circle: Women in the scientific community.* New York: Norton.

Sheila Tobias, an early member of the new feminist movement and a political activist, was a pioneer in women's studies and in the identification of math anxiety and science avoidance as important and surmountable barriers for bright women. She has written numerous books on these subjects and others, taught and done administration on the college level, and currently is working on two books on gender and politics: The Legacy of the New Feminism in America *and* Science as a Career: Perceptions and Realities.

The Red Shoe Dilemma

Lynn Margulis

For as long as I can remember, when someone asked me what I wanted to be when I grew up, I always answered *"an explorer and a writer."* Explorer of what? As a child, I didn't know: Undersea cities,

African jungle pyramids, unmapped tropical islands, polar caves. "Whatever will need exploring," I said without hesitation. Today, nearly incessantly, I explore with passion the inner workings of living cells to reveal their evolutionary history. And, as soon as I learn something new about bacteria or insect symbionts that helps explain the history of life on the Earth's surface, I write about it.

So you see, I am, after all these years, an explorer and a writer. Science for me is exploration, and no scientific work is complete if it has not been described and recorded in an article by the scientist herself (the "primary literature") or in a book or paper by someone else (the "secondary literature"). Much of my day is spent in description: Generating literature that speaks to fellow scientists and graduate students, talking in classes or lecturing to amuse the curious, writing notes and observations, collecting references, and jotting down the insights of others. I have become a mother (four children), a wife (twice), and a grandmother (once, so far).

Because no one in my early life ever even explained the existence of science, I never realized until adulthood that I could participate in the great adventure of science as a profession. Unlike many friends, neither as an adolescent nor as a young adult did I wait for "my prince to come." Rather I expected some—any—opportunity to join serious expeditions. Then, as today, I read nearly everything in sight: Bottle labels, train schedules, recipes, Spanish poetry, and novels. Decades ago, on the south side of Chicago, I used to ride the "IC" (Illinois Central Railroad) some 40 minutes, both in the stifling heat of summer and the freezing cold of winter, at least once weekly to the downtown "Loop" for ballet. Ballet classes (demanding, exhausting, French, and irrelevant) were sufficiently escapist to be captivating before scientists or exploratory missions were available in my life.

Choices

One film moved all of us dancers of those days: We all idolized red-headed Moira Shearer prancing in her *Red Shoes*. Set near Nice on the Mediterranean, close to a place with a marine station (Villefranche-sur-Mer) that I would get to know many years later, this romantic movie mesmerized my dancing classmates. The talent of this beautiful ballerina in the *prima donna* role was exhilarating, as was her true love for her sexy, handsome beau. I remember anger at the melodrama of that movie, however. I thought the dichotomy of her life that led to her self-instigated fate utterly ridiculous.

Why did there have to be "necessity to choose" between devotion to a man or a career? What generated the psychic dissonance that drove her to destruction? Obviously there was no reciprocity: If the star had been male, he would not have been driven to choose. He simply would have taken a wife. Instead, under relentless pressure to be the perfect dancer whose shoes run away with her, the ballerina yields to the dance master's demands that she remain in the spotlight, stage center of his world. But, equally enamored of her man, she is driven by another urgent exigency: Her lover demands that she marry him and have a family.

Caught between the pressure of career and love, she could only resolve the conflict by suicide. Why hadn't she simply married her lover, borne her children, and continued dancing? Hollywood resolved her dilemma tragically, making the young heroine jump to her death from the summit of a sea wall. What infuriated me was the idea that the healthy, beautiful, and ambitious ballerina had to accept the "either-or" notion imposed upon her by the two men who ran her life. Should she simply have opted for *everything*, however, she would have deprived the film of its trumped-up fatal conflict. Wasn't a strong family life *and* a career possible for Moira Shearer's character? Isn't such a full life even easier today in the age of food storage by deep freeze, the private automobile, the dishwasher, and the laundry machine?

Having It All? Hardly!

At age 15 I was certain that the ballerina died because of a silly antiquated convention that insisted that it is impossible for any woman to maintain *both* family and career. I am equally sure now that the people of her generation who insisted on *either* marriage *or* career *were* correct, just as those of our generation who perpetuate the myth of the superwoman who simultaneously can do it all—husband, children, and professional career—are *wrong*.

161

Today many students, especially women, ask me for enlighten-ment, how to combine successfully career and family. When they learn I have four excellent, healthy, grown children and never abandoned science even for a single day in over 35 years, they request my secret. Touting me as an example of an American super-woman, they label me a "role model" (a term I despise). But there is no secret. Neither I nor anyone else can be superwoman.

Aspiring to the superwoman role leads to thwarted expectations, the helpless-hopeless syndrome, failed dreams, and frustrated ambi-tions. A lie about what one woman can accomplish leads to her, and her mate's, bitter disappointment and to lack of self-esteem. Such delusions and self-deceptions, blown up and hardened, have reached national proportions. Rampant misrepresentation of feasi-bility abounds as everyone falls short of the national myth peopled with a happy family, educated children, and professionally fulfilled parents. Something has to give: The quality of the professional life, of the marriage, of the child rearing—or perhaps all—must suffer.

A Dangerous Myth

The unreality of such expectations, coupled with the gross inade-quacy of our educational system—such as it is—often leads to de-spair temporarily relieved by mind-numbing drugs—marijuana, whiskey, cocaine—or other escapes.

Each husband, wife, and child in this sea of false hope suffers the crushing pain of inadequacy. In the United States, we value the beauty and strength of youth, but, as a culture, we disdain love for children as "touchy-feely" and denigrate home-making as trivial and unworthy. We marginalize or expel the elderly and ridicule life on communes. By no means are the homeless on the street the only ones without homes. Unwilling to care for our greatest resource and those in direst need—our infants and children—we, speaking through money, debase their instructors, despising the seriousness needed to acquire a fine education. Our culture laughs at the intel-lectual while lauding the merely acquisitive.

One Woman's Path

I have not in any way overcome these stresses or resolved these common problems. I have just ignored them, as if they were laws that do not apply to me. Looking beyond such social heartaches, I chose intellectual exploration as my way of life and allied myself with nonhuman planetmates, with the scientific quest, rather than devoting myself to an arbitrary integrity of family and human community.

162

And, of course, I never jumped off the ballerina's cliff; the thought of abandoning life itself has always been unthinkable. Be warned, though, I do not offer a recipe for personal fulfillment—superwoman does not exist, even in principle.

Mine is the story of scientific enthusiasm and enlightenment coming to a foolish and energetic girl who turned down dates on Saturday night and who *never* watched television. The point is that I was willing to work. This is not a statement of advocacy, as no single answer or easy path suits every woman. Probably, I have contributed to science because twice I quit my job as a wife. I abandoned husbands but stayed with children. I've been poor, but I've never been sorry.

Children, husband, and excellence in original science are probably not simultaneously possible. Yet women who feel the urge must be encouraged to pursue scientific careers. Such women need our help. If life does not pose its problems as melodramatically as a Hollywood movie, neither does it resolve them so cleanly or definitively.

Yes, women can, of course, be superb scientists, but only at great sacrifice to their social life and its obligations. Most critically productive women and girls must be surrounded by supportive and loving men and boys. We all need a cultural infrastructure that respects the deep needs of our young children and older family members. Let us hope that the provision of such enablers as scholarship monies, family leave opportunities, enlightened health insurance programs, imaginative and indulgent day care for preschoolers, and afterschool play programs will increase the probability that talented and determined women will contribute much more to the scientific adventure in the future than they ever have been able to in the past.

I thank Deborah C. Fort, Dorion Sagan, Landi Stone, and the Richard Lounsbery Foundation for aid in preparing this paper.

Lynn Margulis, Ph.D., Distinguished University Professor of Biology at the University of Massachusetts at Amherst, has written over 100 scientific articles and numerous books. She has worked with atmospheric chemist James E. Lovelock on the Gaia Hypothesis, *which examines how life makes its own environment at the Earth's surface. She has developed the modern molecular-biological version of the evolution of plant and animal cells via symbiosis. She now works on the hypothesized origin of undulipodia (like sperm tails and cilia) from spirochete bacteria and aids in the development of middle school science units on what happens to garbage and trash.*

A Conversation with Bill Moyers[*]

Evelyn Fox Keller

MOYERS: *What are you doing teaching in the department of rhetoric?[†] What does rhetoric have to do with science?*

KELLER: I have had a somewhat checkered career, and I have  written in many different areas. So I pose a problem to the academy. Where can we put Evelyn Fox Keller? They can no longer put me in the physics department. They don't want to put me in the biology department anymore. I'm not formally a historian. And although I think of myself as working in the history and philosophy of science, there are very few history and philosophy of science programs in the country.

So when Berkeley offered me a job in rhetoric and women's studies with an affiliation in history of science, I thought, well, at the very least it's an imaginative solution. But it also made a certain kind of sense, because I realized over the last decade that what I was talking and thinking about kept coming back to the question of language and science. That's what I try to understand—how language works in science. Language is the mediator of human values and human expectations in our descriptions of nature. If we want to understand the ways in which science is reflecting back to us particular expectations, particular values, we have to look at the language of science and see how that works. How the traffic between ordinary and technical language works as a carrier, if you will, of ideology into science.

MOYERS: *One of your chief contributions to this has been to clarify the significant role gender plays in the language scientists use to describe their work.*

KELLER: It has played a very, very powerful role.

*From Bill Moyers: *A World of Ideas,* by Bill Moyers. Copyright © 1989 by Public Affairs Television, Inc. Used by permission of Doubleday, a division of Doubleday Dell Publishing Group, Inc.

†At the time of this interview, Keller was teaching in the department of rhetoric at the University of California, Berkeley. She has since moved to the Massachusetts Institute of Technology.

164

MOYERS: *By gender you do not mean sex, our biological differences.*

KELLER: No, I mean ideas of masculinity and ideas of femininity. We see it at the very beginning of modern science with the scientific revolution of the seventeenth century. The Royal Society of London, one of the first modern scientific societies, was founded in order to "raise a masculine philosophy." What did they mean by a masculine philosophy? Well, Francis Bacon said, "Let us establish a chaste and lawful marriage between Mind and Nature." The purpose of this marriage was to bind nature and bring nature and all her children to your service. Bind her and make her your slave.

MOYERS: *And the purpose of science was to give the mind—the husband—mastery over nature—the bride?*

KELLER: That's right. The central metaphor for the scientific revolution was a marriage between the mind and nature that was modeled on a particular kind of marriage, a patriarchal marriage, the purpose of which was the domination of nature.

MOYERS: *And the Royal Society of London was founded in 1662 but didn't admit a woman until 1945!*

KELLER: Women were excluded from many domains, not just science. But scientists had a particular commitment to the notion that there was something special about what they were doing. It was a special kind of thinking. A special kind of philosophy. A special kind of activity. In the most general sense, science meant "thinking like a man." It was committed to an idea of objectivity that was from the beginning equated with masculinity in a very curious way.

In fact, it was that equation that motivated my entire inquiry. I wanted to understand what it meant to say "thinking objectively" is "thinking like a man." What could it mean? Where does such an idea come from? And more important, what consequences has it had for science? These early scientists used such language for a reason. People would respond in ways that the language intended. The scientists were trying to articulate a form of knowledge and the rules by which you could demarcate correct from incorrect modes of knowing. They were also demarcating who should be engaged in this pursuit and who should not. But it wasn't just the demarcation of men from women. In fact, it was very little about the demarcation of men from women. It was much more the demarcation of *values.* They invoked the language of gender in order to justify the exclusion of a certain domain of human activity, particularly the exclusion of feeling and emotion, from the pursuit of science.

Here is how Joseph Glanvill (1636–1680) described it: "That Job himself cannot be *wise* and in *Love;* may be understood in a larger sense, than Antiquity meant it: Where the *Will* or *Passion* hath the

165

casting voyce, the case of *Truth* is *desperate*. . . . The *Woman* in us, still prosecutes a deceit, like that begun in the *Garden*; and our *Understandings* are wedded to an *Eve*, as fatal as the *Mother* of our miseries." He concludes: "Truth has no chance when the *Affections* wear the breeches and the *Female* rules."

MOYERS: *He was saying that we have to exclude feeling, empathy, intuition from the search into how the world works.*
KELLER: That's right. But he's doing it by attaching these to the female and excluding both. We're excluding "Affections"—feeling and emotion—because they're female, and we're excluding females because they carry these attributes with them. But once you've documented the pervasive gender imagery in the language of scientific development, once you have shown how prevalent these images of masculinity and femininity and domination were, the question remains—so what? That's really the question. Some people might say, yes, but that was just in the seventeenth century; we've left that long since behind. Well, we haven't left it behind. It is still with us. Listen to this passage from C. P. Snow's *The Masters*, written in 1951. He's describing a young scientist, Luke, who has just had a breakthrough.

> "It's wonderful," he bursts out, "when you've got a problem that is really coming out. It's like making love. Suddenly your unconscious takes control and nothing can stop you. You know that you're making old Mother Nature sit up and beg, and you say to her I've got you, you old bitch. You've got her just where you want her."

MOYERS: *So a mythology was created that objectivity, reason, and the mind are male attributes and subjectivity, feeling, and nature are female attributes. But what did that mean to the history of science? Did it change the content of science?*
KELLER: That, of course, is the hardest question of all. Clearly, it mattered to the history of science in that the effect was the exclusion of women. Of course there have always been some women in science. I don't want to contribute to the erasure of the very brave and heroic and talented few women who managed to survive in that history.

But obviously a science that advertises itself in that language is not going to be hospitable to women. So one immediate consequence was that the domain of science was restricted to men, and to a particular world of men, and the development of science was deprived of a pool of talent. But it also meant the exclusion of certain kinds of talent in the men who did become scientists. Did that change the quality of it, did that affect the content of science?

That's the question, but it's a very, very difficult question. We have learned—the hard way, I think—that it isn't true that science gives us a mirror or reflection of nature. We've learned that that picture of science doesn't work. What actually happens is that the descriptions of nature, the theories of nature, are very complexly influenced by all kinds of social, cultural, and psychological presuppositions.

MOYERS: *That kind of presupposition has had a significant impact on a lot of people. Here is a passage from Jacques Monod, a biologist, whom you quote in one of your papers:*

> *If he accepts this message in its full significance, man may awaken from his millenary dream and discover his total solitude, his fundamental isolation, and realize that like a gypsy he lives on the boundary of an alien world. A world that is deaf to his music and as indifferent to his hopes as it is to his suffering or his crimes.**

KELLER: I think that's a wonderfully revealing passage. Monod is arguing for a mechanical universe, for a universe that is devoid of human emotions and human feelings. But he has projected onto that universe emotions that can only be human. It is only a human who can feel alien, abandoned, isolated. Atoms and molecules aren't deaf. They're neither deaf nor hearing; it is people who are deaf or hearing. So it's an interesting illustration of the way in which, despite our greatest efforts to objectify the universe, to remove ourselves from our pictures of nature, we're nevertheless importing our own language, our own expectations, our own categories. No matter how hard we try to eliminate those hopes and anxieties, they are still there.

---

*Keller elaborates in *Reflections on Gender and Science* (1985, pp. 169–170): "Several years [after the discovery of the structure of DNA], Watson and Crick's original model was emended by Jacques Monod and François Jacob to allow for environmental control of the rates of protein synthesis. But even with this modification, the essential autonomy of DNA remained unchallenged: information flowed one way, always from, and never to, the DNA.

Throughout the 1950s and 1960s, the successes of molecular genetics were dramatic. By the end of the 1960s, it was possible to say (as Jacques Monod did say), 'The Secret of Life? But this is in large part known—in principle, if not in details' " (quoted in Judson, 1979, p. 216).

MOYERS: *The physicist Steven Weinberg talks about the universe as being overwhelmingly hostile. Do you feel the universe is hostile?*

KELLER: How can the universe be hostile? Weinberg also says, "The laws of nature are cold and indifferent. We didn't want it to come out that way; it just came out that way." I think in a sense we did want it to come out that way. The language of hostility, of coldness, of indifference is a human language. It's written into the very notion of laws of nature.

MOYERS: *In what sense?*

KELLER: A law of nature is a very curious construct. Whose law is the law of nature? Where does the idea of a law of nature come from? And what is the function of a law of nature? The concept of a law of nature originally comes from the realm of God. They were God's laws to which the material universe must be obedient. So the very idea of a law of nature structures a notion of hierarchy, proscription, law-giving, and obedience to those laws.

Now in a contemporary sense, we don't believe in God's laws. But still, the laws exist in our imagination, somehow above the phenomena, and the phenomena must conform to the laws of nature. This is very important when you think about how physicists actually work, and how we develop our science. Francis Bacon gave us all kinds of memorable expressions about how we have to vex nature. That only under the act of vexation will nature reveal her truths. Well, we do vex nature. We vex nature quite a bit. It is no easy task to make nature conform to the laws of nature. Let me tell you as a scientist, it is very hard work to get nature to conform to the laws of nature. The natural phenomena have to be structured and constrained and twisted and vexed to an astonishing degree before they will obey the laws of nature.

MOYERS: *So when Steven Weinberg (1974) says that the laws of nature are as impersonal and free of human values as the rules of arithmetic, you're not objecting to the formula as much you are to the very language, the very use of the word "law" to describe the operations of nature.*

KELLER: I'm objecting to both. I'm objecting to the language of laws and also objecting to the notion that they are as free of human values as the rules of arithmetic. It's not true. It is a fantasy that any human product can be free of human values. Science is a human product. It's a wonderful, glorious human product.

MOYERS: *But what about nature? Nature is not a human product. The natural world is not a human product.*

KELLER: Yes, but science doesn't give us nature. Science gives us a description of nature. Science gives us scientific theories of nature.

MOYERS: *In the description of nature, we assign to that description our own subjective experience.*
KELLER: There is no way of avoiding that. There is no magic lens that will enable us to see nature uncolored by the values, hopes, fears, anxieties, desires, goals that we bring to it.

MOYERS: *Are you arguing that if there were more women in science, we'd be studying acid rain instead of Star Wars?*
KELLER: I wish that were true. I wish all we had to do was to bring more women into science. But it's much more complicated because these social and ideological patterns get imprinted onto the very structure of science. What I worry about most is the ways in which science is used in the world. If this history of sexism, of patriarchy, of racism, of imperialism, of all the values that I find offensive, has had a hand to play in the actual science that has been developed, then I think that is far more important than the question of women in science.

The question of women in science is important. I don't want to say it's not important. But given the tremendous role that science plays in the world we live in, the idea that we might redirect science, that there could be changes in the way in which science is done and the direction in which it moves—that seems to me of even greater importance.

MOYERS: *Do you think that has cost us something in our creative vision, in the creativity of science? Do we miss certain things about the world because science is gendered masculine?*
KELLER: Well, that's my principal argument. My strongest case for that argument is the story of Barbara McClintock, who won a Nobel Prize in 1983 for her work in genetics. I titled my biography of McClintock *A Feeling for the Organism*. It wasn't for my agenda that I chose that title; the words are hers. It's her deepest belief that you cannot do good research without a feeling for the organism. I argued that it was her feeling for the organism that led her to recognize that genetic elements move within the chromosome.

MOYERS: *What do you mean by "a feeling for the organism"?*
KELLER: I mean the ability to identify with the subject you are studying. To feel kinship instead of a sense of a battle, a struggle, a state of opposition.

MOYERS: *You really feel that's primarily a female mode of approaching science?*
KELLER: No, I believe that's been *called* a female mode of approaching science. I believe it is a human virtue, a human talent.

We are talking about the capacity for empathy. I don't think that women have a corner on the market of empathy; I think all of us are capable of empathy. I do think that it's not a talent that is very well-developed in many men because of the ways in which they're raised. But it is precisely because it has been identified as a feminine virtue, as a feminine talent, that it has been excluded from science.

MOYERS: *You make me think of something you wrote earlier. You said, "We have developed scientific methods and techniques to change the world without asking what we would change the world to. We've never acknowledged we were making choices that could change the world." My question is: what kind of world would you like to change us to?*

KELLER: I'd like to change the world to make it better for humankind—for all people. I have only the most idealistic visions that we all can share. I want a world that will preserve and augment life. I want a world that will promote peace. I want what most people want, really, for the world. I'd like to see a science that serves the ideals of social justice. There's nothing novel in that. But we're not asking what our science is doing—what the knowledge that we're seeking is for. There's no way in which we are going to map all of nature. We are never going to have a complete science. So the question becomes what questions are we asking, what kinds of knowledge, what parts of nature are we seeking to engage, and for what purpose? What guides these choices? It's a selection process in the first place. What aspects of nature are we going to try to model, to develop theories of, and toward what end?

MOYERS: *Assuming that we could move to a science that is gender free, how different would that science be? What would we see differently?*

KELLER: I do believe that there is a history of complicity in science with the forces of aggression that has in part to do with the historic genderization of science. On an institutional level, complicity between physics and the military is well known. This is a social, structural complicity; remember, the military is another domain subject to very sharp gender demarcations. I hope a degenderization of science would break that complicity, would open science to a more erotic engagement with nature, to a more productive deployment of the uses of science toward the goals of life rather than death.

MOYERS: *Is it possible that we could replace the strongly masculine image of the scientist with one that is gender neutral?*

KELLER: Yes. But I don't know if that's enough. When I wrote my book in 1985, I was more optimistic than I am today.

170

MOYERS: *What do you mean?*

KELLER: In the early days I thought if we could just change the stranglehold of this gender ideology on science, it would have a tremendous effect. Not only would it open up the doors of science to women, it would allow men and women alike to think more freely. To make use of the full gamut of their human talents.

Now we have cleaned up the language of science. The gender ideology is not nearly as prominent or explicit as it was 10 years ago, and we have far more women in science. But that's not enough. We can degenderize the language of science and not make very much of a dent in the structures that are in place. Science in the late twentieth century is a product of three hundred years of evolution. It's naive to think that we could just change that structure just by changing the metaphors. The metaphors are built in. They're already embodied in the institutional structures of science. Science is what it is. To change science, therefore, requires a much more complex, long engagement. It's a much more difficult endeavor than I had thought.

MOYERS: *I remember the story of the great Danish seismologist* who talked about her education at the first coeducational school in Denmark where boys and girls were treated equally. They played football alike, and they learned needlework alike. Their intellects were not seen as being different. She said, "It wasn't until I left the coeducational school and went into the world that I realized society was organized differently." So if you're going to change, replace the masculine gender with a gender-free science, you've got to start way back down there.*

KELLER: It's not enough, though, to teach the boys needlework, although I think it's great to teach the boys needlework and the girls carpentry. I'm all for that. I think one has to carry that forward. It's very interesting to think about how it is happening that there are now more women in science. What kinds of arrangements are making that possible? What I had had in mind when I thought we could move more toward a gender-free science was an integration of the laboratory and the nursery. I had in mind a sharing of the responsibilities of men and women by men and women. What we are finding instead—it's a very familiar solution—is that child rearing, the principal task that has traditionally been the task of women, is being parceled off onto other women. The women who become scientists are now becoming scientists because they're liberated from the sphere of domesticity.

---

*Inge Lehmann, who in 1936 was the first person to discover the nature of the inner core of the earth.

MOYERS: *But every woman can't be a scientist just as every man can't be a scientist.*

KELLER: Right. We need people to take care of children. But if you want to degender science then you have to engage men in the spheres that were traditionally those of women. Otherwise, you're not going to redistribute the gendered values in the culture.

MOYERS: *And the world remains very much the way the world is. Recently, I read an article which moves us from science to politics, but I think the analogy is appropriate here. "Is Margaret Thatcher a woman?" the headline asks. And then the subheadline answers, "No woman is, if she has to make it in a man's world." The writer says that not only has Margaret Thatcher been the first Prime Minister since the war not to put a woman in the Cabinet, but she's actually appointed fewer women than any other Prime Minister. Her own children have been sacrificed the same way the families of men are sacrificed when they're consumed by politics. The point is that Margaret Thatcher's arrival as Prime Minister of England has succeeded by political standards because she acted, this author says, as if she were a man. She is a surrogate man; an imitation man, says this writer. What's your reaction to that?*

KELLER: Probably the only thing I would defend in Margaret Thatcher is her right to choose her relation to the stereotypic roles that have traditionally been assigned to women. She is a woman as much as any other woman; she's not a stereotypic woman. She has that right. The major thrust of the feminist movement in the twentieth century has been to struggle for the rights of individuals to choose their courses unfettered by traditional stereotypes. Margaret Thatcher has done that. That she has not appointed women to the Cabinet, that her politics are not good for women in England— that's another problem. That I will not defend. But I don't think one can both saddle her with the responsibilities of traditional womanhood and ask her to be a Prime Minister in the world. I think that those are incommensurable categories.

MOYERS: *Do you think she's acting like a man?*

KELLER: She's acting like a traditional, stereotypic man, yes. She has the right to act like a stereotypic man, just as I want to defend the right of men to act like stereotypic women. I want to break down these boundaries.

MOYERS: *Who first interested you in science?*

KELLER: The long and short of it is that I read a series of books by George Gamow [1904–1968] for a composition class because I had to find something I could write a decent paper on. That was what turned me. Many people were encouraging me very strongly to go

172

into science, but it was George Gamow's books that turned me around. I fell in love with physics.

MOYERS: *You fell in love? That's a romantic notion.*
KELLER: Yes. It was an appropriate notion. I fell in love with the life of the mind. It was a very compelling vision for me. But my career in physics was thwarted by my being a woman, in very conspicuous ways.

MOYERS: *Do you know why?*
KELLER: I was a graduate student in physics at Harvard in 1959, and that was extremely painful—in effect, it was impossible. I was one of three women in a class of a hundred. I could not get my professors to speak to me. I was scrutinized, laughed at, and humiliated. I came with a reputation of being very smart, and so I was an object of enormous curiosity. It was terrible. And very lonely. I couldn't take it. I did actually get my degree in theoretical physics, but only after leaving the actual premises to do my dissertation on molecular biology. Finally, it was teaching my first women's studies course in 1974 that provided the occasion for me to talk about my experiences as a graduate student at Harvard. It had been so painful, and my efforts to talk about it at the time were met with such condemnation and dismissal, that I didn't try again until I was teaching in the State University of New York at Purchase. It became clear to me that it was important for women of my generation who had lived through this kind of experience to say what had gone on. To get it out in the open could serve a political function. I was prevailed upon by my students and colleagues to write that story, which I ultimately published in a book called *Working It Out*.

MOYERS: *Your search invites many more ways of seeing the world. Is that popular in the scientific establishment?*
KELLER: I am advocating a pluralistic vision. I am trying to argue for more tolerance in the scientific community, and that's not popular because it's not seen as efficient. But I think it's just a simple, elementary, logical observation that the phenomena of the natural world are infinitely more complex, are infinitely larger in density and in number than any series of propositions we can articulate. The phenomenology of nature is infinitely more vast than anything that can be encompassed by our theoretical apparatus. Our theoretical representations are of a much lower dimensionality than the phenomena in nature. So there's no way in which any theory can fully encompass that rich array of phenomena. It stands to reason that different perspectives would be very productive, and

173

would suggest other possibilities and other options. They would give us choices.

MOYERS: *A more creative way of seeing the world. Or exploring the world.*
KELLER: Or of seeing what we are exploring. Yes. Or considering the directions in which our explorations are taking us.

MOYERS: *In your early work as a scientist you said you believed in the accessibility of an underlying and unifying truth and that you fully accepted science and scientists as arbiters of the truth. Do you still believe that there is an underlying and unifying truth?*
KELLER: No. I like to think of that as the Truth. I believe in truths, but I don't believe in the Truth. Furthermore, I think that vision of an underlying Truth, with a capital *T*, that scientists are privy to, has been a very counterproductive vision. It has served scientists very well, but what it has done, above all, is enclose the world of science and immunize it from criticism. It has created a kind of insularity which protects the scientific world from the critical examination that I think is very necessary. Most of all, it insulates the scientific community from any examination of the recognition that we are making choices—any examination of the directions in which scientific inquiry is taking us. I think that it's absolutely essential that we engage in such examination.

MOYERS: *What is your starting point now for your inquiry into the nature of this world?*
KELLER: What I'm engaged in is the very difficult problem of trying to find a way of thinking and talking about science that does justice both to the cultural forces that give rise to it and the forces of nature with which science is engaging. To try and find a way of talking about science that both recognizes the force of language and also recognizes that theories do work.

Some theories *do* work. What does it mean to say a theory works? How are we going to account for the extraordinary success of scientific predictions— these extraordinary confirmations to 13 decimal places between experiment and theory—without invoking this very counterproductive and sometimes even dangerous metaphor of science as a mirror of nature? How are we to redescribe it in terms of the negotiation between the language of theory and the experimental phenomena with which we engage? That's the task at hand.

MOYERS: *So you still have a romance with science even though you've fallen out of love with physics.*
KELLER: I wouldn't even say I've fallen out of love with physics. It's one of the most wonderful human endeavors that has ever been.

I think it's marvelous. I want to see it better. It's a deeply satisfying inquiry into reality. I don't know if it's deeper than other kinds of inquiry, but it does seem to me capable of generating more stable accounts of phenomena. More reliable accounts that more of us could agree on if we were given the right place to stand.

References

Judson, Horace. (1979). *The eighth day of creation: Makers of the revolution in biology.* New York: Simon and Schuster.

Keller, Evelyn Fox. (1985). *Reflections on gender and science.* New Haven: Yale University Press.

Snow, C. P. (1951). *The masters.* London: Macmillan.

Weinberg, Steven. (1974, Summer). Reflections of a working scientist. *Daedalus,* 33–46.

Evelyn Fox Keller received her Ph.D. in theoretical physics at Harvard University, worked for a number of years at the interface of physics and biology, and is now professor of history and philosophy in the program in science, technology, and society at the Massachusetts Institute of Technology. She is perhaps best known as the author of A Feeling for the Organism: The Life and Work of Barbara McClintock; Reflections on Gender and Science; *and, most recently,* Secrets of Life, Secrets of Death: Essays on Language, Gender, and Science.

Education—Formal and Experiential

Precollege

Who Is Guiding Our Girls?

Betty P. Preece

Who is guiding our girls? Who is giving them ideas about what they could do with their lives? Who is helping them make plans and set goals for their futures? The answer seems to be "everyone" and "no one."

Many who come in contact with girls send them some kind of message about their lives. It may be accepted as appropriate, rejected as undesirable, or absorbed for later unconscious recall. The message may be spoken or merely an opportunity offered to observe more thoughtfully. It could say, "Look at me. You could be doing what I am doing!" or it could ask, "Do you really want to be as I am?"

Much too often, girls have no one actively exposing them to careers that produce a vision of and a path toward a satisfying future. Only some girls realize that nearly all of them will work for most of their adult lives. Their work can be drudgery, or it can offer rewards in self-esteem as well as money.

Readers of this book are among those who can provide the kind of career guidance that will make the difference for girls. Although we cannot reach many girls individually, we can help bring awareness directly to some of them and indirectly to others by reaching those who do influence them—their families, friends, teachers, community members, and the media, for example.

How Are Girls Being Guided?

A great many things affect girls' career plans or lack of them. Sometimes the influence is planned, but most often it is not and goes unrecognized as a factor in forming lifetime goals.

Girls consistently rate peer pressure as having significant effects on their career choices of school classes and extracurricular activities. Educators and counselors present career images through lessons, texts, comments, resource materials, and role models. Recreation leads many students to try careers that emulate those of popular figures in sports, music, and other performing arts. Families, friends, and the community all serve daily as examples of the work force.

TV programs are powerful sources of good and bad career information. More and more students are being touched by specific programs designed to provide enrichment in the sciences, engineering, or math.

Still, too many are not receiving information that enables them to make their own viable choices.

We women in science- and math-related careers want to see girls—and boys, too—become aware that education can be the key to a better life through planned careers dependent upon choice rather than chance. Only with wider exposure to career information, better understanding of their own capabilities, and knowledge of opportunities open to them can the young make this choice meaningfully.

Opening Doors for Girls—At Home

We can widen girls' choices by making it easier for them to take part in the activities in many arenas that influence career choices. For instance, we can encourage

◆ networking

◆ mentoring and role modelling

◆ curriculum changes

◆ enlightened counseling

◆ community awareness

◆ abolishing bias against science by parents, youth, and the public

◆ better representation in both the popular and the scientific media

◆ family-based science activities

◆ increased and widespread contact with science and technology workplaces

◆ support for postsecondary and vocational education

◆ special programs targeted to give girls experiences that will expand their career outlooks

Spring and early summer are the best times to plan the activities you and/or your group may be able to implement in the coming school year. To raise girls' consciousness about their options, contact organizations like AWIS, the Society of Women Engineers, the American Association of University Women, or technical societies with active career guidance programs for girls and women. Make a list of programs that you thought were successful last year, and gather information on the ones you think might work in the future. Then, stack them against your resources to choose the ones you and/or your organization can best support. After your plans have formed, line up help from your chosen group (for example, your AWIS chapter) before fall schedules fill.

Organizations that can help include school district science coordinators (many of whom work all year), science centers, Girl Scout Councils or girls' clubs, professional organizations, women's groups, and churches with youth programs—especially minority churches, which often have strong community outreach programs. Tell your chosen group what you would like to see happen, how you can help, and see how your priorities relate to theirs. Then jointly proceed to make and carry out plans.

Plan ahead for the regional science fairs that will be taking place in February and March and for the state fairs soon after. If you want to help students, judge, or provide prizes, contact your school district's science coordinator.

Even if you are not part of any formal organization, contribute as much as your resources permit.

Thinking Globally

In recent months I have been talking with educators, scientists, and engineers from many countries at conferences on three continents. We discussed kindergarten through graduate school science and math curriculums, activities to attract students into these courses, and strategies to increase the low participation of women and underrepresented and underprepared groups. The issues and the attempts to find solutions seem similar worldwide.

178

Women in many countries are eager to exchange research and information, especially with their U.S. counterparts. Though I disagree with them, many women in science from other countries don't believe they have much to offer American counterparts, whose significant progress they much admire. The discovery of the common ground among women in science and science education throughout the world provides a strong bond for all, not just for those women who are fortunate enough to attend the international conferences that contribute invaluable opportunities for networks.

Recently, I attended a workshop for counselors at the school district and college level who were working with sex equity programs for single parents, displaced homemakers, and unmarried pregnant women. The workshop was formed to help the counselors to increased awareness of more and better career opportunities for such women. Preparing for such careers by taking math and science classes to give wider options was frequently stressed in the sessions. During a discussion, one of the counselors remarked that she was giving women wider options by advising them to take good liberal arts courses. Others tried to show her that girls who don't take math and science are closing the doors to many career paths. We could not convince her that liberal arts *alone* do not provide a background that will lead to meaningfully broad career opportunities. We still have a lot of work to do with those who are advising young women about career preparation.

In her address to the Ninth International Conference of Women Scientists and Engineers in England (1991, July), Baroness Platt of Writle embroidered a new version of the old saying, "Diamonds are a girl's best friend." She continued, "But they can be sold only once. Science skills can be sold every day for all of one's life."

How Well Are We Guiding?

Unfortunately, evaluating efforts to provide girls with career guidance is difficult. Most of the results occur over a lifetime, and with so many variables it is impossible to determine accurately the influence of one in isolation. Some measurable outcomes indicating changes for the better include increased enrollment of females in science and math courses at the precollege, college, and postgraduate levels and greater women's employment in science, engineering, and math jobs. Most of these indicators record slow increases followed by periods of little growth. It is difficult to assess whether attitudes of parents, peers, and the community have changed to provide more support for girls pursuing nontraditional careers.

These uncertainties do not mean that we should abandon efforts to guide girls. Indeed we must continue in spite of the fact that we cannot always measure the significance of our attempts.

Betty P. Preece, B.S. in electrical engineering and M.S. in science education, has been involved for many years in career guidance for females of all ages through AWIS, the Society of Women Engineers, the American Association of Physics Teachers, and other organizations. She works as a teacher and an engineer.

Undergraduate and Beyond

Letting Nurture Take Its Course*

Shirley M. Malcom

In 1963, I completed George Washington Carver High School in Birmingham, Alabama, and travelled to the University of Washington, where I entered as a premed major. While at the University I

took the standard premed courses, including chemistry (inorganic and organic), physics, mathematics, and biology. Although students converged in these classes from majors across the campus (which enrolled more than 25,000), all too often I was the only black student in my science classes and one of only a few women. At none of the three major research universities—along with Washington, the University of California, Los Angeles, and Pennsylvania State—I attended was I taught by a black science professor. For a while, I was the only black zoology major in a very large department. In graduate school, as a teaching assistant, I found few minority students in my labs or study sections. There were no minority faculty and only a few women. There were three minority graduate students—all women—two black and one Hispanic.

That was in 1968.

I thought that the small numbers of minorities and women in science were peculiar to the institutions I attended. I found out later that the small numbers were not at all atypical.

*An abbreviated version of this paper, based on Malcom's address to the National Colloquium of Project Kaleidoscope February 5, 1991, Washington, D.C., was published in Jeanne L. Narum (Ed.), *What Works: Building Natural Science Communities: A Plan for Strengthening Undergraduate Science and Mathematics* (Vol. 1, Project Kaleidoscope, pp. 25–27). Washington, DC: Independent Colleges Office.

More than 20 years later, in many colleges and universities, this situation has changed little. We see more women faculty and students overall, but research by Sue Berryman (1983) tells us their presence is largely a by-product of their increased participation in higher education rather than their increased attraction to science and mathematics. (See also figure 1 in Betty M. Vetter's paper, page 268.)

The Numbers Speak—Tokens

Data from the National Science Foundation tell us women faculty are more likely than men to be in marginal positions, off the tenure track. (See figure 1.) In 1968, women made up 40 percent of total college enrollment. By 1979, they were slightly over half the population enrolled in colleges and universities, and their proportion has exceeded that of men's ever since. Their representation in science has increased slightly since then, but that improvement has occurred in part because men's participation has decreased. (See figure 2.)

In 1973, 4.2 percent of entering male students said they were majoring in the physical sciences. By 1988 only 2.3 percent of freshman males declared this intention. Entering *females* intending a major in the physical sciences between 1975 and 1991 ranged from 1 to 1.5 percent. (See figure 3.)

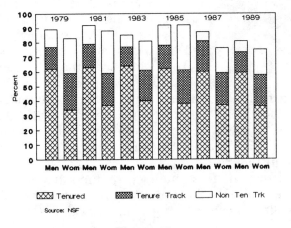

Figure 1*

Tenure Status of Science and Engineering Ph.D.s in Academe, 1979–1989

*All figures provided by the Commission on Professionals in Science and Technology, 1993.

182

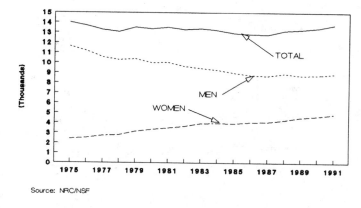

Source: NRC/NSF

Figure 2

U.S. Science and Engineering Ph.D.s by Sex, 1975–1991

Why has women's interest and participation in the physical sciences remained so minimal? And why has men's participation declined?

In the fall of 1987, in all U.S. graduate institutions, 560 black students were enrolled in the physical sciences; 92, in environmental sciences; 445, in mathematics; 693, in computer sciences; and 1,050, in biological sciences. That same year, 610 Hispanics were doing graduate work in the physical sciences; 253, in environmental sciences; 284, in mathematics; 489, in computer science; and 1,083, in biological sciences. (See figure 4 for 1988–1989 data, which show little improvement over earlier enrollment figures.)

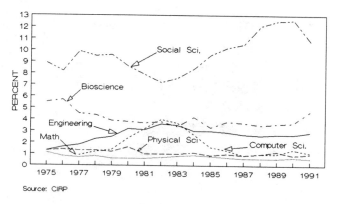

Source: CIRP

Figure 3

Freshman Women Science and Engineering Majors, 1975–1991

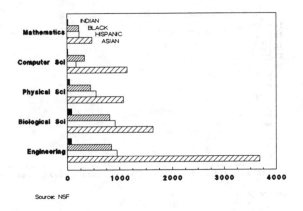

Figure 4

Full-Time Minority Graduate Students, 1988–1989

In 1991, black U.S. citizens received 1,082 doctorates, 21 percent of these in the natural sciences (including mathematics) and engineering, and 21 percent in the social and behavioral sciences. (See figure 5.)

In contrast, 41 percent of all doctorates granted to U.S. citizens in 1989 were in the natural sciences and engineering and 18 percent were in the social and behavioral sciences. Comparable figures for Hispanics are 32 percent of the 569 total doctorates in the natural sciences and engineering and 22 percent in social and behavioral sciences. For American Indians, these values were 40 percent and 19 percent, respectively, of 93 total doctorates. Figures 6, 7, and 8 show similar trends; although the National Science Foundation and

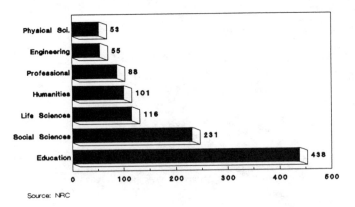

Figure 5

Doctoral Degrees Awarded to U.S. Blacks by Field, 1991

184

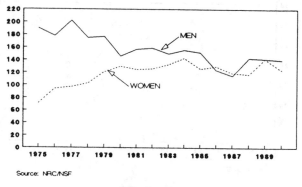

Source: NRC/NSF

Figure 6

U.S. Black Science and Engineering Ph.D.s by Sex, 1975–1990

National Research Council's inclusion of social and behavioral sciences in totals for science and engineering raises the minority totals somewhat overall.

In 1989, American women received 36.5 percent of all doctorates awarded by U.S. universities, almost 19 percent of all degrees in the physical sciences, 8.2 percent of engineering doctorates, 38.2 percent of life sciences doctorates, and 45.2 percent of social and behavioral sciences doctorates. Figure 9 shows percentages of all doctorates from 1950–1990, including those of foreign nationals. Of the 12,510 degrees awarded to women, 30.6 percent were awarded in the natural sciences and engineering and 21.5 percent in the social and behavioral sciences.

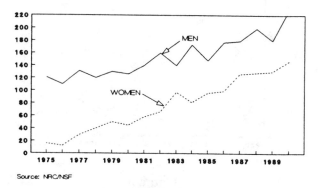

Source: NRC/NSF

Figure 7

U.S. Hispanic Science and Engineering Ph.D.s by Sex, 1975–1990

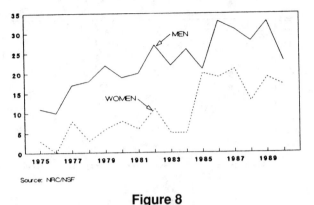

Source: NRC/NSF

Figure 8

**American Indian Science and Engineering Ph.D.s
by Sex, 1975–1990**

Nurturing Schools

Who manages to make it through the system to the upper levels? These are the survivors. What is different about those who made it and those who did not? Elizabeth M. Tidball and Vera Kistiakowsky (1976) documented the disproportionate contribution of women's colleges to the pool of students who go on to complete a doctorate in the sciences. Dorothy M. Gilford and Joan Snyder (1977) made similar observations about science doctorates for blacks and the contribution of historically black colleges and universities. Carol H. Fuller's (1991) collection of information about recent baccalaureate

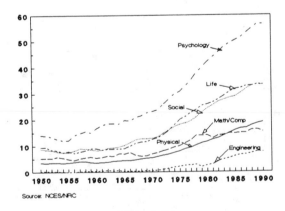

Source: NCES/NRC

Figure 9

**Percent Women Science and Engineering Ph.D.s
by Field, 1950–1990**

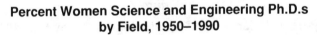

186

origins shows a continuation of such trends but, in more recent years, the data also reveal a broadening base of institutions providing the kind of experience that helps students from underrepresented groups, including, of course, women, to pursue graduate degrees.

These schools that support science outsiders tend to challenge a number of education's traditional assumptions. Such schools

◆ tend not to depend heavily on standardized tests for admission

◆ see the recruitment and retention into science of the women and minorities, who will make up 70 percent of new entrants to the work force in the future (Bureau of Labor Statistics, 1991), as their mission and their responsibility

◆ challenge the status quo in current college-level introductory science classes

Many historically black colleges and universities, finding that success in science with women and minority students does not depend simply on selecting the "smartest" students—those with high Scholastic Aptitude Test scores and high grade point averages—accept students with less than stellar indicators of prior academic achievement and nurture them into scholars. On the other hand, many highly selective institutions, which originally attract high-achieving minority students, find them underperforming in key gatekeeper courses (such as calculus and introductory chemistry and physics) and/or dropping out of their original declared science majors. In such schools, many women and minority students find faculty who are unwilling to accept their interest and ability, who expect little, or who subject their students to demeaning class environments.

Having a poor background does not mean a student is unable to achieve in science. Bringing in an excellent record is no guarantee of success. The success or failure of a future scientist does not rest with the student alone. The institution contributes too. A recent bumper sticker conveys a relevant sentiment: "Humpty-Dumpty was pushed."

Supportive colleges and universities believe that if women and minority students drop out, the institution may be at fault. Often a student's "choice" is not really a choice at all. Further, losing large numbers of women and minorities can eventually impoverish the institution itself in a number of ways. For instance, dwindling numbers of majors make it increasingly difficult to justify and support upper-level courses or faculty positions. Few departments aspire to be service units for other majors. As women and minority students become a larger proportion of the college-aged population, the ability to retain these students as majors may mean the survival of certain fields.

If there is nothing wrong with the science and mathematics courses as they are now, why, typically, are substantially fewer students enrolled at the end of the term compared to the beginning? Of these, why do even fewer take subsequent science courses? What was the gender make-up of freshman majors; of graduating majors? Do the same calculation for racial/ethnic minorities. If, as is usual in most colleges and universities, white males survive much better than minorities or women, something is the matter.

Responsible institutions finding such demographics should conduct exit interviews with their exiting students. Perhaps science drop-outs *have* come to realize that they preferred physical education to physics. On the other hand, perhaps they have been made to feel unwelcome.

If these calculations suggest a problem, Sheila Tobias' book, *They're Not Dumb, They're Different* (1990), and her paper (pages 150–159) offer insight. Tobias' case histories tell a disturbing story about our introductory gatekeeper science courses. These courses seem designed to weed people out, to find those who refuse to be deterred, and to depend on other courses to teach students what science really is and/or what understanding of science they should have.

The supportive college faculty does not ignore the problems students bring from high school and earlier: Everyone knows the K–12 system is flawed, but some institutions take students, problems and all, and move them to a higher level of performance. In addition, the postsecondary community can and must reach out to K–12 teachers. Until professors teach future teachers as they would have those students teach children, the situation will not improve. Somehow, many institutions do not think about teacher preparation as part of the system of readiness that feeds back to their own institutions.

The supportive college knows that engaging women and minority students does not mean lower standards, that equity and excellence are simultaneously possible. In fact, programs that provide meaningful context and rigorous content attract and hold all students. But it is absurd to measure the quality of a program by the number who fail rather than by the number who are enabled to succeed. It is impossible for an excellent program not to be equitable, and it is impossible for an equitable program to give students less than what they need to succeed.

The supportive college rejects the myth that the absence of many students from science is explained by the fact that they "do not have what it takes." There is no evidence to support biological determinism. There is no genetic basis to explain one group's participation, performance, or achievement in science and mathematics (or another's lack thereof). Complex social and cultural factors, the opportunity to learn, and the availability of resources, among other things, have interacted to produce the current distribution of groups in science fields. The existence of programs that can alter the "inevitable" support the idea that there are many interventions we must exhaust before we are allowed to claim biology.

Let nurture take its course.

How Colleges and Universities Can Help

College environments can support the pursuit of science literacy and science careers by people from groups with weak traditions in these fields. With a focus on factors that affect science participation, I am borrowing concepts of *recruitment* and *retention* outlined in a 1988 Office of Technology Assessment report. I flank these concepts with *readiness* and *reconstruction*.

By *readiness*, I mean the set of precollege experiences that enable students to choose undergraduate majors in science, mathematics, or related fields or that permit students to matriculate successfully in college-level science courses.

By *recruitment*, I refer to the activities that attract students to science or related majors or lead them to elect courses in science and mathematics.

By *retention*, I define the actions and programs that seek to hold students' interest in science as a career, to use science in their everyday lives, and/or to prepare a base for lifelong learning in science.

By *reconstruction*, I discuss the process by which students are encouraged and assisted toward further study and toward contributions to the development of science as it incorporates the broadest base of human experience. Their participation, then, reshapes the processes and structures of science.

A number of programs exemplify these elements as we try to increase the participation of women and minorities in science.

Readiness

Perhaps the ultimate partnership that focuses on readiness, though not specifically in science, is that between Boston University and the Chelsea school district. Here, the University has accepted responsibility for running the school district in its entirety. The institution has learned firsthand just how hard it is to put theory into practice in the face of dwindling budget support.

Most colleges undertake more modest efforts to affect what is happening in K–12 science. Many sponsor adopt-a-school programs with area schools; some colleges bring teachers to campus to work with college scientists in workshops, to interact with them in institutes, or to collaborate as research partners. Many of these programs have an urban base and target teachers of inner city schools. For students, weekend, afterschool, and summer programs in science have been developed. Such efforts often give underrepresented students a boost in confidence as they participate in prestige-building programs, acquiring new skills and often new friends with academic interests similar to their own.

Colleges have focused less on targeted students' parents, although research suggests that intervening with parents is important to help them understand their roles as teachers and advocates and to remove some of their own anxiety about science and/or mathematics. The aim is to ensure that early educational decisions do not preempt later informed decision making.

Recruitment

It is a fairly recent idea for colleges and universities to increase recruitment in particular fields such as science and engineering, rather than merely targeting students as potential enrollees. Individual disciplines are much more likely to focus on such activities. But, as the participation of underrepresented groups in science became an issue over the 1970s and 1980s, many colleges and universities expanded their view of recruitment.

Recruitment programs often involve career days, which include meetings with role models, college visits, museum experiences, and science activities; summer programs; and/or specialized publications. College students sometimes become recruiters, not only explaining their experiences to other students but also sharing the responsibilities for continuity of the disciplines with their professors and mentors.

Retention

Perhaps there is no greater challenge than building a community of learners in science within our colleges. Different institutions do it different ways. At Douglass College, the women's college of Rutgers University, a separate residence hall was set aside in 1989 for women students studying math, science, and engineering. Here, the undergraduate students form friendships, support groups, and study groups. Women graduate students also reside in the residence hall and serve as mentors to the undergraduate residents. These women achieve critical mass by clustering to form a smaller community. Does it work? Evaluation at Douglass is ongoing; preliminary results suggest that the experience is positive.

Some institutions tackle the career/marriage conflict for women head-on by offering seminars that help students understand how both are possible and that some people have married, worked, and survived, even thrived. Many minority students participate in pre-freshman summer courses that improve their later retention in college. Most of these programs are aimed at diagnosing un-derprepared students' areas of academic deficiency; providing them with opportunities to remove these problems through course work; orienting them toward the campus to identify and locate services; addressing weaknesses in study skills; introducing them to the pace of college life; and building community among the students.

Prefreshman programs are usually aimed at already admitted stu-dents; therefore, participants have a leg up over other newly enter-ing students. The former "know their way around" and have often established relationships with faculty and other students. The ad-justments of the freshman year are thus moderated. Research from the National Action Council for Minorities in Engineering (Ray-mond B. Landis, 1991) on prefreshman engineering programs sug-gests that such programs are a major component of an effective retention strategy.

No amount of preparation can make up for building a supportive environment for students once they arrive. Courses targeted to minority and/or women students in specific disciplines and "owned" by the faculty in that particular department are the most prevalent models. Such programs achieve community and connec-tion to faculty and allow immediate monitoring of performance and feedback.

Many who initiate such programs report an increasing demand. This shouldn't be surprising—they work. In larger institutions, programs such as the Professional Development Program at the University of California, Berkeley, practice block registration, con-centrating minority students into a small number of sections of calculus, for example, so that they have a built-in study group.

This does not mean minority-only sections. It does mean intervening to make sure students don't go it alone.

Science-oriented clubs and student chapters of professional socie-ties can be excellent sources of support for students. Groups such as the American Indian Science and Engineering Society, the Society for Hispanic Professional Engineers, and the Society of Women Engineers have played a critical role in retention programs in engi-neering. Science does not yet have such a well-developed network of nationally-based, student-oriented professional societies targeted at women and minorities. (See appendix A, however, for a listing of associations and other organizations especially geared to supporting women in science, engineering, and mathematics.)

Reconstruction

Making students a part of the community of science means introducing them to science as it is practiced, sharing with them the pursuit of learning through involvement in research. Existing programs enabling undergraduate participation in research, whether locally stimulated or nationally supported, were created to induct students into science, and research indicates that the greatest predictor of graduate study by blacks is their participation in undergraduate research. This is the aim of programs like the National Institute of Health's Minority Access to Research Careers, the Minority Biomedical Research Support, and the National Science Foundation's Research Centers of Excellence.

Not only do the students gain new and important skills, but also they contribute to understanding within the discipline. Their presence reshapes, that is, reconstructs their departments, their mentors, and their fields. Their deep and sustained involvement can have an even greater effect on science as it evolves to accommodate a more diverse community and expanded vision.

The Family of Science

We must help young men and women of all colors to see themselves as part of the community of science. But that means we must first be able to envision them there ourselves. We have to help them find their understanding by sharing ours and by respecting their need for context.

We must begin to see our introductory courses as an opportunity to recruit, not a place to weed out. If college is our last shot at providing future presidents or congresspeople with a view of science, what image do we want them to have? What do we want them to remember, to understand? Specific specialized terminology or the quest, the dynamism, the energy of science—its place in our lives, and its capacity to empower?

The American Association for the Advancement of Science's report, *The Liberal Art of Science* (1990) and several reports from Sigma Xi, particularly that of June, 1990, on undergraduate preparation in science provide starting places for institutions' self study of science programs. As we listen to these and other voices calling for reform in undergraduate science, we must recognize that, as the demographics change, we are playing to a tougher house. If we do nothing to rethink our programs, if we continue to depend on old strategies of weeding out, we face a troubled future. For we are neither drawing proportionately from the disenfranchised majority nor maintaining the interest of traditional participants.

Women and minorities are the miner's canary signalling deeper problems in our programs. We can take heart in the fact that we know quite a bit about what works for these groups. If applied, approaches like the ones that help them can revitalize our programs for everyone.

References

American Association for the Advancement of Science. (1990). *The liberal art of science: Agenda for action*. Washington, DC: Author.

Berryman, Sue E. (1983). *Who will do science?* New York: Rockefeller.

Bureau of Labor Statistics. (1991, November). *New entrants to the labor force, 1990–2005*. Washington, DC: Author.

Fuller, Carol H. (1991). The national picture: Part II. In Jeanne L. Narum (Ed.) *What works: Resources for reform* (Vol. 2, Project Kaleidoscope, pp. 89–122). Washington, DC: Independent Colleges Office.

Gilford, Dorothy M. and Snyder, Joan. (1977). *Women and minority Ph.D.s in the 1970s: A data book*. Washington, DC: National Academy of Sciences.

Raymond B. Landis (1991). *Retention by design: Achieving excellence in minority engineering education*. New York: National Action Council for Minorities in Engineering.

Office of Technology Assessment. (1988). *Educating scientists and engineers: Grade school to grad school*. Washington, DC: Author.

Sigma Xi. (1990, June). Entry-level undergraduate courses in science, mathematics, and engineering: An investment in human resources. *An exploration of the nature and quality of undergraduate education in science, mathematics, and engineering* [A report of the national advisory group of Sigma Xi, the scientific research society]. Racine, WI: Wingspread.

Tidball, M. Elizabeth, and Kistiakowsky, Vera. (1976, 20 August). *Science, 193,* 651.

Tobias, Sheila. (1990). *They're not dumb, they're different: Stalking the second tier.* Tucson, AZ: Research Corporation.

Tobias, Sheila. (1992). *Revitalizing undergraduate science: Why some things work and most won't.* Tucson, AZ: Research Corporation.

Vetter, Betty M. (1989). *Professional women and minorities: A manpower data resource service*. Washington, DC: Commission on Professionals in Science and Technology.

Before assuming her current post as head of the American Association for the Advancement of Science's Directorate for Education and Human Resources in 1989, Shirley M. Malcom, who holds a Ph.D. in ecology, worked at the National Science Foundation and taught biology in high school and college. She has been actively promoting equity and excellence all her life.

Perspectives on Women and the Sciences[*]

Barbara Furin Sloat

As a college student, I had no idea that I would go into the sciences—or that I would eventually be interested in the issue of women in the sciences. I went from an Ohio town, Youngstown, to

a small Ohio liberal arts college, Denison University, intending to become a public school teacher. This was an acceptable career goal for young women in the 1960s and one encouraged by my parents, both public school teachers themselves. For much of my time in college I thought of myself as an English major who just happened to love biology enough to take at least one science course each semester. It wasn't until well into my third year at Denison that I finally had to choose a concentration—a decision that entailed many sleepless nights. I finally chose biology, with the rationale that I could always read and write, but I would not be able to study and take courses in the sciences as easily once I left the college environment.

I was so busy taking English and science courses that I didn't have time for the education courses that would allow me to teach in the public schools. I had already decided to go to graduate school for the requisite master's degree in education when I saw a bulletin board notice about summer internships in the sciences, sponsored by the National Science Foundation at various research universities. And so it was that I came to the University of Michigan, to spend six weeks in the medical school's department of anatomy. There, for the first time, I was introduced to experimental work and encouraged to think beyond high school teaching. One thing led to another, and, on the way to that putative master's degree, I spent a year in Belgium and became involved in the research on multiple forms of enzymes that would eventually lead to my Ph.D. thesis in Michigan's zoology department.

I recount all this to make the point that I came to study and work in science, not because of pressure from family or teachers (in fact,

*Reprinted with permission from *LSA Magazine* (Spring, 1990). An abbreviated version of this paper appeared in 1990, November/December, in the *AWIS Newsletter*, *9*(6), pp. 4–5.

I was more often questioned about my choices, especially during my undergraduate and graduate years), but because of genuine interest in and fascination with biology. This is what drives my interest in issues of women and science: I don't want to recruit scientists "out of the woodwork," so to speak, but I do want to encourage those with genuine interest to pursue and stay with their interests. It has been my experience that women do not get that kind of encouragement nearly often enough.

Isolation

Throughout most of my educational and working career, I didn't think about the fact that I was a "woman in science." Actually, it wasn't until some years into my working life that I came to a real awareness of how few women there were around me—at Michigan, at Denison, at local and national conferences, and in science classrooms. I realized that I had never had a female science professor in college, in graduate school, or even in high school; that I had not been encouraged toward graduate school or a postdoctoral position to the extent that my male peers had been; and that, especially in graduate school, I hadn't been expected to go on to be a "full member" of the scientific community as much as my male counterparts had been.

I began to realize that, despite my high performance level, an undercurrent always resurfaced, constantly reminding me that I was "working too hard," or that I would "get married and have children anyway." Shortly after obtaining my Ph.D., I was told by a departmental chair at Michigan that "of course you can't expect to earn as much as a male would; after all, your husband has a good job, doesn't he?" Twenty years later, I am delighted that students are alert much earlier than I was to the attitudes underlying such discouraging and destructive comments.

The Scene for Women in Science

In the past few years, the challenge for me has changed from initiating practical programs to increase the numbers of women in the sciences to attempting to determine *why* there are still so few and *what* can be done to make a difference. I find myself trying to understand science as an institution: The social structures of the scientific workplace, its reward systems, and the means by which success is achieved within its framework.

And I have begun to realize that science is an endeavor in which gender differences and role stereotyping show up in especially striking ways. Indeed, the very association of science with masculinity

195

is deeply rooted in our culture and in the structure of science itself. In asking how to increase the numbers of women in science, I am convinced that we must first explore the ways in which women feel like "outsiders" to science and the ways in which their experiences in the scientific disciplines differ from men's. Only when this larger framework is better understood will we be able to make inroads to change the situation by, I believe, changing the institutions in which our students find themselves.

And so I have come out of the lab—out of all that scientific training and experimental work—with an expanding view of the complexities of human experience and, paradoxically, a much greater sense of the potential of opening science to a broader range of people. And I have discovered that the evolution that has occurred in my own thinking in recent years is paralleled by a larger movement in the country as a whole; I perceive that a new attitude is beginning to filter through, and I believe that more of us, as educators and parents, should be aware of it.

The Numbers—Bad but Improving

The bad news is that, despite gains since 1970, women still make up only 16 percent of the science and engineering workforce in the United States (National Science Foundation, 1992, January). Women scientists are disproportionately concentrated in psychology and the life sciences; only 4 percent of the engineering faculty were women in 1992 (Richard J. Bentley and Robert T. Blackburn, 1992). At Denison, my alma mater, women constitute 17 percent of the science faculty in professorial ranks—compared to a national average of about 11 percent.

At the University of Michigan, the numbers are even lower. In 1990–1991, in the College of Literature, Science, and the Arts, where virtually all of our undergraduates attend classes, only 10 percent of the current professorial faculty in biology are female (6/62); 6 percent in chemistry (2/35); 4 percent in geological sciences (1/25); 5 percent in mathematics (2/41); 3 percent in physics (2/64); and none in astronomy. History is in the making, however: Two years ago, the physics department employed its first women (two) in regular faculty ranks, an encouraging development that may portend future changes in the College.

The numbers for students look better: In the College of Literature, Science, and the Arts in the fall of 1992, 42 percent of all undergraduate astronomy majors were women (11/26); 53 percent in biology (478/906); 42 percent in chemistry (141/339); 37 percent in geological sciences (11/30); 38 percent in mathematics (164/430); and 17 percent in physics (28/164). The questions to ask, however, are these:

◆ Where will these students be going?

◆ What are their aspirations?

◆ Will they have a chance of fulfilling them?

◆ What will they have learned at the University of Michigan to prepare them for what lies ahead?

The good news is that the issue of underrepresented groups (women and minorities) in the sciences is now becoming one of national discourse, fueled by projections of a serious shortage of scientific personnel in the decades ahead and cries of national need and international competitiveness. We will hear more and more about this, largely because demographic trends make it abundantly clear that this country is facing a significant drop in the number of white males of college age, who have traditionally made up the pool from which scientists and engineers are drawn (by 2010, white males will make up less than one-third of the college-age population). Even now, we have passed the peak of U.S. graduate students available from traditional pools and, if nothing changes, we are headed towards a potential decrease of 40 percent by the year 2000 (Task Force on Women, Minorities, and the Handicapped in Science and Technology, 1989).

A New Workforce

And so we ask: "Who will do science in the years ahead?" It is apparent that women and minorities form the greatest potential pool from which to repair the projected shortfall: They have been greatly underrepresented in the scientific workforce to date, and they represent an increasing percentage of available undergraduate and graduate students and potential workers (by the year 2000, 85 percent of the net additions to the American workforce will be women, members of minority groups, and immigrants; only 15 percent will be white men [Bureau of Labor Statistics, 1991, November]). Insofar as this attention to national need brings us added resources with which to close the gender gap in the sciences, it is all to the good. My own concern, however, has less to do with projections of national need than with the memory and knowledge of the countless women with genuine interest in the sciences who were, and are, dissuaded or discouraged from its pursuit. It is *their* contributions, born of real and sustained intellectual interest, that we want to encourage and that we so badly need.

197

What is encouraging is that at *this* time prominent scientists and policy makers—including members of the National Academy of Sciences and the American Association for the Advancement of Science—are talking and writing about the underrepresentation of women in the sciences. The topic is no longer just the province of small groups on individual campuses (often generated, I might add, by women's centers and women's studies programs). Because it may translate into funds for programs and support services, this new attention is very important. But what is *really* significant about the current "women in science" discourse is its apparent shift in tone. No longer is there simply a call to increase the numbers of girls and women in the sciences—by making sure that they take more mathematics and science courses, for example—typical responses of the past. Rather, I detect growing recognition that women's experience with science differs from men's and the beginnings of attempts to understand how that is so; there is even a call to *reshape the institutions* in which young women find themselves. I see this call coming now from nationally prominent scientists, administrators, and policy makers, not just from those of us in the ranks, as a sea change in attitude.

Postsecondary Danger Points for Women in Science

It is significant that the 1988 presidential address at the American Association for the Advancement of Science meeting dealt with the issue of women in the sciences. The address, given by outgoing president Sheila E. Widnall, Professor of Aeronautical Engineering at the Massachusetts Institute of Technology, was not only a major address at the conference: It was also published (1990, September 30) as the lead article in *Science,* one of the world's premier scientific journals. Widnall cites data from a recent Office of Technology Assessment study that followed 2,000 female and 2,000 male students from age 14 through attainment of their Ph.D.s. The study discovered two major problem points on the way from junior high school to advanced degrees in science: The early college years, when students decide on a possible major or career choice, and, later, as they negotiate the graduate school system. It is during these years that science seems to lose so many talented and interested young women, and it is at these points that we can, perhaps, make a large difference. Indeed, young women who have gotten as far as college and graduate school with their interest in science intact deserve all the help and support we can offer.

These data—and that of others and my own experience—indicate several findings that may describe a cycle of cause and effect, with

198

the result that one-third as many women as men graduate with B.S. degrees in science and engineering (recall that the numbers of women are also skewed in favor of psychology and against the physical sciences and engineering). The data show that

1. Women often make the decision to drop science concentrations after the first semester of an undergraduate science course. The introductory courses, especially at many large research institutions, apparently serve to discourage undergraduate students at a time when they most need support.

2. Women students are a distinct minority at every level in many scientific disciplines, and especially so in upper-level or graduate courses; consequently, a critical mass of female peers is often lacking in courses and departments.

3. Because women have few female teachers or faculty to serve as role models in the sciences, they rarely have an opportunity to see women who have gone before them into interesting, vital careers in these disciplines.

4. Women ask fewer questions in undergraduate courses and engage less often in debate with other students and faculty members.

5. Women are more discouraged by grades below *A* in the sciences than men in the same classes, and they are more likely to blame their own "lack of talent" rather than problems in the classroom or teaching climate as the cause of their perceived unsatisfactory performance.

6. Women struggle with self-doubt in choosing a science major, apparently believing that they must choose between science and a "normal" life.

(On the undergraduate exodus from science classes, see also Sheila Tobias, 1990, and in this volume, pages 150–159.)

Essential Self-Esteem—Critical Losses

It is relevant to note that all of these factors suggest something about young women's self-concepts or self-images. A study reported at a 1987 conference sponsored by the University of Michigan's Women in Science Program and the American Association for the Advancement of Science indicated that, while the self-esteem of men is raised in college, that of women is *lowered* (Karen D. Arnold, 1987). Despite objective records of similar performance and virtually equivalent grade point averages, women's self-estimates of their intelligence relative to their peers diminished during college, with a particular loss of self-esteem reported in the sophomore year.

Recent surveys of male and female graduate students in scientific and engineering departments at Stanford and the Massachusetts

Institute of Technology report similar findings for students who go on to graduate school. In essence, the surveys indicate that men and women respond differently to the pressures of graduate school and often have different images of themselves and of their advisors' perceptions of them as graduate students.

The Stanford study (Laraine T. Zappert and Kendy Stanbury, 1984) concluded that women were indistinguishable from men in objective measurements of preparation for graduate education, in career aspirations, and in measurable performance in graduate school. Typically, men scored higher on the Graduate Record Exam's math section, while women scored higher on the verbal and analytical portions and had higher undergraduate grade point averages. The grade points of the male and female students as graduate students were essentially identical.

Women and men differed significantly, however, in their *perceptions* of their preparation for graduate school, in their estimations of the ways in which their advisors viewed them, in the pressures and roadblocks they experienced, and in the ways they coped with problems. In *all* the questions in the Stanford survey that measured level of self-confidence in the academic setting, women students scored consistently and sometimes dramatically lower than men. As Widnall points out, the white male students understandably "benefit from the self-reinforcing confidence that 'they belong,' " and it is probable that their self-identification with their predominantly white male mentors serves to reassure them that graduate school is a step on the way to a productive career in science. For women students and minority students, who lack models of those who have gone before them, the environment is clearly not as reinforcing.

Graduate students at the Massachusetts Institute of Technology's School of Science were surveyed both by their graduate school council and by a presidentially appointed committee (Academic Projects and Policies Committee of the Graduate Student Council, 1986, and Presidential Committee on Women Students' Interests, 1987). These surveys supported the results of the Stanford survey: Women reported more difficulty acquiring research skills and less adequate preparation for graduate school than men reported. These surveys also showed that the issues—feelings of powerlessness and of increased pressure and isolation— affecting minority, foreign, and women students seem to be related to their differences from the majority. In an encouraging note, the Massachusetts Institute of Technology studies showed that departments varied widely in terms of their perceived "hospitality" to women students; this points to the notion that specific measures could be taken within departments to improve the attitudes and expectations of students.

More research is also being done on the undergraduate experience of students who enter college with an interest in the sciences. One study reported by the University of Michigan's Women in Science Program and its Center for the Education of Women surveyed the choice of majors in science, mathematics, and engineering among 420 students who entered the University in 1983 and graduated in 1987 or 1988 (Jean D. Manis, Nancy G. Thomas, Barbara Furin Sloat, and Cinda-Sue Davis, 1989). Like other studies of the gender-related influences on achievement and attrition in the sciences, it underscores and calls attention to the importance the "affective atmosphere in which learning takes place" holds for women.

Changing the Educational Climate

How then can we begin to create an academic atmosphere that is hospitable to young women interested in the sciences, one in which they can not only survive, but thrive? There are a number of ways to think about this and a number of points of possible intervention. As a start, science teaching at the K–12 level must be made more engaging and interesting, and colleges and universities can play a role in this process. At Michigan, the Women in Science Program has developed a high school internship program for women students that places high school juniors in the laboratories of University scientists, who also happen to be women, for a six-week period during the summer. A new "Summerscience" program brings seventh-grade girls from throughout the state of Michigan to the campus for a three-week hands-on experience. The program also sends women scientists into junior and senior high schools to serve as role models and to encourage students toward academic achievement. At the same time, more of us have to recognize and respond to discrimination and inequities for women who are already in the work force. We must be sensitive to issues of pay equity, accessible and adequate childcare, availability of part-time positions, adjustable tenure-track timetables, parental leave, and related concerns. All of these affect career choice and retention and are of paramount importance to those who choose to work in the demanding scientific disciplines.

But, if we hope to encourage more women to pursue work in the sciences, we clearly have to work much harder at the undergraduate and graduate levels, for students who get this far in the pipeline with their interests intact deserve all the help we can give them. We must help break the feedback loop of lowered expectations and lowered self-image that leads to discouragement, loss of motivation, and lowering of career ambitions. Widnall in her address and Eliza-

201

beth S. Ivey (1987) suggest that this loop can be broken by constant, conscious awareness and interaction on the part of faculty, administrators, and students. How? As a start, those who want to make a difference can take a number of steps:

1. Provide women students with role models, in classrooms and textbooks, and expose them at an early stage to the many career options available in scientific and technical areas and to the varied and acceptable routes women have taken in their careers as scientists.

2. Give students access to role-playing experiences designed to enhance self-confidence and build independence through exposure to the so-called "hidden agenda" of the academic or work environment. For example, offer opportunities

◆ to engage in research and to present and defend research results in regular and active seminars and group meetings

◆ to evaluate and criticize the work of others, verbally and in groups

3. Provide all students with opportunities for courses, dialogue, and debate about scientific and technical issues as they relate to societal issues and to the humanities and social sciences.

4. Address issues of marriage and family as they relate to the career choices and concerns of young women.

5. Publicly challenge colleagues who make inappropriate or prejudicial remarks about women students and their appropriateness in nontraditional careers.

Looking Beyond the Particular

Finally, to guide us, we need to pull away from the lab bench, administrative desk, or wherever we are, to look beyond our particular disciplines at the development of modern science as a knowledge system. We should look at the gender metaphors that have shaped modern science so that the world is often perceived to be divided into two parts: The "knower" (the mind) and the "knowable" (nature). In assigning "mind" a masculine character and "nature" a feminine one, have we not, in effect, characterized scientific and objective thought as masculine? As philosopher of science Evelyn Fox Keller (pages 164–175) and others have pointed out, the very act by which the knower (male mind) can acquire knowledge—the experimental process—has been genderized. The very thought processes and intellectual postures involved in "knowing"—neutrality, objectivity, separation, power—are vivid images in the scientific milieu. And all of these attributes are traditionally associated with masculinity in our culture (Keller, 1985).

We no longer openly say that women should not do science, but the language and metaphors we daily use to describe science tend to make women "outsiders." Are we not invoking sexual metaphors when we refer to the most objective sciences as the "hard" sciences (physics and mathematics), as opposed to the "soft" sciences (psychology and even biology)? Is it really complimentary to say of a female science student that she "thinks like a man"? Or does this strike at the heart of her concept of herself as a sexual being?

If we can understand the ways in which science itself has been influenced by unconscious mythology and gender associations, perhaps we can free ourselves of some of the constraints that have made science inaccessible and uncomfortable to so many people. One result might be that science would become more hospitable to the public as well.

By broadening the participation of underrepresented groups in science, we can also hope to broaden its scope and the problems with which it concerns itself. As Keller suggests (1988), not only does diversity promote intellectual vitality, it also helps protect against the concentration of special interests in science. What I envision is a coming together of all disciplines around this effort: Those from the physical and natural sciences and from psychology, sociology, women's studies, the history of science, and philosophy will all contribute to the discourse. If we are to broaden the sciences, it will be through an interdisciplinary approach. New national interest in such an approach is an exciting development that is just getting underway.

References

Academic Projects and Policies Committee of the Graduate School Council, Massachusetts Institute of Technology. (1986, November). *Report of the 1986 graduate school survey.* Cambridge: Massachusetts Institute of Technology.

Arnold, Karen D. (1987, July). *Retaining high-achieving women in science and engineering.* Paper presented at the American Association for the Advancement of Science Symposium on Women and Girls in Science and Technology. Ann Arbor, MI.

Bentley, Richard J., and Blackburn, Robert T. (1992). Two decades of gains for female faculty. *Teachers College Record, 93*(4), 697–709.

Bureau of Labor Statistics. (1991, November). *New Entrants to the labor force, 1990–2005.* Washington, DC: Author.

Ivey, Elizabeth S. (1987, Fall). Recruiting more women into science and engineering. *Issues in Science and Technology, 4*(1), 83–87.

Keller, Evelyn Fox. (1985). *Reflections on gender and science.* New Haven: Yale University Press.

Keller, Evelyn Fox. (1988). Comments made as candidate for member of the board of directors, the American Association for the Advancement of Science general election.

Task force on Women, Minorities, and the Handicapped in Science and Technology. (1989). *Changing America: The new face of science and engineering.* Washington, DC: Author.

Manis, Jean D., Thomas, Nancy G., Sloat, Barbara Furin, and Davis, Cinda-Sue. (1989, July). *An analysis of factors affecting choices of majors in science, mathematics, and engineering at the University of Michigan* (CEW Research Report No. 23). Ann Arbor, MI: University of Michigan, Center for the Education of Women.

National Science Foundation. (1992, January). *Women and minorities in science and engineering: An update.* Washington, DC: Author.

Presidential Committee on Women Students' Interests. (1987). *Survey of graduate students.* Cambridge: Massachusetts Institute of Technology.

Tobias, Sheila. (1990). *They're not dumb, they're different: Stalking the second tier.* Tucson, AZ: Research Corporation.

Widnall, Sheila E. (1990, September 30). American Association for the Advancement of Science presidential lecture: Voices from the pipeline. *Science, 241*(4874), 1740–1745.

Zappert, Laraine T. and Stanbury, Kendy. (1984). *In the pipeline: A comparative analysis of men and women in graduate programs at Stanford University* (Working paper number 20). Palo Alto, CA: Stanford University, Institute for Research on Women and Gender.

Barbara Furin Sloat, Ph.D., is a cell biologist and a faculty member in the Residential College of the University of Michigan. She was the founding director of Michigan's Women in Science program in the Center for Continuing Education of Women and has served on AWIS' executive board.

Thriving in Graduate School

Lisa A. Zuccarelli

To *thrive* rather than merely to *survive* in graduate school, a student needs three kinds of support: Guidance from an experienced advisor, a helpful, familiar environment, and freedom from financial worries. These do not necessarily come all at once.

Chances are, for example, unless you are independently wealthy or are being supported by a partner or family, you will not find yourself financially free. You are likely to have more control over the other elements, however. If you can achieve all three conditions, you will find the road smoother—only the academic hurdles remain!

Guidance

Choosing the right advisor—who may become a mentor—is the most important decision you will make in graduate school. Your relationship with him/her will call for a joint investment in energy, time, and vulnerability. Your exchange of ideas must do more than pass on the essentials of the academic discipline. The advisor, with the experience that enabled him/her to progress, can communicate the process of becoming a professional.

A good advisor sets a good example. Observe whether the person you are considering has a strong reputation in the department. What committees is s/he on? A position on the promotion and tenure committee is a good sign that his/her judgement is trusted in sensitive matters. How many students has s/he worked with successfully in the past three years? Does s/he network with other professionals and participate actively in professional societies? Is s/he on the editorial board of a peer-reviewed journal in the field?

And what are his/her work patterns? Early to work? Long hours into the night? Two-hour lunches? No lunch? Will you be compatible?

An advisor needs to be available and active. Is the person in the lab and office on a regular basis? How close is s/he to retirement? If s/he is a well-known speaker often lecturing out of town, does s/he have a lab manager or a senior student taking care of things at "home"? How many students are in the lab and how often does each meet with the advisor? Will you get the necessary attention?

New faculty members are often equipped with enthusiasm, set-up funds, and equipment. Typically, they are still doing bench work. If untenured, they will be under pressure to publish and bring in grants in order to support their promotions. Sometimes, however, those promotions will not happen, and they will have to leave. If you aren't willing to relocate or find a new advisor, then it is probably wise to connect with a faculty member who already has tenure.

The mentor must allow his/her protégée to share experiences. S/he should let you observe him/her in action—at a meeting with colleagues, in the throes of writing an article, or presenting a seminar. The effective guide listens to and reflects back the aspirations and feelings of his/her charge, providing support, giving encouragement, and offering challenges. S/he will be the main source of introductions to collaborators and employers. An effective advisor will engage you in tasks such as going to meetings, writing a review article, coauthoring a text, or presenting a paper.

Make sure that your advisor has adequate funding and a well-equipped lab underwritten generously enough so that you can get on with your projects somewhat independently of departmental red tape. The best situation: Your advisor funds a position for you as a research assistant. If this happens, you will simultaneously have fulfilled the needs for guidance and financial security. Not needing to take on a teaching assistantship or a departmental work position will free time for your own projects.

Supportive Environment

We often have little choice about where we do our graduate work or with whom we interact. But, no matter what your marital or relational status, it is extremely important for your family and your friends to understand that going to graduate school is just like having a job. It has long hours (in classes and libraries), a work load (your reading and/or experiments), clients (your writing), crises (deadlines), and a boss and coworkers (your advisor and labmates). Unless your significant others have lived through this experience themselves, it will be up to you to communicate it to them. Be honest. Tell your friends when you are too full of stress to see them; don't just avoid them. Work out a deal with your partner to take the children to the museum while you write.

Cultivate friends within your department. Go to seminars and parties and talk to others about their progress. Walk the road with companions who are also journeying toward a degree. Always try to do/watch/eat/play/enjoy something familiar each day. If, even though you are busy, you help someone less fortunate, your generosity will shake you out of an introspection which could be debilitating.

Making Ends Meet

It is upsetting to be overworked and underpaid. Yet, this is pretty much the norm for graduate students. (I am not discussing here the way to finance your graduate education, a topic which needs much fuller treatment than I can offer at this point.) Rather, here are some ideas for decreasing the time needed to earn extra spending money.

Think about what you do best and with the most ease. Now, recognize that no one in the world wants to be considered stupid, ugly, or inept. So, if you can reverse any of these conditions for someone, your services are marketable!

Provide personal services in which you alone control your time, and maximize the resources to which you have access. Do not lock yourself into a work schedule or add travel time to your already busy day: Take on steady independent work. For example, if you can balance accounts, hire yourself out to help out a small office on a biweekly basis. If you tutor or provide expert counseling, make the client come to you. Use simple brochures to tout your services; do not waste time going over details again and again. If you are good with computers, use a home-based freelance approach rather than selling your services to a temp agency.

Always calculate the time versus income factor. For example, teaching a course at a local college may seem like a great way to make money. But beware! Count in the number of hours of travel, preparation, photocopying, grading, and counseling, along with the actual class hours. Chances are, it is more lucrative to tutor undergraduates at your own university for $30 an hour than to teach a course meeting three hours a week for a semester for $1,800.

An Institutional Helping Hand

Most universities offer students many kinds of help as they progress toward their degrees. The office of student affairs can alert you to programs for extra funding, mentoring, and emotional counseling. Your own department usually includes a director of graduate studies

207

to advise you. Most departments encourage student groups to provide social outlets.

Avail yourself of every possible opportunity for necessary support—be it academic, emotional, environmental, or financial.

Lisa A. Zuccarelli, a Ph.D. candidate in biology at New York University, does research on the effects of brain hormones on the regeneration of developing peripheral nerves after traumatic injury. She wrote the graduate student column for the AWIS Magazine in 1989 and 1990.

Keys to Success in Graduate School and Beyond*

Virginia Walbot

Choosing an Advisor

The foremost criterion for choosing an advisor is shared interest in a scientific problem. What specific subjects in your field interest you the most? Which technical approaches are most intriguing? When

you have defined your intrinsic interests, talk to potential advisors, postdoctoral mentors, and colleagues about science. Use every opportunity to do so throughout your career.

For example, in graduate school you will take courses and, probably, either do lab rotations or enroll in graduate laboratory courses. Use professorial office hours to ask questions about extra reading, to discuss potential research projects, and to get answers to your specific questions. If you are a rotating graduate student, set up a directed reading program with your professor and meet privately with him/her every week or so to discuss the scientific background and key papers relevant to the lab's work. If you are already a professional, make appointments with key people in your field and keep in regular touch via telephone, by electronic mail, and/or through personal visits.

Direct conversation with a lab director about subjects of mutual scientific interest will allow you to best judge his/her style and how fruitful your interactions will or could be. Are your ideas encouraged or discouraged? Is the competition respected or put down? Does the professor quote with pride the individual contributions of people in his/her lab or merely state that "my lab did. . . ." You should gain insight into this individual's expectations about work habits and schedule, two important things to know about before joining a lab.

And, look carefully at the fate of "graduates" of the lab: Do you want to end up with their kind of postdoctoral appointments or jobs? What percentage of students finish Ph.D.s in this lab, and how long does it take? Are men and women students treated equally— given credit for their ideas and encouraged to take on equally

*This article is based on an oral presentation to women scientists at the University of California, Santa Barbara, May, 1990.

challenging projects? Do the lab members receive support from their advisor and from each other?

Joining a Lab

Participate actively in group meetings and other forums for intellectual/theoretical discussions that provide direction to your lab. It is not sufficient just to do a good job at the bench—technicians can master technical skills. Good scientists are recognized for their abilities to frame questions, to pose potential solutions, and to inspire others to pursue these solutions. Practice these skills through lively discussions, defend your ideas, and help positions evolve. Think about best and worst case scenarios creatively. Don't be afraid to sound overly ambitious!

Arrange a weekly or biweekly private meeting with your advisor, even for 15 minutes, to discuss what you are doing (or not doing). Without being officious, take charge of the meetings and make a presentation on an experimental strategy, a key paper you've read, or the data you've generated since the last meeting.

Prepare for each meeting as if it were a job interview.

Ask yourself the tough questions before you reach the professor's office so that when/if they come up, you will be able to give thoughtful answers. And, if the professor doesn't recognize a potentially fatal flaw, demonstrate that you are self-critical by raising it yourself. Similarly, think of one or two additional experiments that you could do or should do, based on what you will be presenting. Over time, professors expect students to become expert in judging what's hot and what's not and to plan more and more of their own work. A professor forced to suggest key controls or to point out an obvious lead to an advanced student will not be impressed.

Over time, the responsibility for your project should shift from a supervised to a collegial relationship, with you taking the lead in experimental design, analysis, and planning. Accept this change and thrive on the trust that the faculty shows in your abilities.

Schedule a few hours per week to think about your research problem and to make a list of as many projects as you can. Then, cross out the *merely* good ideas, think critically about the remaining *very* good ones, and winnow these to one or two *excellent* ones. Next, spend some time in the library and with lab friends discussing these potential new directions and the types of new techniques that you would need to implement or invent.

You must invest in your own intellectual progress by thinking as well as doing.

It is common for students to become comfortable with a project (often suggested by a faculty member) but, after an initial flurry of reading (as if preparing for a term paper), to cease to think critically about the project. This is a serious mistake.

The project should be evolving as you work on it—you should analyze every piece of data for its obvious message and its various *what if* scenarios. Read widely and think hard. The initial conception of the project may and should change, as you assume more of the responsibility for doing as well as for thinking about the project. In the end, the best students have worked on an original problem, have taken an initial (perhaps even ill-conceived) faculty suggestion, and have nurtured it into a contribution.

As you meet routinely with your advisor and impress him/her with your intellectual commitment and abilities, your level of comfort in bringing up bad news should increase. Your advisor formed a good impression of you before agreeing to let you work in the lab, and your consistent good preparation for meetings should have solidified this impression. Now, when you have technical difficulties or think you should change projects, you should have a sympathetic listener.

Meeting With Your Thesis Committee

This committee will not only advise you during graduate school but individual members will also write letters for fellowship applications, for postdoctoral recommendations, for your first job, and possibly for your tenure or promotion. Choose members with the *clout,* the *time,* and the *interest* to help you now and in the future.

Hold meetings with your committee often—more than the minimum, but not so frequently that you pester busy and important people. Each meeting offers an additional opportunity to impress a captive audience. As with your meetings with your advisor, rehearse what you are going to present before each convening of your committee. Practice your presentation in advance in front of an audience (fellow students, your labmates). Give a polished performance, and be sure to let committee members have time to ask you questions and make comments. Distribute a written outline or agenda, and make sure to thank committee members for their time.

As your results come in, add people to the committee who reflect your evolving interests. Keep all members informed of good news such as manuscripts accepted for publication and your presentations at meetings.

At the postdoctoral stage and beyond, budget your time so that you can volunteer for or accept invitations to write short reviews.

There is no better way to be perceived as a leader in your field than to help define the questions and to prepare a thoughtful assessment of where we stand in seeking the solutions.

Give credit generously.

Joining the Intellectual Life of Your Discipline and Department

Seek Out Chances to Speak

For you to move from et al. status and emerge as a person credited with specific contributions, you need to meet people in your field. Go to all local meetings and as many national meetings as you can. Always wear your name tag, and always make a presentation or take a turn beside the lab's poster.

Within your lab and department, volunteer to give journal club presentations, that is, discussions of new literature in informal settings. If a regular forum for student or postdoctoral presentations does not exist, organize it. Ask an experienced person to preview each of your talks. Consider having yourself videotaped. Solicit constructive feedback about your speaking style and your organization (or lack of it). Learn to speak with self-confidence, but do not change your basic style.

Practice designing effective visual aids, and then practice using them and the blackboard, until you are comfortable and can walk around the front of the room or stage without getting tangled up in cords or dropping overheads. Know not only how to use all of the projector types you are likely to encounter but also how to make simple repairs on them: Learn how to change the bulbs, for example. Even make a kit for speaking engagements: It should contain marking pens, a retractable pointer, forceps (for lifting stuck slides), tape for holding overheads down in a stiff wind, and a lucky charm.

For national meetings, seminar trips, and job interviews, make duplicates of all of your visual aids, and leave one set on your desk in a Federal Express package with the address and instructions on what to do in an emergency attached. Consider having a prepacked carry-on suitcase with everything you need for a trip—duplicate everything (hair dryer, make-up, shoes, clothes, slides, credit card used only for business expenses, etc.). Then, you only need to remember that suitcase and your tickets to have everything you need.

Go the Extra Mile

◆ Write up good protocols, mention that you will have copies at the lab meeting, and distribute them with your name and the date on every page.

◆ When you read a particularly exciting paper or one that provides methods of potential use to your lab group, make an extra copy and give it to your advisor or post it in the lab. Then, make an announcement about the paper at the lab group meeting.

◆ Carry out lab duties as a team member. There are few tasks that women can't do; however, don't be a wimp about asking other people to clean up and do their fair share.

◆ It never hurts to bake cookies for a hungry lab.

Some Final Tips

You cannot expect objective, instant recognition of your success—there are no grades for everyday life. Many women students do obtain excellent grades throughout undergraduate and graduate school, but the importance of these grades declines with each additional day you are a professional.

◆ Recognize that true success in science rests on your abilities in your field, not on your preparation to enter it. And, in many cases, recognition of your contributions can take a long time—months, even years, can pass between your key discovery and the world's catching up to recognize it.

◆ *Don't undervalue your contributions.* Women often give themselves a barely passing C in comparison to the stars in their field, while men with the same credentials view themselves as As, based on their potential for success. Be realistic in your self-evaluation. Then raise your grade because you are committed to make the extra effort to be a success.

◆ Remind yourself that you love science and that the challenges are opportunities. And remember that every person has unique contributions to make. Great ideas—the original and important changes in a field—very often result from the insight of a single person.

Professor Virginia Walbot, Ph.D. in biology, has taught and enjoyed research in plant molecular biology and corn genetics at Stanford University since 1981. Her laboratory utilizes a combination of techniques in molecular biology and plant physiology to understand maize.

Professional Matters

Professional Responsibility[*]

Stephanie J. Bird

As science professionals, we have responsibilities in addition to those we have as adults, parents, and citizens. These additional responsibilities come in various shapes and sizes but fall into two general categories: Those that preserve the integrity of the profession and those that stem from the role that science plays as a component of society as a whole.

As researchers, we must be concerned about the accuracy and reliability of our work. Science is built on the work of others. We count on the veracity of what has been done before. If it is incorrect, not accurately reported, or misinterpreted, then the time and effort, supplies, equipment, and animals that the research has required were wasted. Intentional fraud, however rare, tears the fabric of science. Yet even sloppy science is unethical. If I carelessly contaminate stock solutions or jars of chemicals and drugs, if I don't clean up shared work space, if I fail to return tools and equipment to their designated storage locations, then I waste the time and energy of others. Worse, I expose my research and that of co-workers to unnecessary errors, and potentially all of us may face additional health risks.

Collaboration requires trust. We depend upon colleagues in fields outside our areas of expertise to take the same care as we do to insure that joint efforts are worthy of the energy and resources invested in them. But trust is not enough. We need to take responsibility for the reliability and quality of the work presented in papers that have our names on them. The Council of Biology Editors requires that each author be able to explain the rationale for specific research procedures, that is, be able to say why and how the research

*An abbreviated version of this paper appeared in the (1991, March/April) *AWIS Magazine*, 20(2), 2.

was conducted, and why the conclusions follow from the results. This responsibility is the natural counterpart to taking credit for the work that bears our name and follows reasonably from participation in the development and design of the study, in the collection and analysis of data, and in writing the paper. This high standard does not acknowledge (let alone accept) the all too common emphasis on quantity at the expense of quality, resulting in the phenomenon that William J. Broad (1981) calls the *least publishable unit.* Yet, to accept lower standards wounds our profession and ignores the issue of the interdependence of research. Low standards reflect negatively on all of us. Insistence on high standards is an extension of our mutual and shared responsibility to maintain the quality and stature of our field.

Literacy and Expertise

In our role as educators, we have a two-fold responsibility. The increasing importance of science and technology requires a citizenry that can grasp fundamental scientific concepts that may run counter to intuition or popular wisdom but are essential to making intelligent decisions and choices in a complex and dynamic world. All too often, however, concepts in math and science are made unnecessarily esoteric, as if to serve as a filter to create an intellectual elite who *can,* and thus *should,* make policy decisions that involve science. As educators, we have a responsibility to bridge gaps in experience, background, and socialization to make clear key concepts in science for as many students as possible.

At the same time, we have a responsibility to thoroughly educate and train students pursuing careers in science in the principles and techniques of the field. We need to set high standards for them and for ourselves as role models. But our responsibility to these students extends beyond teaching them the rudiments of science: It includes educating them about the skills, conventions, and mores of the field, as well as their responsibilities as science professionals.

Remembering the Big Picture

Future science professionals need to be reminded of the implications of the basic methodology of science. We need to step back and see that the categories into which we divide our world, and our science, are useful but limited and limiting. We simplify to understand and order our world, to make it possible to function, cope, and progress. In science, we order the conditions of an experiment, eliminate as many variables as possible, in order to solve an equation and assess the influence of various factors on an outcome or process. But our method is artificial and an artifice. It is one of the myriad ways we modify reality and "vex Nature" in order to make it reveal its truths. (See Evelyn Fox Keller's discussion of Sir Francis Bacon on page 168.)

It is important to keep in mind that this simplification is a means to an end and is only meant to be an interim step. The system under study needs to be restored to, or reexamined in, its unmanipulated state so that the function of other factors can be investigated. Unfortunately, too often this crucial step is neglected or intellectually postponed, and we lose sight of the fact that an artificial situation has been created. Yet we have a responsibility to ourselves, our colleagues, science, society, and our students to recognize and address the fact that this is one of the ways in which science is done, that is, we set up artificial situations and perturb the system to see how it works. The ways in which we change things, how we select and delimit variables to be tested and examined, reflect assumptions that are often neither acknowledged nor obvious. But they need to be identified and defined. It is critical that we take serious notice of the wider implications and potentially unintended consequences of this process.

A case in point from the life sciences is the general use of male animals (and exclusion of females) in basic research except when primarily or exclusively female physiology or behavior is being investigated. While this convention in research design was adopted to eliminate the variables of cycling female hormones, experiments have rarely been repeated in females to determine the role of female hormones in the phenomenon and the applicability of research findings for females. This practice reflects and propagates the underlying assumption that only female hormones cycle, perpetuates the erroneous as well as insidious notion that females are simply modified males, and unnecessarily and unethically puts at risk females involved in clinical trials and/or female consumers of compounds, devices, and procedures that are the fruits of biomedical research. This weakness in experimental design, which leads to a serious gap in scientific knowledge, has not been fully addressed. This lacuna is evidenced by women's invisibility in textbooks, funding priorities, reviewers' comments, and student training.

Helping Women Entering Science

As women science professionals, we have a special opportunity to address the particular obstacles and concerns of women exploring and pursuing career options in the sciences. Barbara Furin Sloat (pages 194–204) highlights a number of ways we as science educators can have a positive influence on young women and "break the feedback loop of lowered expectations and lowered self-image that leads to discouragement, loss of motivation, and lowering career ambitions." In addition, we need to help women entering science see a clear picture of the realities of their future careers so that they can determine how best to proceed in their academic choices. Providing such an overview is not easy, because each of us has individual perspectives and experiences that differ widely but that inform our view of reality. Yet, by sharing those perspectives and experiences, we can help women entering science better understand the challenges, obstacles, and rewards that lie ahead, even though both students and professions are changing with a changing society.

As women science professionals, we bring our own experience to these issues. But one need not be established in one's field to serve as a mentor. Mentoring is, in part, sharing our experience and our expertise; it is identifying what we have learned and sharing it with others. Upper-level students can share their experience of courses and instructors with lower-level students; graduate students know what they have learned about selecting graduate schools, thesis advisors, and thesis topics; postdoctoral fellows know about these topics too and about the process and pitfalls of selecting a position. (For additional comments on mentoring, see Bernice Resnick Sandler in this volume pages 271–279).

We are all in this together. We have much to gain, as well as a responsibility to those who have smoothed the way before us.

Working With Our Colleagues

Women science professionals also have a responsibility to each other. In large measure, AWIS itself is one expression of the recognition of this responsibility. As an organization, AWIS works to articulate the concerns and goals of women in science. We join together—combining our talents, skills, and knowledge—to address central issues. At the national and the local levels, in our institutions and AWIS chapters, each of us must do what we can, voting, serving on committees, and taking leadership roles whenever possible, to assure a positive, forward direction. We cannot leave these tasks to everyone else.

Serving Society

As science professionals, we have a responsibility to see that science is not misused, that it does not become a tool for abuse. This is not easy, and it can take time. Often, as scientists, we feel that social commitment is "not our job," and that we are not good at raising and addressing concerns regarding the use of science in public policy. But in our own fields we are far more likely to know of the limits and conditions of our knowledge and, more to the point, the problematic aspects of using this information as the basis for public policy. In addition we recognize—or are most able to sort out and identify—underlying assumptions. By identifying and acknowledging the role of potentially value-laden assumptions in science, we emphasize the way in which social values enter science. We have a right and a responsibility to make our voices heard when our science—our contribution to society—is being misquoted, misunderstood, or misapplied.

As science professionals and as citizens, we have a right and a responsibility to speak out about the effects of war and other destructive applications of technology. Whether the impact is on the environment, irreplaceable archeological sites, the psychological well-being and development of generations, or funding of education, research, and health care, we must speak out on issues and reality as we see them.

Reference

Broad, William J. (1981). The publishing game: Getting more for less. *Science, 211,* 1139.

Stephanie J. Bird, Ph.D., a past president of AWIS and coordinator of its mentoring program, is a laboratory-trained neuroscientist whose present research interests emphasize the ethical, legal, and social policy implications of scientific research. She is currently special assistant to the associate provost of the Massachusetts Institute of Technology where she works on the development of educational programs on the professional responsibilities of scientists.

Applying for Fellowships or Research Grants

Barbara Filner*

With few exceptions, a scientist's professional life from the very earliest stages is filled with grant applications. Whether as a graduate student seeking pre- or postdoctoral fellowship support or as a faculty member seeking support for her research, a researcher's chances of successful applications can be enhanced by following a few simple guidelines.

This paper, based on my experience as a grants program administrator, offers some advice.

Graduate School and Postdoctoral Fellowships

1. Identify Several Possible Fellowship Sources.

There are numerous funding programs available, from government agencies, foundations, professional societies, industry, and other public and private sources. Some are highly competitive, others less so. Try to identify as many sources as possible that might meet your needs, and consider applications to several programs. Use publications and electronic data bases to find some of these programs—your school's library should be able to help you find the right listings. Also seek advice from faculty members and financial aid or graduate school offices. Don't forget to consult AWIS' *Grants at a Glance* (1992) and the listing in each issue of the *AWIS Magazine*.

2. Request Current Program Guidelines.

Once you find the name of an agency that provides relevant fellowships, write or call to request program guidelines. The eligibility, forms, and deadlines may change from year to year, and you should be sure to have the most recent information. You don't want to miss a deadline, and you don't want to waste time applying for a program for which you are not eligible.

3. Contact the Funding Agency.

Grant programs each have their own style. Some are quite willing to provide supplementary information—others will simply refer you to the published guidelines. Ask for a list of previous awards—the

*For Filner's biography, see her interview on page 32.

topics may suggest whether or not your area will be competitive. Priorities can and do change, however, so don't dismiss any program on this basis alone. Ask to speak with a member of the program staff about your particular field of research. You might also ask about award rates—what percent of applicants are funded in your field? If you are considering several possible applications, this information might help you decide where to focus your limited time. Some agencies do not make this information available, but it doesn't hurt to ask.

4. Plan Ahead to Arrange Reference Letters.

Two critical steps lead to good reference letters: First, be sure faculty members know your abilities; second, be as certain as possible, that the requested letters will be positive.

As a student, one of your most serious responsibilities is to have several professors know you well enough to write strong reference letters on your behalf. It's your job to be sure these professors know you and your strengths in depth— beyond your doing well on tests. For science, research is the heart of the matter, and several professors must be able to say convincingly that you think rigorously and creatively and that you know what research is. Seek opportunities to show your capabilities to them, including volunteering or working for pay on research projects. Also, seek opportunities to discuss ongoing research projects with professors in your department.

Ask for reference letters in such a way that someone who is reluctant will be able to decline gracefully. You might believe someone should write a good letter, but will s/he? I know situations in which students completely misjudged the evaluation they received. To avoid this pitfall, don't simply ask "Will you provide a reference for me?" Rather, frame your request along these lines—"Do you think you know me well enough to write a good letter of reference?" This strategy, of course, depends upon having several possible references—hence the advice above. (See AWIS' suggestions for analyzing and screening letters of reference, pages 333–342.)

5. Provide Both Context and Detail in the Research Plan.

Postdoctoral applications will ask for a research plan. Graduate study applications may require a research plan and/or a program of study. If the application asks for the latter, be sure to provide a research plan as part of it—characterize your plan as representative of the approach to the kind of scientific issues you wish to address and that you are preparing yourself to investigate.

Clearly state and develop the research project you wish to undertake, while placing it into a broader context. Right at the beginning, you should articulate the fundamental question you are asking and why it is of interest. Frame questions that probe mechanisms. Do not characterize your research simply as "comparing" or "describing."

Then, present your specific project, and explain how it addresses the fundamental question you described. If you are using a model system, discuss the advantages (and any drawbacks) it offers. Don't get bogged down in technical detail, but present enough information to convince readers that your project is feasible and that you have sufficient expertise to carry it out successfully. If possible, close with a brief paragraph that discusses the next steps after completion of your project: Where is it going?

Reviewers want to see that you can think rigorously and scientifically and that you ask good questions. They will adjust their expectations to the level of training involved—with increasing sophistication and detail expected as you progress from student, to postdoctoral fellow, to independent scientist.

6. Relate the Research Plan/Plan of Study to Your Career Goals.

Fellowship applications often include a section on your long-term goals. You should present fully formulated goals (*not* "I want to do research"). Reviewers also want to see that you are thoughtful (and astute) about the training you hope to receive. Explain how the proposed research or plan of study relates to your goals. Indicate why you have selected this project, mentor, and/or department in the context of your overall scientific aims.

7. Seek Review and Comment on Your Application.

Experience teaches a reasonable balance between context and detail, and you will not necessarily make the right judgements in your first applications. It is vital that you get feedback from people with experience of reviewers' expectations.

After you have drafted your research plan, ask your mentor and/or another professor to read your plan and critique it. Your research plan will be strengthened, based on your responses to their questions. Perhaps the review will also occasion a serious discussion with the professor, who will then be better able to write an informed reference letter.

You might ask some other students to read the application as well. Make it clear that you want honest comments that will help you improve the application. Be prepared to hear that it is boring (too much technical detail?) or not very clear (too much jargon, rationale not well articulated, research question not clearly linked to what you propose to do?). Don't be hurt; instead, thank your readers sincerely and get to work rewriting. Indeed, in a way the least gratitude is due to anyone who simply praises your application. (You feel good, but were you really helped in the long run?)

8. Submit an Application that is Neat and Complies With Format Guidelines.

Remember that reviewers often have to read dozens of applications. Why make it difficult for them to read yours? Word process or type everything, and be neat. Don't use tiny type, compacted line spacing, or minuscule margins. Instead, edit yourself ruthlessly so you make the most important points without pushing the limits of the allotted space.

9. Allow Plenty of Time.

Not only do you need to allow readers time to give your draft a careful review prior to submission, but also you need to plan on time for revision based on their comments. Indeed, if it doesn't take time to respond to your colleagues' comments, the draft probably hasn't had a thorough review, and you should try to find another reader (which also will add more lead time).

Research Grants

Nearly all of the advice for fellowships applies also to research grants; however, there are some additions and/or shifts in emphasis.

1. Identify Several Possible Funding Sources.

In addition to information resources mentioned for fellowships, I would add your institution's office of grants and contracts (or sponsored research, etc.). You might also place yourself on the mailing list for regularly published notices of grant opportunities. Many government agencies have such publications. For information about on-line access to relevant information in the National Science Foundation's Science and Technology Information System, call (202) 357-7555.

2. Request Current Program Guidelines.

National Science Foundation program manager Joanne G. Hazlett notes that some proposals do not fare well simply because they do not follow the suggested content guidelines. Sheila Taube, an administrator for the National Institutes of Health's extramural pro-

222

gram, notes that subject matter guidelines for research grants are usually quite broad. She cautions against artificially tailoring proposals to fit a particular year's priorities. Instead, make the strongest case you can for your area of research, clearly stating the hypothesis and explaining the broad context.

3. Contact the Funding Agency.

In addition to the points made under fellowship applications, you should be aware that some agencies provide feedback on preliminary proposals. Indeed, some require such proposals. If agency policy allows such feedback, advice from program staff can be invaluable.

4. Provide Both Context and Detail in the Research Plan.

The plan for a research grant will, of course, require more technical detail than for a fellowship application. Nonetheless, the research plan still needs to be presented in the context of a fundamental question, to have its importance explained, and to point out the gaps in knowledge that the project will address. The plan should also provide a thoughtful discussion of possible technical barriers and ways around them, and some preliminary data to indicate feasibility and promise. You must show that your research is a logical next step to previous work and that you have both the expertise and the materials the project requires.

5. Prior to Submission, Seek Comment on Your Proposal.

Senior colleagues (with successful records of grant support) may be willing to critique your grant proposal. Seek two kinds of readers: One who is familiar with the research field and one who is not. The former will focus on detail and make sure the technical approach is reasonable. The latter will be able to comment on whether the writing is clear (free of jargon and of unarticulated leaps of logic), whether the hypothesis sounds reasonable, and whether a strong case has been made for proceeding along the lines proposed.

6. If Not Funded, Ask for the Reviewer's Comments, Then Revise and Resubmit.

Many (but not all) funding agencies will give you a written summary of the reviewers' comments on your research proposal. Take the comments seriously—they may have identified an important flaw or gap in your plan. If you think they completely misunderstood the importance of the work and/or your research strategy, still accept much of the blame—you did not make your plan sufficiently clear. Program staff who have heard all of the review discussion may be willing and able to convey additional information. Call them to discuss the review comments: They may amplify and suggest which comments should be taken most seriously.

After due consideration of the feedback from review, revise your research proposal and submit it again—either to the same agency or to another one.

7. Allow Plenty of Time.

Bernice Noble, a professor at the State University of New York at Buffalo with a long record of submission and receipt of research grants, notes that novices frequently misjudge the amount of time needed for others to read the draft and the amount of rewriting that will be required if the readers have been ruthlessly honest and critical (the kind of review you should make it clear you seek). She adds that applicants should not submit a proposal until it is the best they can possibly make it.

If you haven't allowed enough time to revise, it might be better to submit a few months later if there are multiple review cycles in the year.

8. Get Appointed to a Study Section/Peer Review Panel.

The insight obtained by service on such panels is invaluable. Make it known that you would be available for such service. Many agencies publish panel rosters through which you can identify members you know. Don't be modest or shy: Ask colleagues to put your name forward, and ask the agency if it keeps a list of interested scientists. (The National Institutes of Health, for example, maintains a file of potential peer reviewers and publishes notices requesting scientists' participation. Request a Candidate Information Form from the National Institutes of Health Consultant File, 7101 Wisconsin Avenue, NW, Suite 1125, Box 92, Bethesda, MD 20814.)

9. Be Confident and Be Persistent.

My final piece of advice to all fellowship and research grant applicants is not to be unduly discouraged or crushed by an apparent "failure." You may very well have been the applicant one slot away from an award in a very competitive program. Further, the peer review process is neither infallible nor exactly reproducible. Another set of reviewers may rate your application more highly. In addition, the revision, based on the review comments, will be more competitive. Remember that colleagues will readily talk about their funded applications but often forget to mention the one or two rejections that preceded the award. So be confident about your abilities and ideas and be persistent in your determination to find funding.

I would like to thank Joanne G. Hazlett, Bernice Noble, Ph.D., and Sheila Taube, Ph.D., for their thoughtful review and astute additions to this article.

Reference

Association for Women in Science. (1992). *Grants at a glance: A directory of financial resources for women in science* (2nd ed.). Washington, DC: Author.

Pathways to the Podium: Women Organizing, Women Speaking

Marian G. Glenn, Dorie Monroe, and Judith Lamont

Marian G. Glenn   **Dorie Monroe**   **Judith Lamont**

Professional meetings are an important forum for exchanging ideas and showcasing research. In the three professional meetings analyzed here, women biologists contributed talks and posters at almost the same proportion in which they are represented among the membership in the organizations. Our data, however, as well as several recent reports including that by Jessica Gurevitch (1988), have demonstrated that women biologists are often underrepresented as prestigious *invited* conference speakers (as opposed to voluntary contributors). This tendency is prevalent enough that Mary E. Clutter, head of the National Science Foundation's Directorate of Biological Sciences, now refuses to fund meetings where women, who now make up a third of the assistant professors in the life sciences, are under- or unrepresented among the speakers (Boyce Rensberger, 1992).

When Clutter's staff turned down a prominent biologist's request for conference funds because he had invited no women to speak, they were unmoved by his explanation that "some of the men are presenting the work of women scientists." "Some of these guys just don't get it," Clutter laughed.

The visibility and recognition that result from an invitation to address one's colleagues provide a driving force for career advancement. In addition, the motivation and sense of belonging that come from being asked reinforce one's sense of commitment to career development.

We think that mentoring activities can address the gender imbalance at the podium.

In this article we examine women's participation as speakers and organizers in several types of professional gatherings:

◆ a large, formal set of meetings—the American Institute of Biological Sciences, Toronto, August, 1989

◆ a defined but significant component group—the Ecological Society of America—within those meetings, 1983–1992

◆ a small, informal stand-alone conference—the Gordon Conference on Applied and Environmental Microbiology, New Hampshire, July, 1991

Our analysis of all of these meetings follows the model set out by Gurevitch, who wrote:

> From casual observation and conversation it seemed to me that female colleagues were not being invited to participate [in Ecological Society meetings] in the proportion in which they were represented in the field. One person suggested that men sometimes forgot that they had women colleagues who might have interesting work to talk about, and that women were less likely to ignore other women in their field. This was an intriguing and upsetting hypothesis. (p. 156)

Gurevitch's analysis of the 1987 Ecological Society of America's annual meeting revealed that a key factor in fostering women's participation as invited symposium speakers was the presence of a woman on the symposium organizing committee. (See table 2.) For the 12 1987 symposia reported on table 2 in which women were involved in extending the invitations, women made up 23 percent of speakers, a proportion not significantly different from their representation in the membership of the society, and in line with their representation among first authors in the society's journal *Ecology*. The proportion of women speakers in symposia organized by a committee of only men, however, was significantly lower (7 percent). Gurevitch's results do not support the hypothesis that the relative absence of women speakers in invited symposia organized by men was attributable to differences in women's representation among the various subdisciplines of ecology.

With Gurevitch's findings as background, we extended the analysis to the 1989 Ecological Society meetings and those of the other subgroups of the American Institute of Biological Sciences (table 1). At these meetings, as at most large conferences, formal talks fall into

227

Table 1

Participation of Women Biologists at the 1989 American Institute of Biological Sciences Meetings

Society*		Contributed Sessions				Invited Symposia			
	% Women	Total	Women Speakers (%)	Total Sessions	Woman Presiding (%)	Total Talks	Women Speakers (%)	Total Sessions	Sessions w/ Woman Organizer (%)
ESA	22	578	153(26%)	45	15(33%)	113	24(21%)	16	7(44%)
BSA/CBA	30	330	109(33%)	30	11(37%)	54	9(17%)	14	3(21%)
ASPT	23	162	38(23%)	12	3(25%)	46	8(17%)	6	1(17%)
SCB	NA†	76	22(29%)	8	2(25%)	24	2(8%)	5	1(20%)
MSA	30	59	22(37%)	11	3(27%)	26	5(19)	6	2(33%)
PSA	NA	62	15(24%)	7	6(86%)	62	15(24%)	2	2(100%)
ISEM	10	20	1(5%)	3	NA	39	5(13%)	7	1(14%)
ATB	NA	32	15(47%)	3	1(33%)	12	2(17%)	2	1(50%)
AIBS	24	24	12(50%)	2	2(100%)	17	1(6%)	6	0
ABLS	32	29	4(14%)	4	0	8	4(50%)	2	0
AFS	38	21	3(14%)	2	0	12	3(25%)	2	1(50%)

*Acronyms: Ecological Society of America (ESA), Botanical Society of America/Canadian Botanical Association (BSA/CBA) American Society of Plant Taxonomists (ASPT), Society for Conservation Biology (SCB), Mycological Society of America (MSA), Psychological Society of America (PSA), International Society for Ecological Modeling (ISEM), Association for Tropical Biology (ATB), American Institute of Biological Sciences (AIBS), American Bryological and Lichenological Society (ABLS), American Fern Society (AFS).
†NA: Data not available.

Table 2

Gender of Organizers and Speakers at Annual Meetings of the Ecological Society of America, 1983–1992.*

Year	% Women Organizers	Gender of Organizers and Speakers	No. of Sessions	% Women Speakers	% Women Speakers (Contributed Sessions)
		Invited Sessions			**Contributed Sessions**
1983	9% (3/32)	NA†	NA†	10% (16/160)	29% (101/343)
1987		Men Only	17	7% (7/102)	
		Women +/− Men	12	23% (19/84)	
	25% (10/40)	Total	29	14% (26/186)	27% (78/290)‡
1989		Men Only	9	11% (7/61)	
		Women +/− Men	7	33% (17/52)	
	25% (7/28)	Total	16	21% (24/113)	26% (153/578)
1992		Men Only	10	16% (12/74)	
		Women +/− Men	5	41% (12/29)	
	22% (5/23)	Total	15	23% (24/103)	27% (158/576)

*Data for 1983 and 1987 from Gurevitch (1988) analyzed here and in Glenn (1990).
†NA: Data not available.
‡Data based on first 30 sessions.

the two categories already discussed—contributed (voluntary) and invited (more prestigious). Table 1 summarizes data on women's participation in these activities. The societies are listed in the order of the number of speakers who participated.

Trends at a Big Meeting: The American Institute of Biological Sciences

In general, women's participation in the contributed sessions, both as speakers and as moderators, was in line with their representation in the membership of the society. However, in the five societies with the largest number of papers, participation by women as *invited* speakers was lower than the number of women talking in *contributed* sessions. This difference, of 17 percent versus 33 percent, was statistically significant for the sessions of the Botanical Society of America/Canadian Botanical Association.

The American Institute of Biological Sciences, the umbrella organization for the conference, showed the greatest discrepancy between numbers of women in contributed versus invited sessions (table 1). In 1989, it had *no* women symposium organizers and the *lowest* participation of women as invited speakers (6 percent). In contrast, *all* of its contributed sessions were moderated by women, and women made up half of the speakers, a larger percentage than in any of the other societies. This contrast between invited and contributed sessions reflects a dichotomy in subdisciplines: The contributed sessions all concerned teaching, an area in which women are extremely well represented.

This overall trend was not always reflected in particular subgroups of the American Institute of Biological Sciences. For example, the American Bryological and Lichenological Society fielded no women among the symposium organizers, but half of its invited speakers were women. Females were also well-represented among the invitees in several other small societies (such as the International Society for Ecological Modeling and the American Fern Society). In these small groups, women colleagues may have greater visibility. But this plus is not universal. For example, it did not apply at the Gordon Conference discussed below.

Trends Over Time: The Ecological Society of America

Only the Ecological Society of America had enough women symposium organizers that we could examine the influence of this factor on women's rates of invitation. Table 2 shows that the representation of women among invited speakers has increased steadily, from 10 percent in 1983 to 23 percent in 1992. The presence of a woman on the organizing committee appears to be important. In all the years studied, this Society's committees consisting only of men invited women at a rate significantly lower than that of committees including a woman.

It is encouraging to see that symposia organized only by men *have* seen a steady increase in women speakers—from 7 percent in 1987 to 16 percent in 1992. It is nevertheless true that the symposia whose organizers included a woman account for the growing numbers of invited women speakers: Invitees are now nearly proportionately equal to contributors.

Trends at a Particular Small Meeting: The Gordon Research Conference on Applied and Environmental Microbiology

Increased visibility does not always occur at small meetings. At the 1991 Gordon Conference, for example, women scientists made up 21 percent of the 119 participants. At this week-long conference, 19 invited speakers addressed 8 sessions, and all participants at the meeting were encouraged to make poster presentations. That women were first authors of 13 of the 44 posters (30 percent) indicated that the women at the conference were active investigators. Among the invited speakers, however, only one woman was scheduled, and she canceled. One session was moderated by a woman.

At the conclusion of the conference, a general meeting evaluated the week's work. The conference chair appeared sincerely upset by the absence of women speakers, and assured the group that he *had* invited several, but that they had been unavailable. A number of participants (mostly women) agreed to furnish a longer list for the next conference.

The next order of business was nominations for a new member of the organizing committee who would in two years' time become the conference chair. Although several women were nominated, each of them declined for sensible reasons, including major responsibilities for organizing other professional meetings.

Maybe their choice will increase the number of women at the podium at other scientific conferences, if not directly at subsequent Gordon meetings.

Acknowledgment: We thank Sara Webb of Drew University for help in data collection.

References

Glenn, Marian G. (1989, November/December). Making colleagues visible—Women leaders are effective. *Association for Women in Science Newsletter, 18*(6), 14–15.

Gurevitch, Jessica. (1988, September). Differences in the proportion of women to men invited to give seminars: Is the old boy still kicking? *Bulletin of the Ecological Society of America, 69,* 155–160.

Rensberger, Boyce. (1992, August 26). Women's place: On the podium: Science Foundation official makes antisexism a policy for conferences. *Washington Post,* p. A21.

Marian G. Glenn, Ph.D., is an associate professor in the biology department and coordinator of academic advising for nonmajors at Seton Hall University. She does research on the role of microorganisms in ecosystems.

As a biology major at Seton Hall, Dorie Monroe carried out the research for this project. Since graduation, she has been working at the research facility of the New York State Department of Health at Albany.

Judith Lamont, Ph.D., works for Orion Enterprises, Inc., a Fredericksburg, Virginia, consulting firm specializing in technology transfer and technology security. She is active in AWIS locally and nationally.

Women Speakers: Make the Most of Your Moments*

Heidi B. Hammel

It is the afternoon of the third day of the meeting. Hundreds of talks have been given already. The lecture hall is dark; the only sound is the droning voice of the man giving the talk. He's the fourth speaker in a row, and they are all starting to sound alike. You fall into a semiconscious daze.

Applause momentarily jars you to consciousness, but the voice of the male moderator announcing the next talk quickly lulls you back to somnolence. Suddenly, a woman's voice starts speaking clearly and strongly. The sound of her voice—so much higher in pitch than the previous speaker's—catches your interest. . .

This moment is critical for the woman speaker. The sound of her voice is unusual and catches the attention of the audience. By virtue of women's limited representation in science, these moments occur with some frequency at scientific meetings. Women in science, especially female graduate students giving their first public presentation, need to be aware of the importance of this recognition.

A male colleague of mine, speaking about a woman student, once told me, "Boy, she really blew it at that last conference. It was her first talk, and she gave a horrible presentation. Since there were only a few women there, everyone knew exactly who she was and for whom she was working, and her performance didn't do her reputation any good, that's for sure." Another colleague put it this way, "A young female speaker just can't just fade into the 'yet another bearded male graduate student' horde."

This is reality—women speakers can make a startling impression. Instead of bemoaning this fact, the woman speaker should turn it to her advantage. Below are some tips for tightening a talk. While geared toward short presentations at scientific conferences, these principles can (and should) be applied to longer colloquia and speeches.

*This paper is based on Hammel's piece in the 1991, July/August *AWIS Magazine*, *20*(4), 6–7.

Memorize Your Introduction and Conclusion

These are, by far, the most important sentences of your entire presentation. If you prepare nothing else, at least prepare these sentences. "You never get a second chance to make a first impression," warns a TV commercial. So make that impression a good one. One woman I know always had a tough time getting her talks started. Once she was a few minutes into them, she relaxed, but often she had already lost her audience. When she memorized her first five sentences, she was able to stand up, take a deep breath, and start talking loudly, clearly, and without hesitation.

If you lose the audience's attention during your talk (and this happens to the best of us), the words "to summarize" or "to conclude" will usually bring it back. Make sure you exploit your advantage by providing a concise, clear conclusion or summary. Don't babble for another five minutes and fade out with something timid, such as "Well, I guess that's all I have to say." Such an anticlimax leaves listeners feeling cheated, frustrated, even annoyed. Leave them instead with a pithy summary.

I literally write out, on paper, my first and last couple of sentences. I rarely read them—they are usually fixed in mind as I think through exactly what I want to say. But, once in a while, I have a train wreck, and having my well-worded conclusion written in front of me has salvaged a potentially gruesome experience.

Talk to Your Audience

Face your audience: *Do not talk to a screen or blackboard.* If you are unamplified, your voice will disappear the moment you turn (that's why actors cheat their bodies toward the audience during stage performances). If you are speaking without a microphone, you should be especially aware of volume, always speaking so that the people in the back of the room can hear. If you are unsure, ask: "Can you folks in the back hear me?" But, even if you are amplified, don't talk to the screen. Both regular mikes and clip-on types lose your voice the minute you turn your head.

In the best of all possible worlds, you won't need to point out specifics on your slides because they will be clear and self-evident (see below). In reality, though, it is sometimes necessary to use the pointer. If you must point to the screen, try to pause, turn and indicate, revolve back to your audience, and continue talking. Doing this gracefully—while keeping the "flow" of the talk going— is not easy. That's why you need to practice. Pay attention to how other speakers—especially good ones—handle this.

Watch the Clock

If your paper is too long, *cut it.*

The moderator usually has a timer, but s/he will only signal when your time is running out. It's much better to keep track yourself, so you can adjust if you spend too much time early on. I often take my watch off and set it on the podium where I can see it with a glance. That way, I'm not constantly looking at my wrist (a distraction for the audience). Practice your talk ahead of time to check the length.

If you still run out of time, jump immediately to your prepared concluding sentences and end gracefully as you planned. *The worst thing to do is to speed up.* Resist the temptation. It's better to leave something out. (You may be able to bring it up during questions afterward.) One way to control time variables: Prepare your talk in "modules," and be prepared to drop the second to last two, if necessary.

Never drop your conclusion, however, and make sure that your final sentences are appropriate if you do have to end earlier than you expected.

Use Visual Aids Carefully

I highly recommend slides, and I prefer them to view graphs (overheads). Slides force you to organize your talk well ahead of time, if only because it takes time to make them. It is too easy to wait until the last moment and then scrawl out overheads, which are also messier to handle than slides.

If you must use view graphs, have someone else change them during the presentation. (You will have plenty to concentrate on during the talk.) Also, when someone else is changing your view graphs, you have to be well-prepared; you won't be able to rearrange the them during the talk. If you must change them yourself, be careful. Nervous hands can knock over a pile of view graphs.

Whatever form of visual aids you use must be carefully checked before use. Look at them from the back of a room comparable to the size of the one in which you are talking. Is the text legible from a far corner? I have been at talks where view graphs were unreadable even from the front row. Such "illustrations" are worse than none at all: Not only do they add nothing, they actually distract the audience. At another presentation, the slides were entirely unintelligible. The speaker apologized—"Well, this slide would show the X instrument, but it's kind of old, so you really can't see the apparatus. This next slide would show our setup if it weren't so dark." The slides were a waste of time and an impediment to understanding. If the presenter didn't care enough to get decent pictures of his work, why should his audience care about what he was describing?

Practice, Practice, Practice

First, practice the talk itself, checking its content. Volunteer to give it as a lunch talk. If several of you are going to a conference, arrange a preconference minisymposium. Or, even better, do both. Ask for constructive criticism after your first attempt, on both the content and on your presentation. Apply what you learn to your second try, and solicit comments after the second try, too. If you are a mentor, strongly suggest that your graduate students give practice talks before they go to a conference.

Second, practice the physical logistics of the talk. When you get to the conference, find out where you are speaking, and go look at the room. Get the feel of the room. Try using the pointer. Pretend to talk in the microphone. Practice adjusting the mike to your height. Gauge the size of the room, thinking about the person sitting in the last row (what can s/he see and hear?). Put up a view graph or a slide. I usually do this the morning before I give my talk, early enough so that most people aren't up yet. (I feel silly sometimes, but I'm more comfortable later on during the real thing.)

Suddenly, a woman's voice starts speaking clearly and strongly. The sound of her voice—so much higher in pitch than the previous speaker's—catches your interest. She speaks precisely, introduces her material neatly, and sets it carefully into her talk's context. Her slides are readable, colorful, and concise. You feel as if she's talking to you personally; she even seems to look straight at you for a while. She doesn't seem rushed, and she reaches a logical conclusion, which sums up her argument in a few words. You will be able to explain the gist of her remarks exactly to your friend later.

Next time, that speaker is going to be you.

Heidi B. Hammel, Ph.D., is a principal research scientist in the department of earth, atmospheric, and planetary sciences at the Massachusetts Institute of Technology. Her main areas of interest are ground-based astronomical observations of outer planets' atmospheres and satellites in the visible and near infrared.

Go Where You Are Wanted, and Go Where You Can Work: Thoughts for Women Starting Out in Science

Florence P. Haseltine*

All of us have dreams. All of us have values that we live by. All of us have a sense of right and wrong. We balance each of these elements as we move through our work. The dreams about our future keep us going and determine our actions. Many of us can state with great certainty when we decided what we would do when we grew up. That decision is part of our identity. We will think of ourselves in terms of that decision, either because we live up to it or because we deviate from it.

The Sweep Versus the Details

Overall generic goals are often met, specific goals rarely. I knew by the time I was six that I would work in science and that I would always work. That mission has been accomplished. The specifics of my dreams have not been fulfilled and will not be: My desire was to be a physics professor at Berkeley, and I clearly did not do that. As a result, the way I think about myself is not the same as the way other people think about me. I can enumerate the many little hits that knocked me into another field until I ended up as a government bureaucrat. That may or may not happen to you.

Each of you have general and specific aspirations. You have educated yourselves or are doing so now. Now you need to plan the next batch of years.

First Principles

At the beginning of training, whether graduate level or residency, certain principles are essential.

First, you must do your own work, and what that is depends on the level of your expertise. In the laboratory, this rule means that,

*For Haseltine's biography, see her interview on page 38.

when you are starting out, you do not ask the technician to do your tasks. In a hospital, it means you draw your own blood. In a library, you do the searches yourself. Why? You need to gain the experience so that you know what to believe and what to question as you progress.

Second, do not believe everything that you are told. Question statements and check them out. Repeat other people's experiments if your work depends on it, and, most importantly, *believe your own results*. They may differ from those reported in the literature.

Third, it is usually best to look at an aspect of a problem that does not simply disprove other people's work. Move on to something else. The reason is pragmatic: You do not become a leader by merely disproving something someone else did. You need to add to knowledge, and, if you choose, you will have many opportunities to disprove work later.

As a junior person, your job is to develop your abilities, not just to uphold the honor of science by pointing out its many errors.

Brass Tacks

How do you find a position that balances your principles, dreams, and needs? First, you must look for a job—they will not come to you. You must apply, make calls, and cultivate contacts. Those around you will be important.

You will need everyone you meet professionally: You never know who will be called for references. One thing is certain, however: If you are being interviewed and someone mentions they know someone who works at your current place of employment, that person will receive a call about you. The world of science is very small. If you are able, contact anyone who you think might be called and let him/her know that you met someone who brought up his/her name.

Most superiors try to be helpful. But, as you quickly move from junior to senior student status, those behind you will look to you for help. Do not just bow to the top. Once you enter a field, the most rapidly growing group of your colleagues will be the people behind you.

The most important judgments about you will be made based on your curriculum vitae. You must be able to document your activities, but it is important to know which ones to list when. When you are junior, list invited speaking engagements and abstracts. When you become more senior, leave them off.

No matter how much time you put into your personal life, it counts only for you, not for your professional development. You will remember your personal achievements, but the other members of the professional community do not. In addition, it is what you write, not with whom you interact that is judged.

Setting Priorities

When you are starting out, your work has to be the most important guide for your life.

When you look for a job, typically, you take your work and peddle it. Make it as perfect as possible: For example, practice your lectures with your friends and in department seminars.

When you take your first independent job, make sure you have time to do the work that gains promotions. You need enough time that, if you do have people working with you, you can train them and keep them long enough to make progress. The most important people to train are the technicians who can finish what you start. The next set of people that you want to recruit are usually people who are stuck in the area for personal reasons. Universities are rich sources of such people. If you are the person who must find a job because of location, then these young labs are often interesting places to work. This is the one time I would advise working with people without a track record rather than working in a famous but miserable lab.

One of the problems young scientists get into is not negotiating a real working situation. Space and full-time equivalent help are the most valuable commodities that you will need. A location that offers space and technical support wants you.

You must be willing to move. It is much more important that you work in a productive environment than in a specific city. You cannot afford to be picky about your locale. (Because many of you will have a family to consider, luxury items that are not critical to both your career and that of your spouse must be tossed.) Often you will have to compromise on side issues. You can live anywhere, so *go where you can work.*

To give you a perspective on time, think about the most senior people in your field. Most will have moved around the entire country. In addition, you will live and work long enough that you will not refer to anything written this year. Keep a long-range time perspective on yourself. You will be around a long time. And so will your friends but, more galling, so will your enemies.

Once you have identified your field and some places where you can do the work, you can make a choice. All things being equal (but I have never found them to be so!), *go where you are wanted.*

Another important criterion is to determine how well others who have gone to your contemplated position have done. If your predecessors have not succeeded, do not go. If you are choosing an

239

academic career, you will need to publish, so you need a supportive environment. You set the criteria for success, because you know what you want.

Choosing a Work Environment

Often, big name places are attractive because, over a long period, people who have gone there have done well. If you feel that you are not as good as people already established in that august place, however, look again. Did you talk to an unsupportive group, or were you intimidated?

Do not chose a laboratory because it is politically correct. Instead, go into a group—a man's or a woman's—because it is good. As a junior person, you cannot change the system. Put changing that on hold until you are the boss: Then, you will truly have the opportunity to help other women. If a laboratory is new, no matter who is running it, you risk inexperienced supervision. Young laboratories are often exciting, however, so that if the science is compelling, the risk is often worthwhile. But do not go into the laboratory unless the project is irresistible.

Try to pick the most exciting group in your field and go there. The competition for the attention of the lab or program chief will be intense, but it will also force you to maximize your potential. People running laboratories or programs know that some individuals do well in their group and others do not. The boss usually does not want to admit that someone s/he chose is not working out any more than the person who is not producing wants to admit failure.

Just because a person does badly in one laboratory, however, does not mean s/he will not do better elsewhere. If people do not make the right choice, and that happens, they need to change. If they are encouraged, the move is called a *push.*

Changing

One of the main reasons anyone changes jobs is because of the *push,* not the pull of an attractive position. When you graduate, you clearly are pushed. When you finish postdoctoral training, you are again pushed. When you come up for tenure, you are nudged again.

Typically, only once or twice in your life will you receive an offer to do a job not on your career path. It is hard to advise anyone what to do when such an opportunity comes along. Whether you take the opportunity or not depends on whether there is any *push* from your present position or whether a rare position has opened up. I was fortunate to have one of those opportunities at a time when there was a *push*. It was relatively late in my career. Making a dramatic change closes a lot of classical career doors, so if you do so, make it late, not early. Although reentry into your chosen field is often impossible, do not refuse an exciting opportunity because you cannot go back. There are a lot of ways to live and work on your goals.

Gender Issues on the Job and in Our Lives

Sexism in the Guise of Acceptance: A Case Study*

Anonymous

The AWIS member who wrote this piece, as relevant today as 15 years ago, accompanied her paper with this introduction:

> *My conversion to the women's movement and this article on my experiences are the results of a job that lasted a short time. I resigned because I couldn't take it any longer. I want very badly to take legal action against the company. I feel that I have lots of evidence, but I don't think I could handle the backlash in terms of time, money, and emotions. Getting into a controversy will not necessarily destroy you when your career is established. But, if you are like me, just starting out, then you have to be careful.*
>
> *So I try to find other ways to discharge my anger. I am submitting this article, and I make small donations to AWIS as my budget will permit. I have signed up for an assertiveness training course. I donate to the Equal Rights Amendment, and I send in the names of potential donors. All of these things help, but inside, I still feel angry. In reading this article you may wonder if I am exaggerating to gain your sympathy; I most certainly am not.*

The traditionally male-dominated professions of science and engineering are beginning to open up to women, largely because of the rise in women's consciousness over the past few years. It would be a serious mistake, however, for a woman entering these professions to assume that, because things have changed since her mother's time, she automatically will be accepted by her colleagues. It is my thesis that many men resent the influx of women into "their" domain and will continue to hold sexist beliefs. Men feel that they must be careful not to show evidence of their sexism because of the ever present danger of lawsuits. Thus, they will disguise it in "safe" forms, so they "won't get caught" (i.e. sued, fined, fired). A woman entering science professions today will face discrimination, but it will take subtle and indirect forms.

*This paper originally appeared in the 1977, July/August *AWIS Newsletter*, 4(4), 6–8.

I had an experience [15 years ago] with an employer which illustrates the problem of disguised discrimination. Prior to the beginning of my work period, this employer had come under heavy attack because of underutilization of women. As a result, this company established a very aggressive affirmative action program and began actively recruiting women. On the first day of work, I was told by the supervisor that they were glad to have me on their team and that they believed that women were as talented as men. In retrospect, I understand the deception in their words. They made these statements because they were afraid of getting into trouble if they displeased me, not because they really liked and accepted me. I was a token, the person they could point to when women's groups approached them. Since my only function was to make "women's lib shut up," I was denied full responsibility and opportunity.

Yes, I experienced sexism, but it came in the guise of acceptance. What were some forms of the deception? What advice would I give you?

Guidelines for Self-Protection

Don't Blindly Trust the Affirmative Action Program

The management dramatically had formed an "equal opportunity committee." This was a group of 10 company employees whose sole purpose was to advance the careers of female workers. I was told that if I ever experienced discrimination, I was to approach the committee. I was assured that the committee would then solve my problem. Unfortunately, the committee members were appointed by the company president, a man who had no sympathy for women's rights. So he filled many of the committee seats with his "buddies" who, like him, were male chauvinists. One of the women on the committee privately told me that the committee was useless. The committee was so horrendously bureaucratic that a woman with a complaint was ensnarled in meaningless red tape. The woman committee member suspected that the company president used the committee as an easy way to form a blacklist for purposes of retaliation. Any woman that trusted the committee enough to file a complaint was added to the list of "troublemakers" and harassed by the old boy network.

Don't trust any such committee until you have solid evidence of its sincerity. Concentrate on developing anti-sexist techniques. Get close to a woman's group run by women.

Don't Be Willing to "Serve"

When you are a new worker trying to build up a career, it's natural to feel a desire to prove yourself. You want to work especially hard to gain recognition and acceptance. You want to serve the company. Has it occurred to you that some men will take advantage of this willingness and give a woman degrading tasks? I was so eager to serve that, initially, I accepted such tasks. Naively, I thought that serving the company well would win its administrators' favor. Instead, they came to think very little of me. I was the "girl" in the office who got the bad jobs nobody else wanted.

Don't let this happen to you. Make it very clear that you will work hard but don't overdo your offer. Be very sensitive about what your bosses ask you to do. Is it true scientific work, or is it something a motivated high school student could do? If the task is demeaning, tell them that you are not there to do personal favors for them and don't do it.

Be Sensitive to the Reasons for Praise

Praise can be a manipulative psychological weapon. After I was conned into doing clerical work, I was praised intensely for doing it. Interestingly, on those rare occasions when I made valuable contributions, my bosses treated me with total indifference. What was going on? They were trying to pressure me into doing degrading work by convincing me that I was a genius for doing it. They hoped that I would be so thrilled by their lavish praise that I would continue to handle the bad jobs. They did not want me to move into a responsible position, so they did not praise me when I did good work.

Be sensitive to praise. If you are complimented for genuine brilliance, that's a good sign. But if you are praised for the neatness of your handwriting when you take telephone messages, or for your marvelous efficiency on the copy machine, beware. If you think you are being manipulated in this way, tell your bosses politely but firmly that the work is not appropriate and you would like increased responsibilities. Never act delighted when others lavish manipulative praise on you.

Be Aware That You May Be Set Up for Failure

Your bosses yielded to affirmative action by hiring you, paying you more than a secretary, and giving you a "man's" title. But now that the affirmative action pressure bearing down on them has eased, you will not be allowed to advance. They don't want to advance you beyond the trainee stage, so they may assign you to a project with so many negative aspects to it that your career will be hurt.

I was the only woman in a large group of newly hired trainees. All the male trainees were assigned to a project I will call X. Project X was well-managed, productive, stimulating, and, most important, had excellent advancement possibilities. I was assigned to another project, which I'll call *Y*. Project *Y* was disorganized, behind schedule, and run by a man called *Z*. *Z* was incompetent and kept his job only because of seniority. Professionally, he was an outcast with no credibility. I was not aware of these things at the time project assignments were made. But, after a few months had passed, I heard that the male trainees in *X* were being offered salary increases and increased responsibilities. I, on the other hand, had been hurt because my professional name was now associated with project *Y*, a scandalous disaster.

Be aware that men may sometimes set up a woman for failure. In the work assignment stage, speak up! After work assignments, be on the alert for a set-up. If you have doubts, approach the management. Do this early, before your professional name is hurt.

Don't Show Signs of Insecurity

All of us feel insecure from time to time. This is especially true when we are new to a field. But, in the professional world, people want an aggressive, confident person who will contribute to the company's success. If this is true for a man, it's doubly true for a woman. If you show insecurity, your opponents will drive a wedge into the crack. Your admission of weakness will be exaggerated and spread.

Don't show signs of insecurity. If you make a mistake or don't know something, be objective and businesslike about it. Don't falter, look unhappy, or apologize.

Be Aware That You May Be Excluded from Important Information

When working as part of a scientific team, you must know the important information on your project. After a while, I noted that colleagues spoke freely with me on nontechnical matters, but they never brought me into discussions about our work. If I joined a group, conversation would shift from professional to social matters. I was once denied receipt of a valuable report. All the mail baskets except mine contained it.

Be aware that this can happen. Actively seek out information and ask questions. Don't passively wait for information to be volunteered. State that you want to receive all reports. Be firm.

Don't Let a Man Establish Personal Dominance Over You

On the third day of work, without warning, a man told me that I was being taken to see a contractor to present a talk on my work. When I told him I was so new to the job that I could not be expected to know it well enough to present a talk, he said "being new is no excuse." He then applied pressure, treating me as an incompetent for failing to master a complex project in three days.

What was happening? He was trying to establish personal dominance over me. By making unreasonable demands, he hoped I would become frightened and submissive. In this situation, a direct counterattack is needed. Tell him "You're making outrageous demands, hoping I'll be afraid of you, but you're just an employee like the rest of us!"

Beware of Chivalry

Chivalry says that you are a "lady," to be catered to and pampered in a lot of little ways. You're supposed to be so thrilled by the gallant little deeds that you aren't interested in a good assignment.

Do not act grateful when they perform their "gallant deeds." If the favor is useless or you never requested it, say so.

Beware of the Father Figure

The father figure typically is an older man who tries to convince you that as a more experienced, wiser person, he will protect you. This is nonsense. The two of you are colleagues competing for professional recognition. A woman who falls into this trap will have her professional life manipulated by this man.

When sexism takes the form of benevolent paternalism, insist on getting the "scary" assignments. If you disagree with the would-be father, speak up! Silence makes him think you are agreeing with his "wisdom."

Camouflage Can Be Dangerous

Note that in none of these nine cases did a man overtly say "no woman has the brains to be a good scientist." That would have been blatant sexism, and the speaker would have been vulnerable to disciplinary action. So "safe" ways were found to express the opinion.

I hope any woman reading this article will take my advice to heart and benefit from it. We *have* come a long way since the days when we weren't allowed to vote. But we still live in a sexist society and equality in the scientific fields remains an elusive goal. By allowing yourself to become a company's "token female," you are hurting the cause of all women.

The woman who contributed this piece to the AWIS newsletter in 1978 wished to remain anonymous to avoid the professional retaliation she feared would result from signing her work. Fifteen years later, she continues to prefer to withhold her name because, having recently changed scientific fields, she finds herself happily embarking on a new career path, and, as a newcomer, does not want to be labelled a complainer.

Affirmative Action in Perspective: When It Works and When It Doesn't

Anne M. Briscoe

Since the end of my tenure as AWIS national president in 1976, I have been its affirmative action advisor, serving as a resource for women wanting help with problems related to their professional

status. These problems have involved sex discrimination of every variety and have often included sexual harassment. In 99 percent of the cases, the women have suffered through no fault of their own. Perhaps 1 percent of the women in jeopardy are themselves at fault; *perhaps*.

Each woman who is a victim hopes to fight for justice and win. Unfortunately, at present there are few absolute victories. It is difficult to accept the fact that in this great country "liberty and justice for all" is an ideal to be pursued, not a present reality. The name of the victory game is power. Law enforcement is weak. Law suits are prohibitively expensive, and, through them, the individual woman is rarely truly vindicated. In the process, she loses precious time, peace of mind, status, and faith in herself.

Individually, she *rarely* wins because the wider women's movement has not raised the status of women sufficiently. That is to say, there are not enough women judges; there are too many reactionary judges and unpredictable juries. This is the reality. To be forewarned is to be forearmed.

Affirmative Action: History and Promise

Affirmative action is the term coined to describe positive actions required of federal contractors to combat sex and race discrimination. These steps, defined in Executive Order 11246 in 1965 and amended by 11375 in 1967, resulted from the turmoil of the civil rights and women's movements of the 1960s. Affirmative action was designed to correct the unequal opportunities for women and minorities in the workplace and in education. Enforcement of these regulations was the responsibility of the Office of Federal Contract Compliance (Department of Labor), which relegated enforcement

247

in academic institutions to the Office of Civil Rights, then part of the Department of Health, Education, and Welfare.

In addition to executive orders, Congress passed statutes prohibiting sex discrimination, such as the Equal Pay Act of 1963 (amended in 1972), Title VII of the 1964 Civil Rights Act, and Title IX of the 1972 Education Amendments. There were goals and time tables for implementation of plans that the responsible officers of companies, government agencies, and academic institutions were asked to formulate, and, after acceptance, those plans were legally binding. Mandated sanctions called for withholding federal funds from federal contractors for noncompliance.

The political climate of the 1970s was such that most companies and universities responded to what seemed inevitable and established offices for monitoring their own compliance. Because there was undue delay in the Office of Civil Rights' investigations of complaints, AWIS, together with other women's groups, initiated legal action that resulted in short, well-defined time tables for federal investigation and resolution of complaints against academic institutions. While the clout of federal law resulted in definite improvement in opportunities for women and minorities, it had little impact in the higher echelons of government and industry and among the ranks of tenured faculty. Professional women nationwide were optimistic 20 years ago that affirmative action policies would be a more powerful incentive for rapid progress than, in retrospect, they have in fact been.

Although complaints were often not heard in a timely fashion, verdicts were usually delayed, and sanctions were rarely invoked, some degree of compliance occurred when the government in Washington gave its moral and actual support to this system, which improved fairness in educational opportunities and in the workplace.

In 1980, the election of Ronald Reagan ushered in an era not only of retrenchment in protection of civil rights but also a posture of government deregulation in general. This atmosphere stiffened the resistance in executive suites of academe and industry to compliance with the statutes and executive orders.

Affirmative action as a concept, however, had brought great changes. It had facilitated the progress of women and minorities across barriers that were previously insurmountable. It was educational in a white man's world, a consciousness-raising device that may have forever changed the workplace. University policy now requires that women be hired. In-house grievance or review committees have played a positive role. Married couples can often now find appointments in the same institution. Companies with an eye on both the market place and the consumer try to present an

248

equal-opportunity-employer image, a concept unknown before 1970.

Familiar Dramas

Perhaps you will recognize some of these situations. Similar ones are reported to me weekly by women graduate students and professional scientists in every employment setting all over the country.

Case 1:

You are a graduate student working in the laboratory of an abusive, exploitive chief. He creates an impossible situation by making your progress dependent on the whims of his long-term technician.

Case 2:

You are an assistant professor with a heavy teaching load working in research facilities inferior to those of the men in your department. The equipment promised at the interview or stipulated in the letter of appointment has never materialized. Your chief "regrets" that an unexpected cut in funding has and will result in more teaching hours and less facilities for you.

Case 3:

You work for a chief who suggests that all your problems can be solved by granting him sexual favors; the understanding is that you can refuse and resign.

Case 4:

Your chief makes you, his female colleague, the co-principal investigator on a research proposal into which he then incorporates your most ingenious ideas. After he is awarded the grant, he finds a pretext to fire you. Under the National Institutes of Health's regulations, he has absolute power. The co-principal investigator has no rights.

Case 5:

You are denied promotion and tenure although your record with respect to publications and teaching evaluations is as good as that of a male colleague to whom the department awards tenure.

What does affirmative action do for victims like these in 1993?

In many instances, affirmative action requirements do *not* effectively serve as the route to justice, nor do they restore a woman's status or career opportunities.

Hard Lessons—Uphill Battles

The good news is that the majority of women scientists today operate within reasonable working conditions and have certain opportunities. Most women, however, are still almost invariably paid less and promoted more slowly than men with comparable qualifications. But the majority are neither harassed nor humiliated.

The bad news is that some people in positions of authority abuse their power and harass and exploit subordinates with impunity. Some of the women unfortunate enough to be victims of such men eventually request help from AWIS; usually, however, they do not ask soon enough. The rule is—the sooner the better. My advice is not to wait until there is a crisis.

No case is unique, but each woman is. Here are some composite lessons.

◆ Deans, college presidents, and chief executive officers usually back their deputy,* even when they know s/he is at fault.

◆ There is a difference between what is true and what can be proved. There are often no witnesses to abusive conversations or to false promises. Even if witnesses *were* present, they may not support the victim because of their own precarious situation or their dependence on the chief for funds, recommendations, status, and/or hassle-free working conditions.

◆ In-house grievance committee decisions that favor the complainant are often overruled by the dean, president, or trustees.

◆ Few law suits are successful. And, even when they are, the victim pays a high price in time and personal cost. When a large financial settlement is made in her favor, it is usually also stipulated that she leave the institution. She has been bought off, in effect. Her career is a part of the price because of the time taken to get a judgment, because of the reputation she acquires as a so-called trouble-maker, and because of the emotional consequences of seeing the perpetrator win. And win he usually does, often staying in his position, sometimes even being promoted, while she is cast out.

◆ Very few women can on their own afford the cost of a law suit. And women whose parents or companions are able to provide for them often find their private life disrupted and their combined financial position compromised.

Deputy is used as a generic word for midlevel administrators—department chairs, associate chairs, assistant deans, division chiefs, laboratory directors, and so forth.

250

◆ Becoming a complainant is emotionally damaging. The case, whether legal (external) or in-house, usually becomes the dominant concern of the victim's life, her *raison d'être*. It is difficult for her to maintain a sense of proportion. Communicating with other victims may seem a solution, but she will find that they cannot really help each other with specific resolutions to particular situations. She may lose faith in herself and in others, when her colleagues, once friends, appear to desert her.

◆ The kind of men who harass, cheat, and/or exploit women are dangerous adversaries. When a woman encounters such a man, she is unlikely to be his first victim. He is ruthless, adept at deceiving his superiors, skilled at intimidating his staff, and not to be underestimated.

Words to the Wise: Minimizing the Damage

In the 1980s and early 1990s, the best strategy has been to anticipate and if possible avoid events that can lead to a crisis situation.

In a more progressive era, I trust and expect that the women's and civil rights movements will overcome the present stalemate. Class action lawsuits can accomplish what individuals cannot. Meanwhile, we must survive. Many men have helped us; many men in positions of power are sympathetic to our aspirations.

During my lifetime of 74 years, there has been enormous improvement in the status of women, but I have appreciated this change only in retrospect. When I was in the midst of the fray, I did not appreciate the progress.

Now, in a spirit of cautious optimism that we shall overcome, I offer some interim advice.

Start Out Right

Whether you are a student or a qualified scientist in a new job, put your best foot forward. Aim

◆ at friendly, detached (i.e. not personal) relationships in the department or lab

◆ to make tentative initial judgments about people and situations (first impressions are often wrong)

◆ to have few confidants and none among professional colleagues

◆ to participate in department social events (which are really part of one's professional life)

◆ to cope with some inequality based on gender in this less-than-perfect world and to keep a sense of proportion about what matters and what does not, keeping a distant goal in focus and avoiding diversion by trivia

◆ at discretion, "the better part of valor": Everyone does not have to know what one is thinking, disapproving, liking, or disliking

◆ at a dispassionate reaction to an annoying person by dealing with him or her as one would a psychiatric patient: Dislocate the problem from the hypothalamus, solve it in the cerebral cortex, and, following Plato's advice, *never make an unnecessary enemy*

◆ at excellence in effort and performance to establish one's credibility as student or scientist

Remember to take into account the consequences of being an eccentric, an individualist, or a nonconformist: Expect to pay a price, decide if it's too high, and—perhaps—postpone extensive self-expression until later.

What If . . .

In spite of your best efforts, if you encounter unequal treatment (i.e., sex discrimination) by your chief, take this advice into account.

If you find yourself a victim of discrimination, seek advice before taking action and, if possible, before expressing anger to anyone.

◆ The first law of self-preservation is to protect your notebooks, records, computer files, specimens, personal property, and so forth. Remove everything of value to you from the institution before taking a stance—or you are likely to regret it. Packing up personal valuables at the first sign of trouble is a professional application of the term "streetwise" that young women on the brink of their careers must learn.

◆ Keep notes on conversations and events. Document whatever you can.

◆ Evaluate the situation and decide whether it prevents you from doing your best work. Give your present position a chance. It may not be the best time for you to move to another job. Remember that an aggravating job is better than no job at all.

◆ Find another more objective perspective by discussing what's going on with your family, a trusted friend, a mentor, or an AWIS representative.

◆ Present a calm facade. Try not to let your attitude reveal your feelings. If you decide to negotiate with your chief, do so in the most friendly, unemotional manner you can affect.

◆ Look for a better situation quietly if you think your position is hopeless or unbearable.

◆ Watch out if you are starting a new job and your chief makes inappropriate remarks about your appearance or your physical attributes. Such a posture is a common opening by a habitual harasser. At that stage, a posture of polite but tough rejection may cause him to look elsewhere. But he will not forget the rebuff.

◆ Expect that the perpetrator of sexual harassment may not yield to pleas or reason. Particularly if he is married, however, it may be possible briefly to intimidate him and eventually to obtain evidence admissible in a court of law. There has probably already been a succession of secretaries, lab technicians, and female junior colleagues who could provide damaging evidence against him. But often previous victims cannot be found or are unwilling to become involved.

◆ Be alert and try to side-step an unequal battle before your status in the scientific community is established.

◆ Remember that, even if others can and will support your accusations, your best possible solution—whether or not you decide to prosecute—is to become professionally independent of him. Then, when you have safely moved to another job, if you have the means and the will, you may choose to go after him.

◆ *Do not allow your career to be hostage to the outcome.*

The Path of Change: Individually and Collectively

Women in science must be alert not only to every opportunity for professional advancement but also to every chance to move sideways if the situation is unsatisfactory or potentially dangerous: You are never

◆ too old to move

◆ too young to accept responsibility

◆ a prisoner

◆ unable to gamble on change

Collectively, women's advocacy groups are the major instruments we have to challenge the system, to be the women's presence in the arena where changes in society are forged. The student in a university or the woman at an early stage of her career will not change the system by sacrificing her career. Progress is not made by martyrs, but

253

by an army of women, more competent than their male peers, united in a common cause.

Occasionally, circumstances occur in which senior-level women such as Anita Hill, Esq., or Frances K. Conley, M.D., choose to speak out. When they rise to the occasion, they greatly enhance the cause of us all.

You too join the battle by supporting AWIS, the National Organization of Women, and all the other organizations supporting women and their needs through group action and class action.

And remember, with Milton, that "they also serve who only stand and wait."

Anne M. Briscoe, Ph.D., a biochemist retired from the faculty of medicine of Columbia University, is a feminist (neither retired nor repentant) who has long been active in AWIS activities. She has served as AWIS' president, head of its Educational Foundation, and chair and cochair of its Affirmative Action Committee; she has also been vice-chair of the New York City Commission on the Status of Women and chair of the Committee for Women in Science of the New York Academy of Sciences.

Tacit Discrimination and Overt Harassment: The Toll on Women, Minorities, and the Nation*

Linda S. Wilson

Mentoring students and colleagues is one of the most important responsibilities of all whose talents and opportunities have enabled them to achieve. Part of that mentoring responsibility is to share information and thoughts about the way the "system" works. Another part is to try to improve the system for those whose careers are still developing. Such mentoring is an investment in our nation's future. It brings the personal satisfaction known to all who give of themselves and their resources for the greater good.

From the vantage point of one whose roles have provided and provide many direct opportunities to observe the environment for women in what are often called nontraditional fields and to review the reports of studies of their experience, let me share what I have learned.

The nature of the economic base of this country presents a growing need for skilled and knowledgeable workers, for intellectual talent, and for ingenuity. Substantial progress has been made in changing the rules that previously barred women and minorities from entering education, the workplace, and many social environments. Our nation's future economic security will depend on how well we have educated, trained, and incorporated women and minorities (as well as men) into full and effective participation in society.

Women and minorities, as new entrants to the workforce in nontraditional occupations, represent an important source of *renewal*. New entrants bring questions, fresh ideas, new energies and skills, and innovative and different perspectives to old problems.

*Wilson's paper is based on the testimony she gave June 25, 1992, to the Oversight Hearing on Sexual Harassment in Nontraditional Occupations before the Subcommittee on Employment Opportunities, Committee on Education and Labor, of the U.S. House of Representatives.

They can learn the existing strategies, but they are not blinded by the familiar.

Furthermore, many of the challenges we now face will not yield just to knowledge and innovation. Progress requires concerted public will—a broad and sustained commitment to make short-term sacrifices where necessary for long-term gain—in the development of viable policies for energy, education, health care, and the environment. We need to develop, now more than ever, *an informed, scientifically literate citizenry*. We cannot succeed without the full participation of women and minorities, both in the development and in the support of effective policy and action.

These facts lead to some vital questions: *Are the United States' science and engineering enterprises hospitable to women, to men, and to all people, no matter what their race and ethnicity? Were we to evaluate the design and operation of these professions and courses of study, would we conclude that their intention is to make women and minorities full participants or to continue to treat them as guests or outsiders?*

Postsecondary Science for Women: What Welcomes and What Inhibits

There is mounting evidence that our institutions are less than hospitable in important ways.

A recent report from the University of Michigan (Susan Frazier-Kouwassi, et al., 1992, March) reviews studies on women in science and mathematics and publishes the results of a new study about the experiences of women and men in mathematics and science programs at a major research university. The latter focuses on what students believe enhanced or inhibited their decisions to pursue or not to pursue academic work and careers in math and physics. The information presented below summarizes, excerpts, or quotes findings in this excellent report.

Among the important results noted in the literature review are the following:

◆ Prestigious liberal arts colleges are especially effective in producing women who subsequently earn Ph.D.s.

◆ Self-confidence affects whether men and women choose to go into science and math and may well be the distinguishing characteristic between the approaches of men and women to the latter.

◆ Even women who perform as well as men in science and math report lower confidence in their ability to do science and math, and women's confidence drops during the critical early years in college.

♦ Women students must have unusually strong confidence in their abilities to counter prevailing notions that science and math are inappropriate fields for women.

♦ Women are especially sensitive to cues from the environment that reflect the quality of their performance and the likelihood of their success.

♦ Studies of classroom dynamics suggest that men and women have quite different levels of positive experiences. Women receive less direct encouragement, are taken less seriously, are given fewer opportunities, and are less likely to enjoy a comfortable relationship with counselors and teachers.

♦ The negative classroom dynamics seem to be worse for women majoring in mathematics and science. The women studied were nearly unanimous in believing that women receive less positive treatment. They report being "put down," patronized, called on less frequently, and ignored.

♦ Teachers who are particularly successful in encouraging women to pursue science and mathematics include information about women scientists in the curriculum, avoid gender-stereotyped views of science and scientists, and are sensitive to sexist language.

♦ Women generally respond negatively to what is perceived as an *overly* competitive environment. Typically, they find cooperative atmospheres more helpful and competitive atmospheres more harmful than do male students.

♦ Of the programs colleges have designed to increase the number of women who complete degrees in math and the physical sciences, very few focus on restructuring the academic environment or changing the discouraging attitudes and behavior of faculty members.

At the University of Michigan, three new research projects have provided snapshots at varying temporal points along the pathway to advanced education in mathematics and physical sciences: At the initial entrance into an accelerated undergraduate curriculum; at graduation with a bachelor's degree in math or physics; and in doctoral work in math or physics. The studies showed that

♦ Academic performance and ability are clearly *not* what limit women's achievement.

◆ The critical factors are students' *perceptions* of science and math, of the educational environment, and of their own abilities.

Encouragement, whether by faculty, family, or peers, appears to be the critical link in the chain that helps build and maintain the self-confidence needed to persist on the path to a higher degree in math or science.

The Stacked Deck Against Women in Science

Several major research universities have undertaken serious self-assessments of the academic environment for women in the sciences at the graduate student level and at the faculty level. Some of the findings follow:

◆ With few exceptions, women in science are but a small minority in their peer groups, and their proportion drops sharply as they advance through their careers. The resulting isolation impedes research, increases stress, and may lead to abandonment of the profession.

◆ The period when successful scientific careers are usually forged (in the general career pattern developed when the enterprise was almost exclusively male) corresponds to the time of childbearing.

◆ Experimental work, which makes extraordinary demands on availability in time and/or location, raises conflicts with the family responsibilities that continue to be disproportionately borne by women.

◆ Women graduate students are often dissuaded from pursuing certain areas of science. In some disciplines, they are discouraged by faculty and student colleagues from pursuing mathematical or theoretical investigations; in other fields, women are discouraged from pursuing experimental work.

More subtle forms of discrimination also continue, including, for example, treatment of women as outsiders and negative attitudes of faculty toward women's family commitments. The predominance of males among the tenured science faculty in major research universities results in many nontenured women feeling powerless. Many nontenured women do not have positive, collegial relationships with senior members of their departments; they are deprived of the mentoring relationships often critical to advancement in a field. In some cases, junior faculty feel exploited, and, in many instances, women perceive their situations to be worse than those of their male junior colleagues. The failure to integrate junior faculty into their own departments has at times been a longstanding problem.

Many institutions have recently undertaken studies of access and the environment for women. These efforts are commendable, but the studies frequently show that the barriers and problems found in similar reviews 20 years ago persist.

◆ In addition, a recent study by Louise F. Fitzgerald, Lauren M. Weitzman, Yael Gold, and Mimi Ormerod (1988, September) reveals that the power dynamics involved when faculty engage in sexual relationships with students—graduate and undergraduate—are still widely misunderstood. Many institutions have now established policies on sexual harassment and unprofessional conduct. Many have procedures for resolution of complaints. Overt sexism is less pervasive than in the past. Nevertheless, serious instances of sexual harassment and gender-specific academic harassment do occur.

Evening the Odds for a New Workforce

Most of these problems reflect a culture that has insufficiently recognized the capabilities and contributions of women and their potential. They reflect a culture that has kept pace neither with women's changing employment patterns nor with society's increasing need for women scientists' talent. These problems are a result of our tendency to imagine the ideal scientist as a man who can singlemindedly devote 60 to 80 hours a week to science because he has no conflicting familial obligations.

Such a picture is now anachronistic. The assumptions on which it is based are not valid. Women constitute a substantial proportion of the workforce. Because families are now most often supported by multiple wage earners, the family support system at home, which previously permitted men to concentrate their energies on work with intensity and without distraction, is now less available to men and rarely available to women. Institutional designs that fail to accommodate this altered circumstance—the changed nature of the workforce and the real situations workers face—cannot yield the quality and productivity the future requires.

The United States is the only industrialized nation in which basic workplace policies assume that women are not present. Yet America educates its women more than do other nations. Women's talent, education, and productivity represent major advantages for this country, advantages we are squandering by clinging to old assumptions about ability, about appropriate roles, and about how to teach and develop talent. Our assumptions reflect too inadequate an understanding of our talent pool, too limited a view of the path to achievement, and too narrow a set of assumptions and criteria for identifying and assuring excellence.

A Mandate for Change

The dilemmas, the conflicts, the competing claims on human, physical, and financial resources are real and difficult. But our working and learning environments do need change, both for the sake of the women and men who study and work in them and for our society's future well-being.

The new environments we design, which will develop and nurture the talent we need, can eliminate the harassment women now experience. Their resulting self-confidence, which will also reduce their vulnerability to harassment, points a pathway to a win-win situation for all.

Reexamination of the assumptions on which institutional designs are based, in light of current economic and social realities, should begin immediately. The improvements in the environment for women in science and engineering will bring a boon to men as well and broaden the base of talent that can contribute successfully in a knowledge-intensive society.

Many of the barriers to achievement have been identified. What is needed is a broader vision of productive enterprises, leadership to signal the value of change, and innovative strategies to preserve core values as we transform the workplace for a new century.

References

Fitzgerald, Louise F., Weitzman, Lauren M., Gold, Yael, and Ormerod, Mimi. (1988, September). Academic harassment: Sex and denial in scholarly garb. *Psychology of Women Quarterly, 12*(3), 329–340.

Frazier-Kouwassi, Susan, Malanchuk, Oksana, Shure, Patricia, Burkam, David, Gurin, Patricia, Hollenshead, Carol, Lewis, Donald J., Soellner-Younce, Patricia, Neal, Homer, and Davis, Cinda-Sue. (1992, March). *Women in mathematics and physics: Inhibitors and enhancers*. Ann Arbor, MI: Center for the Education of Women, University of Michigan.

Linda S. Wilson, Ph.D., trained as a chemist, is president of Radcliffe College and was previously vice president for research at the University of Michigan. She serves on numerous national boards and committees, including the American Council on Education's Commission on Women, the National Science Foundation's Advisory Committee for the Directorate for Education and Human Resources, and she chairs the National Research Council's Office of Science and Engineering Personnel.

Dismantling Internalized Sexism

Sheella Mierson and Francie Chew

Sheella Mierson

Francie Chew

Many discussions of women in science focus on external events: Our representation, our status, our treatment. We focus in this article on our internal responses to some of those events. In particular, we discuss two issues that affect women scientists—self-esteem and isolation. Each of us is a wonderful, smart, unique person, woman, and scientist. Unfortunately, many of us forget our strengths and focus on our perceived limitations. We may become preoccupied with insignificant criticisms and quickly dismiss praise. One reason for this behavior is that we have been given misinformation about our true natures, resulting in a distorted view of ourselves and of our places in the world.

What Is Internalized Sexism?

Both women and men can lose self-esteem compared to what they had as children due to a variety of factors. Some factors, however, affect us specifically as females. At an early age, many of us get the message that we aren't as capable as males in certain areas of endeavor. We receive messages like these: Our power is limited; our bodies don't look right; our expectations for our careers and for our lives should be limited. We internalize these messages as we grow up. The messages arise from *sexism;* when we accept them they become part of *internalized sexism*. The result is that we believe this misinformation about ourselves and each other and act as though it were true.

As an example, take an elementary school girl who enjoys math and excels in it. In junior high, people tell her that girls can't think about math as well as boys can, that boys won't like her if she gets better grades in math than they do, or that she should concentrate on more "feminine" subjects. In high school, she doesn't sign up for the advanced math class. Even if a guidance counselor doesn't actively discourage her, she now believes that she can't think very well about math. Fortunately, this girl's story is not all of ours.

Internalized sexism has some particular effects on women as scientists. For instance, many of us have nagging doubts about our intelligence and competence which may persist despite all evidence to the contrary. Have you ever noticed how little correlation there is between a woman scientist's level of accomplishment and her self-confidence? Sheila E. Widnall (1990, September 30) documents studies showing that female scientists' self-esteem drops relative to that of males in high school, undergraduate, and graduate school. This occurs even though males' and females' academic records are comparable. Studies summarized by Gloria Steinem (1992) indicate that this drop in self-esteem occurs for females relative to males in all fields, not just in science. In high school and college, even when women's records are better than men's, men's expectations are higher (see Mary Beth Ruskai, 1991). For further documentation of females' experiences in high school and college classrooms, see Kathleen Weiler (1988) and Roberta M. Hall and Bernice Resnick Sandler (1982, and in this volume, pages 271–279).

Steinem points out that one reason females may learn not to take themselves seriously is that they are often not taken seriously by teachers. Numerous studies show that

> boys are called on more often and talk more in their average response [than girls], yet [in one study] when [teachers were shown] films of classroom discussions in which boys outtalked girls by a ratio of three to one, the teachers—including feminists—still perceived the girls as talking more. We are so culturally trained to think that females talk too much, that we should be "good listeners," that we seem to measure ourselves against those expectations, not reality. (p. 120)

Internalized Sexism Makes Us Forget Our Accomplishments

We function at our best when we feel good about ourselves and about our intelligence, so we need to counteract the internalized sexism which keeps us from feeling proud and delighted with ourselves. Unfortunately, we have lots of practice in focusing on negative occurrences: "Another paper was rejected," "I asked a stupid question," or "Why did I say that to my boss (or to my technician)?" Often, even typically, we don't allow ourselves the time to remember the positive events.

How long did you allow yourself to celebrate when you had a paper accepted, received a teaching award, won a grant, were given a favorable annual evaluation, or asked a critical question that set off a good discussion? One week? Five minutes? To focus on positive events, we should build a personal support network of people to whom we can relate our most recent accomplishments on a regular basis. In doing this, we can start noticing and remembering them ourselves. We can be sure to compliment colleagues when we notice that they have done something well. We can encourage each other not to put ourselves down and to focus on our strengths and accomplishments.

Our scientific institutions, still predominately male, may leave us feeling that we don't quite belong. Add to this whatever doubts we have about our scientific competence, and the result is we feel that we always have to prove ourselves and that we are always starting over. The energy required to prove ourselves over and over and to counteract internalized sexism that argues "I don't belong here" is enormous. It is energy that could much better be spent doing creative science, enjoying our work and our colleagues, and building personal lives where we flourish.

Internalized Sexism Isolates Us From Other Women

Lack of self-esteem is one component of internalized sexism; a second is often isolation from other women. What reaction do you get from nonscientist women when you tell them you are a scientist? Two typical reactions: "You must be smart," or "I was never good in science in school." As scientists, we spend our lives thinking in areas where many females are taught they shouldn't and/or couldn't venture. When other women not in science meet us, out come all their doubts about their own intelligence—*their* internalized sexism.

Additional complications occur when stereotypes about scientists intersect with internalized sexism. One such stereotype is that scientists are more intelligent than other people. This belief, which has no basis in fact, keeps others feeling stupid and powerless. A second stereotype is that scientists don't have the same needs or skills for close contact and nurturing that other human beings do. This piece of misinformation seems to affect men and women in different ways. For men, it reinforces conditioning that they are supposed to be emotionally independent and that they cannot think as well as females about relationships. For women, something different happens. In our society women are regarded as the nurturing sex. Indeed, some consider that the responsibility for nurturing is ours alone, and that *only* we can be successful at it. If women scientists are seen as *not* being nurturing and as not needing close relationships, however, we are set apart from other women.

The reality is that both men and women flourish when they feel good about themselves and about their intelligence, and when they are surrounded by the close relationships they desire. We needn't resign the human ability to participate in loving, nurturing relationships in order to enjoy another part of being human, namely our curiosity and intelligence. The reality about women is that there need be no conflict between being fully contributing scientists and being fully female.

Not All Difficulties Are Our Fault

Feeling isolated, in combination with any internalized doubts about our competence, can make us tend to take difficulties personally. Our isolation stems both from what we carry inside as internalized sexism and from external isolation resulting from our often low representation and unequal status in science. This isolation makes it harder to remember that many of the difficulties each of us faces do not arise from personal defects. Examining surveys of students in science, Widnall discusses differences in responses of men and women to experiences in graduate school. "The men most often expressed anger, even rage, at the system and suggested ways that it should be changed," she summarizes, "whereas the women more often described the effect that the current system had on them and expressed feelings of frustration and discouragement" (1990, p. 1743). The cumulative effect of unequal treatment, resulting in lowered self-esteem, can make women more vulnerable to any challenge that might weaken their self-image. If criticism reinforces feelings of inferiority, for example, women might take criticism harder and require longer to bounce back. We suspect, from discussions with a number of successful women scientists, that, in general, women tend to take rejections from journals and funding agencies more personally than do men and, therefore, take longer on average to resubmit manuscripts and grants.

Sexism affects women differently depending on background. Many of us belong to other groups that receive unequal treatment in our society. We may be working class, women of color, Jews, lesbians, or older women. Unequal treatment from multiple sources can further reinforce isolation and undermine self-esteem. When we realize what we have been up against, we can give ourselves full credit for persevering and flourishing as women scientists. Can you imagine what our personal and professional lives would be like if we no longer carried internalized sexism? Eliminating external factors that contribute to our unequal status is only half the work; eliminating the hurt we carry inside will make us less vulnerable and better able to respond effectively to any unequal treatment we do encounter.

We Can Dismantle Internalized Sexism

So how can we change the situation? First, as part of a support network, set up a regular meeting with a friend. Get together with her once or twice each week (a half-hour in person or by telephone is a good start). Agree to socialize some other time. Each person takes a turn (about 10 minutes each; we use a laboratory timer). When it's your turn to talk, focus on your achievements for that week, and think out loud about next steps for yourself— in any area of your life. When it's your turn to listen, do so attentively and supportively, but don't interrupt with questions, comments, or advice, and keep confidences. Give the other person a chance to set her own agenda. Each of us has found that this dyad format helps to put us in charge of our decisions to act, to seek advice, and to choose.

Second, work at counteracting the effects of internalized sexism in the classroom by promoting active participation by all students. If you teach, engage shy students (many of whom are female) with eye contact. Request questions or responses from people who haven't spoken in class recently. Structure some thinking activities using student dyads to encourage reflection. In these reflection/ thinking aloud activities, one student takes a turn for two minutes while the other listens; then, they reverse roles. This approach is similar to the longer dyad described above, but the assignment focuses on a specific topic such as "What did I just hear and what seems unclear?" (For more information, see Chew, 1992.) Refuse to buy the internalized sexism in students' views of themselves—that, for example, as females, they shouldn't face challenging work or courses, compete for scholarships and prizes, or do certain kinds of work because their test scores in a large introductory course weren't as good as they'd hoped. These methods require a teacher's self-awareness. Tufts biologist Saul Slapikoff (1985, May) describes his discovery—through observations made by his colleague Sara Freedman (Department of Education)—of his own unaware focus on the men, despite the fact that his course included a major section on debunking the scientific basis of sexism, and that a slight *majority* of the students were women. For a discussion of how teacher support groups increase self-awareness, see Julian Weissglass (1991). Both men and women teachers have found that these methods promote greater active participation by all students.

Third, we can counteract internalized sexism in our colleagues by noticing when they do things well. We can tell our colleagues when we learn from their seminar presentation or from their questions. We can tell our colleagues when students compliment their courses. Nearly everyone, including male scientists, has been consistently told "You haven't done enough" and "You could always do more or better." What an antidote to our personal doubts when someone notices we've done something well! We have found, in addition, that others tend to notice our work in return.

Setting up a support network, including regular dyads with a friend, and working against internalized sexism in our classrooms and among our colleagues, will help us end whatever isolation we have. These steps, by helping us regain our self-esteem so that we do not sap our energy by taking difficulties personally, will free more energy for doing science. They may also give us more time to improve the situation for women in science in general.

References

Chew, Francie. (1992). Peer interaction boosts science learning. In Tom Warren (Ed.), *A view from the academy: Liberal arts professors on excellent teaching* (pp. 156–165). New York: University Press of America.

Hall, Roberta M., and Sandler, Bernice Resnick. (1982). *The classroom climate: A chilly one for women?* Washington, DC: Association of American Colleges.

Ruskai, Mary Beth. (1991). Comment: Are there cognitive gender differences? *American Journal of Physics, 59*(1), 11–14.

Slapikoff, Saul. (1985, May). Teacher's unconscious sexism improved. *Radical Teacher, 7*(28), 33.

Steinem, Gloria. (1992). *Revolution from within: A book of self-esteem.* Boston: Little Brown.

Weiler, Kathleen. (1988). *Women teaching for change: Gender, class, and power.* South Hadley, MA: Bergin and Harvey.

Weissglass, Julian. (1991). Constructivist listening for empowerment and change. *Educational Forum, 54,* 352–370.

Widnall, Sheila E. (1990, September 30). American Association for the Advancement of Science presidential lecture: Voices from the pipeline. *Science, 241*(4874), 1740–1745.

Sheella Mierson, Ph.D. (biophysics), is an associate professor in the School of Life and Health Sciences at the University of Delaware, where she teaches physiology and does research in membrane physiology and biophysics. She uses student-centered, problem-based learning to teach physiology to medical and graduate students; she also teaches courses in leadership development and multicultural issues.

Francie Chew, Ph.D. (biology), is a professor of biology at Tufts University, where she teaches biology, education, and American Studies, and directs an active lab in plant-insect chemical ecology. She helps teachers to use collaborative learning methods, with particular attention on counteracting the effects of sexism and racism in the classroom, and leads programs on multicultural issues.

Mentors

Status of Women in Science: Mentors Needed

Betty M. Vetter

Women haven't yet achieved full equity in science with men—at 45 percent of the work force and over 50 percent of the population, they should appear in the profession in similar percentages. They

have increased their participation at every degree level, particularly since the 1950s, however. But their progress has been far from steady.

The women's movement of the 1920s saw women increase their percentage of all science doctoral degrees to 12.6 percent of the total awarded in that decade. But the depression of the 1930s dropped their participation slightly, to 11.5 percent. In the 1940s, as the World War II GI Bill helped educate American servicemen (and a few women), the standards for admitting women were raised higher than those for men. This again reduced the percentage of degrees awarded to women—to 9.6 percent. The 1950s carried this trend further, so that women earned only 7.5 percent of the science doctorates awarded during that decade.

The 1960s saw the beginnings of the present women's movement and a slight increase in women's science degrees—back to 9.6 percent of the total. Momentum continued to build throughout the 1970s, when women almost doubled their share of the science doctorates to 17.5 percent. The 1980s continued the increase, averaging 30.2 percent across the decade, and in the first two years of the 1990s, women earned 34.8 percent of science Ph.D.s.

A Growing Presence

Although women's participation has continued to grow faster in the social and behavioral sciences than in the physical and mathemat-

267

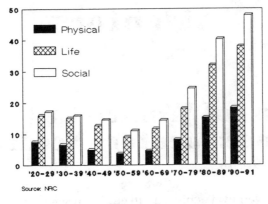

Figure 1

Percent Women Science Ph.D.s by Decade, 1920–1991

ical sciences, or even in the life sciences, all fields now include at least a few thousand women who are making their way slowly up into the professorial and/or managerial ranks. The days when women were not allowed to register in any graduate schools are over, and the tokenism of the early decades of this century is also over.*

Women's contributions to science slowly are being recognized, although it appears difficult for many men in organizations like the National Academy of Sciences to find women worthy of joining their august company. While about a century elapsed between the election of the Academy's first woman member, Marie Mitchell, in 1848, and the second, in 1943, 69 women (4 percent) are now active members.

One reason that women find it so difficult to breach the walls of the Academy is that they lack mentors among the members. Individuals must be nominated before being considered for membership. Often, the nominator is their mentor, who then extols their accomplishments to fellow members. Although the majority of successful women in science have had mentors—largely male ones—there are still too few who think first of their female students or assistants when asked for recommendations. The emergence of more women mentors, as well as the continued increase in the

---

*In 1921, the Women's Committee of the American Chemical Society noted that 34 universities were willing to admit women to a doctoral program in chemistry; today, 188 graduate schools grant Ph.D.s in chemistry, all of them to both men and women.

numbers of women scientists, will hasten the day when scientists will be judged by their work, not by their gender.

Rising Confidence: A Priority

The most important thing a woman needs to become a scientist, besides the brains and the interest, is the sense of self-esteem that makes her believe that she can do whatever she sets her mind to. By the time a young woman reaches the age when this decision is necessary, however, she has already gone through several years of school in which her male classmates were

◆ assumed to be better in science and mathematics than she

◆ offered more attention and more assistance

◆ provided more recognition for their insights

◆ given permission—tacitly or explicitly—to interrupt or steal ideas from girls

Except in girls' schools, boys often do the laboratory experiments, and girls take the notes. The recent American Association of University Women report *How Schools Shortchange Girls* (1992) documents this pattern in detail.

Without realizing it, girls often lose self-confidence during the high school years, and some find it very difficult to recover later. But self-confidence is vital for the scientist, who must be able to trust her theories and results. A good mentor can help to instill self-confidence.

Equity

Like boys, girls should be encouraged to satisfy their curiosity, to find out how things work. They should learn that girls are as good in mathematics as boys—even if some studies show that among the very highly gifted in mathematics, males, left-handers, and the near-sighted appear more frequently than they do in the general population (Camilla Persson Benbow, 1986).

Girls who are curious about the world around them and show it are likely to be interested in science. A mentor can stimulate that curiosity, whether in a child or a young scientist, by indicating interest, asking questions, and listening carefully to answers and explanations.

The woman who has reached an early milestone such as a bachelor's degree in science already has overcome some of the handicaps and barriers placed in her way by society and school.

269

There are more ahead at the graduate level; at this point a mentor becomes even more important, often being instrumental in whether a student goes on to graduate school.

The rewards of mentoring are so great that it is surprising that more people are not involved in it. For the mentor, the achievements of the person encouraged are akin to the victories of one's own child.

Mentoring is a gift that gives.

References

The American Association of University Women. (1992). *How schools shortchange girls.* Washington, DC: Author and National Education Association.

Benbow, Camilla Persson. (1986). Physiological correlates of extreme intellectual precocity. *Neuropsychologia, 24*(5), 719–725.

Since 1963, Betty M. Vetter has been the executive director of the Commission on Professionals in Science and Technology (formerly the Scientific Manpower Commission) in Washington, D.C. She is editor of the periodical Scientific, Engineering, Technical MANPOWER COMMENTS; *author of more than 150 published reports, book chapters, and articles on some phase of production and/or utilization of scientists and engineers; and a frequent speaker on aspects of these subjects.*

Mentoring: Myths and Realities, Dangers and Responsibilities*

Bernice Resnick Sandler

What happens to women in academe, as students and as faculty, and to women in workplaces outside of academe may depend not only upon how hard a person works, the quality of her work, and how much she knows, but also upon whom she knows and how much guidance, support, information, and advocacy others provide.

The process of mentoring used to follow this pattern: An important older male takes on the education of a young man and teaches him the tricks of the trade. Eventually the young man also becomes powerful; he then has a falling-out with his mentor and leaves his symbolic father. Occasionally, a happy ending ensues when the young man, now middle-aged, makes peace with the mentor who made success possible in the first place.

This scenario dates back to Homer when Odysseus' trusted friend, named Mentor, began to educate Odysseus' son, Telemachus, whose father was off, variously, fighting and wandering. Mentor protects and nurtures Telemachus, introduces him to other leaders, and guides him to his rightful place. The relationship is between men— the word *mentoring* was rarely applied to female interactions until the birth of the new women's movement in the 1960s. But although we never had a *label* for relationships between young and older women, the latter have been guiding the former since time immemorial.

What Is a Mentor and What Does One Do?

A mentor is someone in the institution or organization who coaches, teaches, advises, supports, guides, and helps the mentee†

---

*This paper is based on an address to the AWIS chapters' conference June 7, 1991, in Washington, D.C.

†Apologies for this dreadful but unavoidable word. Mentee and protégée are interchangeable in this paper.

or protégé achieve his or her goals. Especially in colleges and universities, a mentor initiates the mentee into the adult world. Mentors also help further the development of their charges' personal and professional identities. Mentors help in the long process of career development; they initiate mentees into the occupational world by introducing them to its formal and informal parts, its values, customs, resources, and players. Mentors teach both how to get things done and what not to do.

A woman mentored by a man is in some instances almost anointed. By guiding her, the mentor has tacitly proclaimed her worth, has asserted that she is "not like the others," and should be accepted by the inner circle of men. His protégée is one with whom *they* can be comfortable. She is probably less likely to be harassed, sexually or otherwise, by other men because she "belongs" to the mentor.

Career workshops and much of the literature aimed at helping women emphasize mentoring and networking. Typically, mentoring involves a close relationship; networking is more casual. They are part of the same continuum. But one can gain similar kinds of help from both—some types, more easily from mentoring; others, more easily from networking. Most people need both strong and weak ties in order to survive. Sometimes mentoring projects include networking. In this paper, mentoring means a traditional long-term, one-on-one relationship.

The number of people with mentors varies because the concept is now popular. It is comforting to be able to say "I have a mentor." Not all helping relationships with friends, colleagues, or bosses are described as mentoring. They may instead be personal relationships, especially when women guide women. As few as 25 percent of professionals enjoy intense mentoring relationships. Nevertheless, most of us participate in relationships that help our careers.

Mentors' Availability

Most important people in important jobs in important organizations are white males, and, because people are most comfortable with clones of themselves in gender, race, and social class, men find it easiest to mentor men—and women, women. If equal numbers of men and women existed at all levels, this would balance out. Unfortunately, the discomfort that many powerful older men have with women leads often to their reluctance to mentor women, producing a mentoring gap for women: There are few women at high ranks, and those who are there have less time available. They typically have more home and committee duties than most senior men, as well as additional informal responsibilities, such as advising or representing women's interests and concerns.

Some male professionals in science and mathematics are uncomfortable around women, in part because when the men were in school, women were rare. As a result, this male generation may still be uncomfortable with women as colleagues. And even younger men remember few women in their classes.

This discomfort factor, coupled with the fact that there simply are not very many women in important places, means that most of the people available to serve as mentors are males. It is hard for women and people of color to establish relationships with white males as mentors. It is especially hard for minority women, disabled women, and older women.

Male professors are more likely to mentor "sons" than "daughters," and those chosen fall into a very few categories: The cheerleader/mascot, the dutiful helper, and, occasionally, the woman whose brilliance cannot be ignored. Women may become protégées for reasons that do not apply to men seeking mentors. If the institution's commitment to affirmative action needs demonstrating, for example, the mentee may be viewed as a token rather than a capable member of a group of excellent students deserving special attention. In some instances, her potential as a sexual partner may also enter the equation.

Fighting Devaluation

Another factor in the selection of mentees is the devaluation of women. Numerous studies (among them, that by Michelle A. Paludi and Lisa A. Strayer, 1985) have shown that papers, works of art, and résumés attributed to women receive lower ratings from both genders than objects attributed to men. This general devaluation of women (in our culture and others) means that women are less attractive as potential mentees than men. The familiar placard announcing that a woman has to be twice as good as a man to be paid half as much pokes fun at a real situation.

When women are not seen as having potential like men's, they are less likely to be chosen as suitable candidates for mentoring. In addition, when men mentor women, other men may not value their work because their protégées are not viewed as being potential colleagues or achievers. In one study by Janice R. Mokros, Sumru Erkut, and Lynne Spichiger (1981), when male professors were asked what was special or distinctive about their mentees, most described them as unusually bright, enthusiastic, and hard-working. Male professors did not describe their male protégés' weaknesses or deficiencies, but they did, on occasion, criticize those of their female mentees.

273

Mentoring—Some Risks

Not all aspects of the mentor/protégée relationship are positive.

◆ Mentoring relationships are generally exclusive and one-on-one. In contrast, social networks include large numbers of people—all of one's eggs are not in one basket. Thus, one can gain a variety of kinds of information rather than having it all funnelled through one person.

◆ The more intense the mentoring relationship, the harder to make a necessary break, and the more potential that such a rupture will be disruptive and potentially damaging. The casualness of networking relationships makes beginnings and endings easier.

◆ The mentor/protégée relationship is not casual; it takes time, energy, emotional commitment, and involvement. The investment in a mentoring relationship may mean isolation from other equally productive and valuable interactions.

◆ The mentoring relationship typically involves a hierarchy. Mentoring relationships do not take place between equals. Social networks may involve unequals, but they may also include reciprocal exchanges of information. The social network involves people at all levels of the organization—some higher, some lower, some equal—as well as individuals outside it. Anyone who may help advance one's career may participate. John P. Kotter (1982) found that the people judged most effective on the job had the largest social networks.

◆ Mentors often set the agenda, and it is *their* agenda rather than that of the protégée. Mentors decide if they want the role and set the terms of the relationship. In contrast, social networks allow input into what kind of help one needs and how to best find it.

◆ Finally, relying primarily on a mentor for emotional support, as well as for information, evaluation, coaching, and introductions, means that the mentor has to be superior on all fronts—a hard role for both participants. Support can come from many relationships in one's social network.

Ten Myths About Mentoring

◆ ***Having a mentor is the best way to succeed.*** Many complex factors are relevant to success. Mentoring is important but not necessarily essential.

◆ ***Mentors should be older than protégées.*** Ageism intrudes here—the assumption is that a relationship is determined in large part by a gap in the ages of the participants rather than other factors. In addition, mature adults, whether they are returning students or already established professionals, may also need mentors.

◆ ***A close, intense relationship is the best primary way to learn about one's profession and to move up the ladder.*** Such relationships can indeed be helpful. But social networks can also be helpful in providing information, support, and many of the benefits mentors provide. Some networks may be *more* helpful than some mentors.

◆ ***Mentoring relationships must be long-lasting to be truly useful.*** Not so, they can last a few days (such as at a conference), weeks, months, or years. The criteria is not the length but the kind of relationship. Was it nurturing and helpful? Did it provide information, guidance, and assistance?

◆ ***A person can have only one mentor at a time.*** Multiple mentors and a variety of social networks expand one's ability to develop allies. Relying on a number of people means some of the mentoring functions can be split. For example, one person might provide informal advice about the organization or the school; another might offer insights and information about a particular field. Relying on multiple mentors can preclude a futile search for the "perfect" mentor and give one the opportunity to evaluate advice from more than one source. Some men's discomfort with mentoring women might dissipate if they were performing only some of the mentoring functions. Seeking multiple mentors may make it more likely that women will have some access to male mentors.

◆ ***Mentoring is a one-way relationship, benefitting only the mentee.*** On the contrary, both participants gain. For example, through this relationship, mentors may fulfill their professional obligation to teach and help newcomers. Men may find mentoring one of the few roles where they feel it acceptable to nurture. Mentors also receive new information from their protégées and other forms of direct help, such as assistance with research. To the extent that the relationship is open and nonhierarchical, an exchange of ideas can take place.

◆ ***Mentees must be invited.*** Unlike at an old-fashioned dance, women do not have to wait passively to be chosen. Candidates can actively seek mentors:

275

1. Prospective mentees may introduce themselves and make the first contact in relationship to a professional subject. If students, they may ask questions not only during but also after class.

2. They may also begin to ask for advice on the strengths and weaknesses in their work, pleasantly but persistently, always expressing appreciation for help and criticism.

3. Would-be protégées should try to increase opportunities for spending time with proposed mentors. Formal interactions can offer time for informal mentoring. Working with a mentor on an independent-study or honors project, or becoming a research or teaching assistant, a junior collaborator, a proposal writer, an intern, or another type of "apprentice" will provide opportunities where teaching, evaluation, and general guidance can naturally occur. In addition, such situations can offer candidates the opportunity to demonstrate their abilities and commitment.

4. Prospective mentees may ask colleagues to mention them or their work to potential mentors.

5. The search for mentors should not be limited to candidates' institutions. Hopeful mentees should, if appropriate, send papers with a letter asking for comments to mentors who work in the same area; whose work they have cited (or who have cited them); whom they met at conferences; or who have been recommended by their home institution. Candidates should *not* send dissertations or book-length manuscripts without specific prior encouragement.

6. Would-be candidates may volunteer to serve on a task force, committee, or project where potential mentors are members. Candidates may also offer to take on a major piece of the mentor's work, such as coordinating a project or writing a report, which will require significant collaboration.

7. They might also invite potential mentors to be guest lecturers in their classes or before other groups.

◆ *When men mentor women, a sexual encounter is inevitable.* Is it possible and does it happen? Yes. (It's somewhat cold comfort that sexual harassment can also happen with same-sex mentoring.) Certainly, women need to be aware of any sexual messages from the mentor. If such overtures can't be deflected, it's time to get out of the relationship as gracefully and as quickly as possible. If you need help ending it, seek out someone who is familiar with sexual harassment issues and strategies. Also problematic when men mentor women are others' preconceptions about the relationship. It is hard for most people to believe that any interaction between a man and woman is not sexual.

Women should hesitate before engaging in a sexual relationship with a mentor:

1. Having sex with a mentor can lead to self-doubt: Is he my mentor because of my intellectual abilities or my sexual attractiveness?

2. Sexual "indiscretions" are usually forgiven men but held against women. The hint of a sexual liaison can undermine a woman's professional reputation and reinforce others' views that women's intellectual abilities in professional pursuits are secondary.

3. A woman involved in a sexual relationship with a senior colleague is likely to lose her peers' support. They may envy her access to a senior person, and/or they may attribute her achievements to him. Moreover, they may see such a liaison as a violation of conflict-of-interest rules.

4. If a sexual relationship ends (and it usually does), the protégée loses both her lover and her closest advisor—who may, if he has been rejected, purposely use his status and power to hamper her advancement.

◆ *Men are better mentors for women.* While men may be powerful, able to open doors, and have more information to share, male mentors often have different styles than women. Mokros, Erkut, and Spichiger's study shows that male mentors were more likely to direct students and, therefore, to be disappointed if they did not choose what the professor wanted. In contrast, women mentors were more likely to affirm, encourage, and give examples, rather than directions. Finally—and this quality could be a plus or a minus, depending on the personal preferences of the protégée—male mentors were likely to be work-focused and disinterested in the personal lives of their mentees, while women mentors often showed concern for the personal lives of their students.

◆ *The last myth: The mentor always knows best.* It hardly needs saying but mentors can make mistakes and may deliberately exploit their mentees. For example, some mentors misperceive their mentees' potentials and set goals that are too high or too low. Or, as the protégée grows and develops professional stature, her mentor may find it difficult to let go and to move to a more collegial relationship. This stance will increase the likelihood that the mentee's development will be stifled and/or that a severe breach will occur. And certain unscrupulous mentors may—deliberately or inadvertently—use the mentoring relationship to gain help and recognition for their own projects at the expense of the mentee's recognition, interests, and achievements. Finally, the mentor may give well-intentioned, even correct, advice on a project, but at the expense of the protégée's research interests, such as dissuading her from investigation of new and/or controversial areas.

The [Woman] Mentor's 10 Commandments

I. Almost anyone can be a mentor to someone else. Many women underestimate how much knowledge they have about their system, academic or other, the number of their contacts, and the avenues they can open. One doesn't have to be boss to be a mentor. Teaching assistants can mentor other graduate students, graduate students can mentor undergraduates, undergraduate majors can help those just beginning.

II. Recognize and evaluate what you can offer a protégée, keeping in mind that you cannot and should not fulfill every mentoring function.

III. Clarify expectations about how much guidance you will offer concerning personal as well as professional issues.

IV. Give criticism as well as praise when warranted. Always present criticism with specific suggestions for improvement. Do it in a private and nonthreatening context—over lunch or coffee are good times.

V. Where appropriate "talk up" your protégée's accomplishments to others. Good forums are in the department, organization, laboratory, or institution, at conferences and at other meetings.

VI. Include protégées in informal activities whenever possible. Invite them to lunch, to discussions following meetings or lectures, and/or to dinners at academic conferences.

VII. Help mentees learn what kinds of available institutional support junior persons should seek in order to further their own career development. Tell them about funds to attend a workshop, for example, or released time for special projects.

VIII. Tell your protégée if she asks for too much or too little of your time.

IX. Remember that you can't mentor everyone or be all that anyone needs. Work within your institution to develop formal and informal mentoring programs as well as encouraging social networks. Work also to develop ways for information and facts to be shared formally through printed materials and meetings, such as having senior faculty do a panel for junior faculty on how to get tenure.

X. Help not only those who are like you but also those who are not. I have always believed that it is far easier for women than for men to cross boundaries such as race, color, ethnicity, class, and religion. And we can do that when we mentor each other.

A New Biblical "Revelation"

"Discovered" recently by a woman archeologist, accompanied by an all-female team of assistants, a fragment from the prophetic scrolls* reads:

> And they shall beat their pots and pans into printing presses
> And weave their cloth into protest banners
> Nations of women shall lift up their voices with nations of other
> women
> Neither shall they suffer discrimination anymore.

We don't yet know for sure if this will be proved to be apocryphal or prophetic. But probably the latter: Women are learning the power of politics and the power of change. The campus, the nation, and the world will never again be the same.

References

Kotter, John P. (1982). *The general managers*. New York: The Free Press.

Mokros, Janice R., Erkut, Sumru, and Spichiger, Lynne. (1981). *Mentoring and being mentored: Sex-related patterns among college professors* (Working Paper No. 68). Wellesley, MA: Wellesley College.

Paludi, Michelle A., and Strayer, Lisa A. (1985). What in an author's name: Differential evaluations of performance as a function of author's names. *Sex Roles, 12*, pp. 353–361.

Bernice Resnick Sandler, Ed.D., is a senior associate with the Washington, D.C.-based Center for Women Policy Studies, where she consults with and speaks at colleges about what she calls "chilly climate" issues relating to equity. She played a major role in the passage of Title IX and has written extensively about the problems faced by women in academe.

*Mary Chagnon's words, reproduced on a poster, no date.

Part IV
Resources

Resources

National Organizations of and for Women in Science

Many of the organizations below may help women pursuing careers in science by providing information about potential careers in specific fields and/or through referrals. Other organizations not listed will also assist—AWIS here lists only groups (or the divisions within them) explicitly devoted to supporting women in science and mathematics. This section includes relevant and updated listings from *A Directory of National Women's Organizations.**

Most groups listed have membership directories, which can serve as networking tools, and many offer essential publications. Professional journals not only publish scientific breakthroughs but also, like the *AWIS Magazine,* often list job opportunities both in general and in specific fields.

Many items on this list were compiled by Heather A. Multhaupt in 1990 and updated by AWIS staff.† Additional entries come from the *Bibliography of Science Education Resources* (1989, February) prepared by AWIS' Chicago area chapter and, eclectically, from resources at national headquarters. The list divides into field-specific and general resources.

A concluding section compiled from materials at the national office lists some of the federal programs that are especially supportive of women and minorities in science.

---

*(1992). New York: National Council for Research on Women.

†(1992). The Women in Science Program, Center for the Education of Women, University of Michigan, 330 East Liberty, Ann Arbor, MI 48104-2289. Telephone: (313) 998-7225.

283

Field-Specific Resources

ANTHROPOLOGY

American Anthropological Association
1703 New Hampshire Avenue, NW
Washington, DC 20009
(202) 232-8800

Committee on the Status of Women in Anthropology of the American Anthropological Association
Contact: Harriet E. Manelis Klein
Department of Anthropology
Montclair State College
Upper Montclair, NJ 07043
(201) 893-4119 or (201) 893-7556

Publications of interest: Reports on the status of women in anthropology.

ASTRONOMY

American Astronomical Society
Executive Office
2000 Florida Avenue, NW
Suite 300
Washington, DC 20009
(202) 328-2010

Publication of interest: Status: A Publication on the Status of Women in Astronomy.

BIOLOGY

American Association of Immunologists
Committee on the Status of Women
Contact: Eleanor de Marcario
Department of Microbiology
Uniformed Services University of the Health Sciences
4301 Jones Bridge Road
Bethesda, MD 20814
(301) 295-3413

Publications of interest: Newsletter and report on the status of women in immunology.

American Physiology Society
Committee on Women in Physiology
Contact: Donita Garland
The National Institutes of Health
9000 Rockville Pike
Building 3, Room 102
Bethesda, MD 20892
(301) 496-2492

> *Publications of interest:* Newsletter, computer printout of members by gender.

American Society for Biochemistry and Molecular Biology
Committee on Equal Opportunities for Women
9650 Rockville Pike
Bethesda, MD 20814
(301) 520-7145

> *Publications of interest: Career Opportunities in Biochemistry/ Molecular Biology,* directory of women members of the Society, special registry for women and minority students.

American Society for Cell Biology
Committee on Women in Cell Biology
Contact: Ursula W. Goodenough
9650 Rockville Pike
Bethesda, MD 20814
(301) 530-7153

> *Publications of interest: How to Get a Job in the 1990s* (pages 313–331 of this volume publish a condensed revision of this document), *The Women in Cell Biology Newsletter,* pamphlets, opportunities/programs for underrepresented groups in cell biology.

American Society for Microbiology
Contacts: Amy Chang, Assistant Director, Education and Training
Janet Shoemaker, Assistant Director of Public Affairs
Committee on the Status of Women Microbiologists
1325 Massachusetts Avenue, NW
Washington, DC 20005
(202) 737-3600

Publications of interest: Reports on the status of women, biographies, sources of grant support, survey of women members in the Society, newsletter: *Communicator*.

Biophysical Society
Contact: Emily Gray, Executive Director
9650 Rockville Pike
Bethesda, MD 20814
(301) 530-7114

Committee on Professional Opportunities of Women
Contacts: Elizabeth S. Rowe
Virginia Medical Center
4801 Linwood Boulevard
Kansas City, MO 64128
(816) 861-4700, extension 3541

Publication of interest: Newsletter.

Ecological Society of America
Contact: Marge Holland
2010 Massachusetts Avenue, NW
Suite 420
Washington, DC 20036
(202) 833-8773

Women in Entomology
Contact: Diane M. Calabrese
22 Anderson Avenue
Columbia, MO 65203-2673
(314) 874-4143

Publication of interest: Newsletter; women meet informally at professional entomologic meetings.

Women in Plant Physiology
Contact: Mary Jo Vesper
College of Arts and Sciences
University of Dayton
300 College Park
Dayton, OH 45469-0800
(513) 229-2611

Women's Caucus for the Endocrine Society
Contact: Julane Hotchkiss
Physiology Department
University of Texas Medical School
University of Texas
PO Box 20708
Houston, TX 77225
(713) 792-5891

> *Publications of interest:* Newsletter, *Report to the Society on Women in Endocrinology.*

CHEMISTRY

American Chemical Society
Women Chemists Committee
Contact: Eileen Reilly, Staff Liaison to Committee
1155 Sixteenth Street, NW
Washington, DC 20036
(202) 872-4456

> *Publications of interest:* Newsletters: *Woman Chemist, Women on College Chemistry Faculties.*

American Institute of Chemists
7315 Wisconsin Avenue
Suite 525 E
Bethesda, MD 20814
(301) 652-2447

> **Women Chemists Committee**
> Contact: Rubye Torrey
> Tennessee Technological University
> Derryberry Hall, Room 305
> PO Box 5012
> Cookville, TN 38505
> (615) 372-3374

American Society for Biochemistry and Molecular Biology
(See BIOLOGY.)

287

Iota Sigma Pi
National Honor Society for Women in Chemistry
Contact: Martha Thompson
Oregon Health Science University
Department of Physiology and Pharmacology
Portland, OR 97201
(503) 494-8770

COMPUTER SCIENCES

Association for Women in Computing
41 Sutter Street
Suite 1006
San Francisco, CA 94104
(415) 905-4663

Women in Information Processing
Contact: Judy Beckman
Lock Box 39173
Washington, DC 20016
(202) 328-6161

> *Publication of interest*: Data on the status of women in information processing.

EDUCATION

American Society for Engineering Education
(See ENGINEERING.)

Center for Women Policy Studies
2000 P Street, NW
Suite 508
Washington, DC 20036
(202) 872-1770

> *Publications of interest:* Newsletter, *On Campus with Women,* and other publications, including *Looking for More Than a Few Good Women in Traditionally Male Fields, Recruiting Women for Traditionally Male Careers.*

Women in Mathematics Education

Education Department
George Mason University
4400 University Drive
Fairfax, VA 22030
(703) 323-2264

Publication of interest: Newsletter.

ENGINEERING

American Indian Science and Engineering Society

Contact: Norbert Hill, Executive Director
1630 Thirtieth Street
Suite 301
Boulder, CO 80301
(303) 492-8658

Publication of interest: Winds of Change.

American Society for Engineering Education

Contact: Kirstin Peters
11 Dupont Circle, NW
Suite 200
Washington, DC 20036
(202) 293-7080

Publications of interest: Women in Engineering, Directory of Engineering and Engineering Technology Undergraduate Programs, Directory of Engineering Graduate Studies and Research, Engineering Education.

Electrical Women's Round Table

Contact: Ann Cox, Executive Director
PO Box 292793
Nashville, TN 37229-2793
(615) 890-1272

Publications of interest: Newsletter, directory.

Institute of Electrical and Electronics Engineers, Inc.
Anti-Discrimination Committee
Contact: Scott Grayson
1828 L Street, NW
Suite 1202
Washington, DC 20036
(202) 785-0017

> *Publications of interest:* Reports on women in engineering.

National Action Council for
Minorities in Engineering, Inc.
Contact: George Campbell
3 West Thirty-Fifth Street
New York, NY 10001
(212) 279-2626

National Consortium for
Graduate Degrees in Engineering
Contact: Howard Adams
PO Box 537
Notre Dame, IN 46556
(219) 287-1097

> *Publications of interest: Negotiating the Graduate School Process, Graduate Financial Resources, GEM* fellowship recruitment materials and applications.

Society of Women Engineers
Contact: B. J. Harrod
345 East Forty-Seventh Street
Room 305
New York, NY 10017
(212) 705-7459

> *Publications of interest:* Pamphlets: *Women in engineering, What are you doing the rest of your life?, Womengineer, U.S. Woman Engineer,* bimonthly magazine, newsletter, and report on the status of women in engineering.

Women in Engineering Program Advocates Network
Contact: Jane Daniels
Purdue University
West Lafayette, IN 47907-1286
(317) 494-3889

**Women in Science, Engineering, and Math
Consortium of Ohio**
Contact: Lynn Elfner
Ohio Academy of Science
1500 West Third Avenue
Columbus, OH 43212
(614) 488-2228

> *Publication of interest: Exemplars.*

**Women in Science and Engineering
of the New England Area**
Contact: Miriam Schweber
22 Turning Hill Road
Lexington, MA 02171
(617) 862-9251

> *Publications of interest:* Newsletter, lists of job openings in the
> New England area.

GEOGRAPHY

Association of American Geographers
Committee on the Status of Women in Geography
Contact: Susan Cutter
Department of Geography
Rutgers University
New Brunswick, NJ 08903
(201) 932-4103

> *Publications of interest:* Newsletter, informal file for networking.

Society of Women Geographers
Contact: Lareen Miller, President
1619 New Hampshire Avenue, NW
Washington, DC 20009
(202) 265-2669

> *Publication of interest:* Newsletter.

GEOSCIENCE

Association for Women Geoscientists
Resource Center for Associations
10200 West Forty-Fourth Avenue
Suite 304
Wheat Ridge, CO 80033-2840
(303) 422-8527

> *Publications of interest:* Bimonthly newsletter, membership directory.

Society of Exploration Geophysicists
PO Box 702740
Tulsa, OK 74170-2740
(918) 493-3516

> *Publications of interest: Careers in Exploration Geophysics, Women Exploring the Earth.*

Women in Mining
1801 Broadway, #400
Denver, CO 80202
(303) 298-1535

> *Publications of interest:* Newsletters, reports on the status of women in earth science.

Women in Natural Resources
Contact: Dixie L. Ehrenreich
University of Idaho
Bowers Laboratory
Moscow, ID 83843
(208) 885-6754

> *Publication of interest: Women in Natural Resources.*

MATHEMATICS AND STATISTICS

American Economics Association
*Committee on the Status of Women
in the Economics Profession*
Contact: Nancy Gordon, Chair
Congressional Budget Office
Room H2-418A, Annex #2
Washington, DC 20515
(202) 226-2669

> *Publications of interest:* Newsletter, roster of women
> economists, membership directory.

American Mathematical Society
PO Box 6248
Providence, RI 02940-6248
(401) 272-9500

> *Publications of interest:* Bradley, John S. (Ed.). (1991,
> September). Women in Math [Special issue]. *Notices of the
> American Mathematical Society, 38*(7).

American Statistical Association
1429 Duke Street
Alexandria, VA 22313-3402
(703) 684-1221

> *Publications of interest: Careers in Statistics,* report on the status
> of women in statistics, directory, journal, and magazine.

Association for Women in Mathematics
Contact: Patricia N. Cross, Executive Director
Box 178
Wellesley College
Wellesley, MA 02181
(617) 235-0320, extension 2643

> *Publications of interest:* Newsletter, career resource materials.

Caucus for Women in Statistics
Contact: Stephanie Shipp
2 Massachusetts Avenue, NE
Room 3985
Washington, DC 20212
(202) 272-5060

293

Joint Committee on Women in Mathematical Sciences
Contact: Mary W. Gray
Department of Mathematics, Statistics, and Computer Science
American University
Washington, DC 20016
(202) 885-3120

> *Publications of interest:* Report on the status of women in mathematical science, membership directory.

Math/Science Network
Contact: Cherrill Spencer, Treasurer
Mail Stop 12
Stanford Linear Accelerator
PO Box 4349
Stanford, CA 94309

MEDICINE AND HEALTH

American Association of Women Dentists
Contacts: Peter C. Goulding, Executive Director
Cheryl Kraus, Executive Secretary
111 East Wacker Drive
Suite 600
Chicago, IL 60601
(312) 644-6610

> *Publications of interest:* Bimonthly newsletter, *American Association of Women Dentists Chronicle.*

American Medical Women's Association, Inc.
Contact: Lilian Gonzalez-Pardo
801 North Fairfax
Suite 400
Alexandria, VA 22314
(703) 838-0500

> *Publications of interest: Medicine—A Woman's Career, Journal of the American Medical Women's Association.*

The American Pharmaceutical Association
Committee on Women's Affairs
Contact: Patricia Schultheiss
2215 Constitution Avenue, NW
Washington, DC 20037
(202) 429-7540 or (202) 628-4410

> *Publication of interest:* Report on the status of women in pharmacy.

American Psychiatric Association
Committee on Women
Contact: Yvonne B. Ferguson
Women Psychiatrists
Contact: Miriam Rosenthal
1400 K Street, NW
Washington, DC 20005
(202) 682-6000

American Public Health Association
Women's Caucus
Contacts: P. Ellen Parsons
Center for Health Statistics
Residential Building
Room 850
6525 Belcrest Road
Hyattsville, MD 20782
(301) 436-7089

Shauna Heckert
Federation of Feminists
Women's Health Centers
3401 Folsome Boulevard
Sacramento, CA 95816
(916) 451-0630

Association of American Medical Colleges
Women in Medicine Program
Contact: Janet Bickel, Director for Women's Programs
1 Dupont Circle, NW, Suite 200
Washington, DC 20036
(202) 828-0575

> *Publications of interest:* Quarterly newsletter, *Women in Medicine Update, Building a Stronger Women's Program.*

Association of Women Psychiatrists
Contact: Ruth T. Barnhouse
PO Box 190179-350
Dallas, TX 75219-0179
(214) 855-5104

> *Publication of interest:* Newsletter: *Women in Psychiatry.*

Lambda Kappa Sigma
Contact: Mary R. Grear
Executive Director
6250 Mountain Vista
Henderson, NV 89014-2318
(702) 456-3186

> *Publication of interest*: Newsletter: *The Blue and Gold triangle.*

National Alliance of Breast Cancer Organizations
Contact: Amy Langer
1180 Avenue of the Americas
Second Floor
New York, NY 10036
(212) 719-0154

Society for Menstrual Cycle Research
Contact: Mary Anna Friederich
10559 North One-Hundred-and-Fourth Place
Scottsdale, AZ 85258
(602) 451-9731

> *Publication of interest:* Newsletter.

Society for the Advancement of Women's Health Research
Contact: Joanne Howes
1601 Connecticut Avenue, NW
Suite 801
Washington, DC 20009
(202) 328-2200

> *Publication of interest: Journal of Women's Health.*

Society of General Internal Medicine
Women's Caucus
Contact: Ellen Cohen
Department of Medicine
Montefiore Medical Center
111 East Two-Hundred-and-Tenth Street, Centennial 3
Bronx, NY 10467
(212) 920-4784

> *Publication of interest:* Column in the *Society of General Internal Medicine Newsletter.*

Women's Veterinary Medical Association
Contact: Chris Stone Payne, Secretary
32205 Allison Drive
Union City, CA 94587

> *Publication of interest: Association of Women Veterinarians' Bulletin.*

METEOROLOGY

American Meteorological Society
Board on Women and Minorities
Contact: Susan Zevin
45 Beacon Street
Boston, MA 02108-3693
(617) 227-2425

> *Publication of interest:* Report on the status of women in meteorology.

PHYSICS

American Association of Physics Teachers
5112 Berwyn Road
College Park, MD 20740
(301) 345-4200

Committee on Women in Physics
Contact: Martha Takats
Department of Physics
Ursinus College
Collegeville, PA 19426
(215) 489-4111

> *Publication of interest: Making Contributions: A Historical Overview of Women's Roles in Physics.*

American Physical Society
Committee on the Status of Women in Physics
335 East Forty-Fifth Street
New York, NY 10017
(212) 682-7341

> *Publications of interest:* Newsletter, directory, report on the status of women in physics.

Science and Women's Organizations With Special Focus on Equity

Below are listed some organizations and special programs geared towards the needs of women, sometimes in particular minority women, working in science. Some of the entries were updated from the American Association for the Advancement of Science's *Sourcebook for Science, Mathematics, and Technology Education* (1992).*

American Association for the Advancement of Science
Committee on Equal Opportunities in Science
Directorate for Education and Human Resources
Contact: Shirley M. Malcom, Director
National Network of Minority Women in Science
1333 H Street, NW
Washington, DC 20005
(202) 326-6400

Girls in Science
Contact: Marsha Lakes Matyas

Publication of interest: Linkages.

National Network of Minority Women in Science
Contact: Audrey B. Daniel or Yolanda George

Proyecto Futuro
Contact: Margaret E. Tunstall

Publication of interest: Annual Network News.

American Association of University Women
Contact: Amy Swauger
Associate Director for Program and Policy
1111 Sixteenth Street, NW
Washington, DC 20036
(202) 785-7761

*Washington, DC: Author.

ASPIRA Association, Inc.
Contact: Janice Petrovitch, Director
1112 Sixteenth Street, NW
Washington, DC 20036
(202) 835-3600

> *Publication of interest: Communities Count.*

Association for Women in Science
1522 K Street, NW, Suite 820
Washington, DC 20005
(202) 408-0742

Association of Science–Technology Centers
Teacher Educator's Network
Contact: Andrea Anderson
1025 Vermont Avenue, NW
Suite 500
Washington, DC 20005
(202) 783-7200

Commission on Professionals in Science and Technology
Contact: Betty M. Vetter
1500 Massachusetts Avenue, NW
Suite 831
Washington, DC 20005
(202) 223-6995

> *Publications of interest: Scientific, Engineering, Technical*
> *MANPOWER COMMENTS* and other publications.

Dartmouth College
Women in Science Program
Contact: Mary Pavone
Thayer School of Engineering
No. 8000
Dartmouth College
Hanover, NH 03755-8000
(603) 646-2230

Douglass College
Contact: Ellen Mappen
PO Box 270
Chemistry Annex
New Brunswick, NJ 08903
(903) 932-9197

Educational Equity Concepts, Inc.

Contact: Barbara Sprung
114 East Thirty-Second Street
Suite 701
New York, NY 10016
(212) 725-1803

> *Publication of interest:* Gender equity curriculum kits.

Girls Incorporated

Contact: Evelyn Roman-Lazen
30 East Thirty-Third Street
Seventh Floor
New York, NY 10016
(212) 689-3700

National Coalition for Women and Girls in Education

National Women's Law Center
1616 T Street, NW
Washington, DC 20036
(202) 328-5160

National Research Council
Committee on Women in Science and Engineering

Contact: Linda C. Skidmore
2101 Constitution Avenue, NW
Suite 2133/211a
Washington, DC 20418
(202) 334-1841

> *Publications of interest*: Women in Science and Engineering:
> Increasing their Numbers in the 1990s, Science and Engineering
> Programs: on Target for Women?

Quality Education for Minorities Network

Contact: Shirley McBay
1818 N Street, NW
Suite 350
Washington, DC 20036
(202) 659-1818

Sigma Delta Epsilon
Graduate Women in Science
111 East Wacker Drive
Suite 200
Chicago, IL 60601
(312) 616-0800

Publication of interest: The Bulletin.

University of Michigan
Center for the Education of Women
Program for Women in Science
Contact: Cinda-Sue Davis
330 East Liberty Street
University of Michigan
Ann Arbor, MI 48104-2289
(313) 998-7240

Wider Opportunities for Women
Contact: Donna Milgram
1325 G Street, NW
Washington, DC 20005
(202) 638-3143

Working Opportunities for Women
Contact: Cindy Benolkin
2700 University Avenue, West
Suite 120
St. Paul, MN 55114
(612) 647-9961

Federal Programs to Encourage Women to Enter the Science and Math Professions

Below is a partial list of federal agencies with programs that create opportunities for underrepresented groups in science. Most of the agencies listed run programs that are specifically geared towards women; however, AWIS also notes some agency programs directed to increasing opportunites in science in general. The American Association for the Advancement of Science's *Sourcebook for Science, Mathematics, and Technology Education* (1992)* provides a more general and extensive list of federal programs.

Although AWIS made every effort to compile a full list, the nature of the federal bureaucracy, particularly in the aftermath of the recent election, means that programs and contacts change frequently. AWIS attempts to offer here useful starting points rather than a definitive description of available resources.

Most of the programs listed provide grants to individuals pursuing careers in science and to institutions developing projects designed to promote women and minorities in science. Some of the programs encourage the participation of girls and women in science through educational programs. Also listed are information dissemination services that provide information on federal funding and resource opportunities.

NATIONAL AERONAUTICS AND SPACE ADMINISTRATION
300 E Street, SW
Washington, DC 20546
(202) 453-1000

Equal Opportunity Programs

Minority University Research and Education Division
Contact: Sheree Stovall-Alexander
(202) 358-0973

Women in Science and Engineering

*Washington, DC: Author

NATIONAL OCEANIC AND ATMOSPHERIC ADMINISTRATION
Educational Affairs Division
Contact: Arva J. Jackson
1825 Connecticut Avenue, NW
Universal South Building
Washington, DC 20235
(202) 606-4380

NATIONAL SCIENCE FOUNDATION
1800 G Street, NW
Washington, DC 20550
(202) 357-7500

Cross Directorate Programs for Women
Contact: Peter E. Yankwich
(202) 357-9549

Career Advancement Awards

Research Planning Grants
These grants and awards are part of many Foundation programs. For more information contact the appropriate program officer.

Directorate for Education and Human Resources

Elementary and Informal Science Education Division
The following programs, although not specifically geared towards girls, emphasize and promote the participation of girls and minorities in science.

Informal Science Education Program
Contacts: Barbara Butler or Hyman Field
(202) 367-7076

Young Scholars
Contact: Julia V. Clark
(202) 357-7538

Graduate Education and Research Development Division

Faculty Awards for Women
Contact: Sonya Ortega
(202) 357-7456

303

Graduate Women in Engineering Research Fellowship
Fellowship Office
National Research Council
2101 Constitution Avenue, NW
Washington, DC 20418
(202) 334-2872

Visiting Professorships for Women
Contact: Margrete S. Klein
(202) 357-7456

Research Initiation and Improvement Division

Minority Programs
Contact: Susan Duby
(202) 357-7856

Program for Persons with Disabilities
Facilitation Awards for Persons with Disabilities
Contact: Larry Scadden
(202) 357-7461

Women's Programs
Model Projects for Women and Girls in Science and
Engineering
Contact: Lola E. Rogers
(202) 357-7734

Directorate for Engineering

Engineering Infrastructure Division

Supplemental Funding for Support of Women, Minorities, and Disabled Engineering Research Assistants
Contact: Sue Kemnitzer
(202) 786-9631

NATIONAL INSTITUTES OF HEALTH
9000 Rockville Pike
Bethesda, MD 20892
(301) 496-2351

Office of Education
Contact: Gloria Seelman
(301) 402-2437

Reentry Postdoctoral Training

Inservice and Preservice Teacher Academy Fellowship in Biology

Office of Research on Women's Health
Contacts: Judith LaRosa and Rosemary Torres
(301) 402-1770

Division of Research Grants
Contact: Majorie A. Tingle
Westwood Building
Room 10A11
5333 Westbard Avenue
Bethesda, MD 20892
(301) 496-6743

Science Education Partnership Award

Science Teacher Enhancement Award

Minority High School Student Research Apprentice Program

National Institute of Neurological Disorders and Stroke
Contact: Edward Donohue
Federal Building
Room 1016
750 Wisconsin Avenue, NW
Bethesda, MD 20892
(301) 496-4188

Research Career Award Program

Clinical Investigator Career Award Program

Reentry into the Neurological Sciences

SMITHSONIAN INSTITUTION
National Science Resources Center
Contact: Patricia McClure
Arts and Industries Building
Room 1201
Washington, DC 20560
(202) 287-2063

U.S. DEPARTMENT OF AGRICULTURE
Fourteenth and Independence Avenues, SW
Washington, DC 20250-2200
(202) 720-USDA

Office of Higher Education
Contact: K. Jane Coulter
(202) 720-7854

Office of Science and Education
Contact: Assistant Secretary
(202) 720-5923

U.S. DEPARTMENT OF THE ARMY
Army Research Office
Contact: Donald Rollins
PO Box 12211
Research Triangle Park, NC 27009-2211
(919) 549-0641

Research in Engineering Apprenticeship Program

Uninitiated Introduction to Engineering Program

Junior Science and Humanities Symposia

Science and Engineering Apprenticeship Program

U.S. DEPARTMENT OF EDUCATION
400 Maryland Avenue, SW
Washington, DC 20202
(202) 401-1576

Office of Elementary and Secondary Education

Equity and Educational Excellence Division

Desegregation Assistance—Civil Rights Training and Advisory Services
Contact: Sylvia Wright
(202) 401-0358

Women's Educational Equity Act Program
Contact: Caroline Andrews
(202) 401-1342

School Effectiveness Division

Dwight D. Eisenhower Mathematics and Science Education State Programs
Contact: Rick Davis
(202) 401-0841

Office of Postsecondary Education

Division of Higher Education, Incentive Programs

Patricia Roberts Harris Fellowship Program
Contact: Charles Miller
(202) 708-9438 or (202) 708-7389

Minority Science Improvement Program
Contact: Dr. Argelia Velez-Rodrigues
(202) 708-4662

Special Service Projects Program
Contact: Dorothy Marshall
(202) 708-6104

Fund for the Improvement of Postsecondary Education
Contact: Joan Straumanis
(202) 708-6119

Office of Educational Research and Improvement

Fund for the Improvement and Reform of Schools and Teaching

Dwight D. Eisenhower Mathematics and Science Education National Programs
(202) 219-1496

U.S. DEPARTMENT OF ENERGY
1000 Independence Avenue, SW
Washington, DC 20585
(202) 586-5000

National Programs
Contact: Donna Prokop
(202) 586-8910

High School Student Research Apprenticeship Program
This program supports summer research apprenticeships at national laboratories for women and minority students.

Research Laboratories and Facilities

Brookhaven National Laboratory
Contact: Donald Metz
30 Bell Avenue, Building 490
Upton, NY 11973
(516) 282-3054

Programs of interest:
Renate W. Chapman Scholarship for Women, Science and Engineering Opportunities for Minorities and Women, and Women in Science Speaker's Bureau.

Idaho National Engineering Laboratory
Contact: Tiajuana Cochnauer
785 DOE Place, MS 1214
Idaho Falls, ID 83401
(208) 526-9586

Programs of Interest:
Women Scientists' Outreach Program, Young Women's Career Day.

Inhalation Toxicology Research Institute
Contact: David Bice
PO Box 5890
Albuquerque, NM 87185
(505) 845-4514

Programs of Interest:
Minority and Women Student Programs.

Lawrence Livermore National Laboratory
Contact: Laurel L. Egenberger
PO Box 808
Livermore, CA 94550
(510) 423-4142

Programs of Interest:
National Physical Science Consortium for Graduate Degrees—Minorities and Women, summer employment opportunites.

Los Alamos National Laboratory
Contact: Judith Kaye
PO Box 1663, MS P-278
Los Alamos, NM 87545
(505) 667-1919

Program of Interest:
Women in Science University Coop.

Mound Facility
Contact: William Taylor
PO Box 3000
Miamisburg, OH 45343
(513) 865-5092

Program of Interest:
University of Dayton Women in Engineering Scholarship,
Mound-University of Dayton Women in Engineering.

National Renewable Energy Laboratory
Contact: Linda Lung
1617 Cole Boulevard
Golden, CO 80401-3933
(303) 231-7044

Program of Interest:
Expanding Your Horizons Conference.

Northwest College and University Association for Science
Contact: Bryan Valett
100 Sprout Road
Richland, WA 99352-1643
(509) 375-3090

Program of Interest:
Women in Math, Science, and Engineering.

Pacific Northwest Laboratory
Contact: Irene Hayes
PO Box 999, MS Kl-66
Richland, WA 99352
(509) 375-2584

Programs of Interest:
Women in Science and Engineering, Women's College
Internships.

U.S. DEPARTMENT OF LABOR
Women's Bureau
Contact: Director of the Women's Bureau
200 Constitution Avenue, NW
Room S3002
Washington, DC 20210
(202) 523-6611

U.S. ENVIRONMENTAL PROTECTION AGENCY
401 M Street, SW
Washington, DC 20460
(202) 260-2090

Office of Environmental Education
Contact: George Walker
(202) 260-5335

Office Of Environmental Equity
Contact: Doña Canales
(202) 260-8448

Office of Exploratory Research
Contact: Virginia Broadway
(202) 260-7664

Minority Institutions Student Fellowship Program

Office of Toxic Substances
Contact: Carol Glasglow
(202) 260-8164

Women in Science and Engineering, Environmental Protection Agency

U.S. DEPARTMENT OF THE NAVY
Office of Naval Research
Contact: Debra T. Hughes
Code 11SP
800 North Quincy Street
Arlington, VA 22217
(703) 696-4111

High School Apprenticeship Awards

Naval Science Awards Program

Young Investigator Program

Graduate Fellowship Program

National Defense Science and Engineering Graduate Fellowship Program

U.S. GEOLOGICAL SURVEY
National Center
Reston, VA 22092
(703) 468-4000

Minority Participation in the Earth Sciences Program
Contact: Jane H. Wallace
2646 Main Interior Building
1849 C Street, NW
Washington, DC 20240
(202) 208-3888

Graduate Intern Program
Contact: Mary F. Orzech
(703) 648-6631

Interagency Resources

Federal Coordinating Council for Science, Engineering, and Technology (FCCSET)
Office of Science and Technology Policy
Contact: John Gibbons, Director
Old Executive Office Building
Seventeenth Street and Pennsylvania Avenue, NW
Washington, DC 20506
(202) 456-7116

FEDIX
National Technical Information Service
U.S. Department of Commerce
5285 Port Royal Road
Springfield, VA 22161
(703) 487-4778
On-line database retrieval service of government information for colleges, universities, and other organizations.

Minority On-Line Information Service (MOLIS)
Federal Information Exchange, Inc.
555 Quince Orchard Road, Suite 200
Gaithersburg, MD 20878
(301) 975-0103
On-line database retrieval service lists black and Hispanic colleges and universities' capabilities and provides information on federal agency education, research equipment, and employment opportunities.

Landing Your First Job*
Women in Cell Biology

Finding a Job in Academia

In the last 20 years, it has become much easier for women to locate academic jobs, because affirmative action laws require that jobs be openly listed and publicized. Twenty years ago, information about available jobs circulated primarily by telephone between tenured male professors. This handicapped not only women, whose male thesis advisors frequently did not take them seriously as candidates for tenure track positions, but also those men who either did not get along with their advisors or who came from the less prestigious institutions.

The fact remains that the easiest way to get a job at a first-rate university is to be recommended by a thesis advisor who was a graduate student or postdoctoral fellow there. Despite the complaints by some white males that today women have an unfair advantage, it still helps to be a white male. (If all of those complaints were true, many more women would have tenure track jobs.) But, at least now women are able to locate the jobs and apply for them.

The office of the department in which you are a graduate student or postdoctoral fellow probably has job listings. Your field's professional societies (which are well worth joining) often maintain their own registries. They may keep the registry at their office, publish it in their journal,† and/or display it at meetings. (These sources are often more fruitful for postdoctoral positions than for academic jobs, but they do list some of the latter.) General journals, such as *Science*, provide extensive advertisements of job opportunities.

Your major professor, however, remains one of the best sources of information about employment opportunities. In addition, if you let people know that you are job hunting, faculty members in your department, or even some you get to know at meetings or seminars, may unexpectedly help you.

---

*This section, published in 1976 and revised in 1989 as *How to Get a Job*, appears here in a condensed version with permission of the Women in Cell Biology, c/o American Society of Cell Biology, 9650 Rockville Pike, Bethesda, MD 20814, Copyright © 1989.

†AWIS lists positions and grants both in the *Magazine* and through the national office.

Because the job grapevine has been limited primarily to males in the past, some women have, reasonably, felt bitter and excluded. Often the most angry were women who cultivated men exclusively, and found that it did not work. Remember, women can and do have a powerful network of their own through which many have found their jobs. All of us should be working to make it even more powerful. Even departments without women faculty members will almost certainly include other women as graduate students, postdoctoral fellows, and research associates. They will have contacts in many other settings. It's not unusual, as the years go by, to find yourself helped, often immeasurably and on many different occasions, by women who received their Ph.D.s before or after you and are now out in the academic or business world. This picture changes with time, field, and institution.

The point is, that while it is foolish not to stack the deck in your favor, the cards in question are human beings whose behavior is unpredictable. You never know from which direction help or harm will come. Most likely, people you know will empathize with your problems, place a high value on your work, and help you out. It's important to make an effort to get to know the women in your field by joining women's groups in your specialty and in science in general, and by attending women's caucuses at scientific meetings.

Paving the Way With the Ph.D. and Postdoctoral Years

If you are an undergraduate who is really hungry for a top-notch job in a first-rank institution, do everything possible to ensure that you get your Ph.D. and do your postdoctoral work at one of the most prestigious 10 institutions in your field and, if possible, with one of the best-known researchers. Such an institution may not accept you for graduate work for a variety of reasons (your grades, the college you are attending, etc.), but you will never be accepted if you don't apply.

If you are rejected, you have two alternatives. One is to go to a less prestigious university and work hard for a solid master's degree, at which juncture you can reapply to the top places for a Ph.D. The other is to earn a good Ph.D. and apply for a postdoctoral fellowship with a well-known person. The first strategy is by far the best.

One practical way to increase your chances for a good job is to research how your prospective advisor's former graduate students and postdoctoral fellows have done in the job market. You may discover a very clear pattern. There are laboratories where every person passing through seems to do a nice piece of research, publish it, and find a good job. There are others where people consistently

314

drift, fall away, fail to publish, and have spotty employment records. There are also some where males follow the first pattern and females the second.

It is up to you to maximize your chances by working with a professor who has a reasonable record with women. Beware of the mentor whose former female graduate students have only succeeded by overcoming tremendous handicaps. If this person seems genuinely interested in having you in the lab, what makes you think you will be different from your predecessors? Some advisors want only willing workers for the research problems and are indifferent to their students' future.

If the professor with whom you would like to work is young and has a short record to evaluate, trust your own judgment. In general, a nontenured faculty member is a good bet, because s/he is as committed to publish and make a name as you are. The young professor is likely to be in the lab, will work you hard, and will probably do whatever s/he can to help you to a good position. Your success will help gain prestige for him/her and future collaborators.

This strategy has its risks, however. If the assistant professor does not receive tenure in the next two to three years, you could be in trouble. Also, there will probably be fewer crumbs from his or her table. For example, if you are working with a well-known professor, you may substitute at the talks that your advisor was originally invited to give or to write reviews in his/her stead. Doing so can be helpful in meeting other people in the field and making your name known. The fact that your advisor feels you *can* do a good job as a stand-in speaks well.

Applying

Having located a job, you must now start the application process. Usually, you begin by your sending out a curriculum vitae (c.v.), discussed in the next section, and a cover letter. It will help a great deal at this stage if a colleague you know can write or telephone someone s/he knows at the institution and recommend you as a superior candidate. This will help differentiate your application from the others. If you can't arrange an advocate, do not despair. This strategy can sometimes even backfire in the machinations of departmental politics.

Do not assume that universities are courting women applicants. You must make the best possible impression on paper, in order to make it to the final round of consideration—the interview.

The C.V.

For a first job, your c.v. is unlikely to be longer than one or two pages. Make sure that those pages are neat, clear, easy to read, and accurate. The c.v. should include the following information:

◆ name, address, and current telephone number

◆ degrees

◆ where and when the degrees were awarded

◆ positions held

◆ membership in professional societies

◆ fellowships, grants and honors

◆ publications (including theses and advisors)

◆ areas of interest and experience in research and teaching

◆ three to five names and addresses of highly regarded people in your field who have agreed to provide letters of reference (*be sure to ask permission first*)*

Check the final draft carefully for typographical errors. If you have any doubts about format, ask some of the assistant professors in your department to show you their c.v.s and look yours over. (Even if you are confident, have colleagues check your document.)

The c.v. does not have to include personal data. How much you include is up to you. Gender (if not obvious from the name), citizenship, and date of birth are generally included; however, if you started college late, you may not wish to include your birth date. Let them extrapolate from your degree dates. You do not have to provide marital status, nor do you have to list the number and age of your children. Males sometimes include such items to show that they are "good family men," but if *you* do, employers may wonder how you can have three children and still work full-time, something that is none of their business!

Keep your c.v. professionally focused. Do not include your height, weight, hobbies, etc. A selection committee reading hundreds of c.v.s may, consciously or unconsciously, use such factors as elimination mechanisms. Candidates often forget, or are unaware, that in the last stage of the hiring process, c.v.s go to college-wide committees and/or presidents and trustees, many of whom are conservative, even if the faculty that you hope to join seems liberal. If you feel

*See AWIS' advice on letters of recommendation on pages 333–342.

that you must acknowledge a nonprofessional political, religious, or personal commitment, save it for the interview.

Women often penalize themselves by leaving professionally relevant data off their c.v.s. Be sure to include

◆ invited talks at other universities, including those that were job seminars (but do not list them as such)

◆ book chapters and proceedings of meetings (either included under "publications" or listed separately)

◆ abstracts (usually listed separately to avoid padding and usually dropped after several publications)

◆ articles in press (at best you have returned the proofs; at least, you have made all revisions for an accepted paper)

◆ articles submitted for publication

◆ articles in preparation (used for a first job only: Do not list anything you cannot produce)

◆ community work (keep this brief and omit anything, such as P.T.A., which looks like "women's work," no matter how unfair this is)

Keep your c.v. up to date. If a submitted manuscript is rejected, drop it or call it in preparation. Do not include honors (or indeed anything) from high school, with the exception of such prestigious, college-oriented awards as Westinghouse or National Merit Scholarships.

The Cover Letter

The cover letter, which almost always accompanies the c.v. in a job application, can, on one hand, be tricky to write because there is no standard format to follow. On the other, flexibility is an advantage. Here is your chance to present yourself to the search committee as an individual. Use this opportunity with discretion and care.

These letters often make fascinating reading for a search committee, because applicants can make revealing errors. The major point to keep in mind, as you write this letter, is that a seduction is occurring: Mutual wooing and ego-inflation are going on between the candidate (you) and the institution. (You may find this metaphor distasteful, but it works.) Never forget that institutions, as well as the individuals that make them up, have egos and can be insulted. The aim of the letter—and, indeed, the whole elaborate ritual of searching and hiring—is to suggest that this particular institution is so well-known and so highly regarded that you—in all of your superiority—have been attracted by it and wish to improve it further by joining it. Naturally, you will show the humility appropriate to a junior faculty member, but behind it is this tone.

Don't insult the institution by sending out a form letter. And don't explain that you would like a job at the institution because your spouse has a job in that area or because you have always wanted to live in a small New England town. While both statements may be true, it does not help to say so.

A problem in many women's cover letters is an overly humble manner. Sometimes, women offer to teach low-grade or beginning courses that no one else wants. Such letters may stem from misery, desperation, or the loss of self-esteem which comes with repeated rejection; however, they do not work. As in personal relations, institutions tend to take you at own self-evaluation. Try to write cover letters when you are in a good mood and feeling self-confident.

The Dual-Career Hunt

Many couples find themselves looking for jobs together. If you plan to move to an area with your mate, do not wait to apply for a job! If you will not accept a job unless your spouse or significant other has been offered one as well—or vice versa—then you both may wish to state this fact. Wait for the interview to go this far, however. Should an institution really want one of you, it may help find a job for the other one.

The Interview

With luck, at least some of the institutions to which you have applied will invite you to visit them, at their expense, for one to three days. Because of affirmative action guidelines, departments often still need to list the number of female and minority candidates interviewed. This fact can give you a better than average chance of being invited.

Finances can be a problem in traveling to multiple interviews. If you are interviewing for several jobs within a short time frame, it may help to apply for several credit cards for charging airline tickets. Some schools will take six weeks or more to reimburse you. You should not expect honoraria.

It is possible that a particular institution, under pressure to interview women, could be cynical enough not to take your candidacy seriously or to invite you to interview for a blatantly unsuitable job. Should this be the case, regard it as useful experience. Remember, you will almost always be invited to give a departmental seminar. An excellent presentation will give you valuable time to impress the audience. You may not be offered the job (indeed, with a department of that sort, would you want it?), but you will have made a start at undercutting some of the prejudice against women. It is reasonable to assume that if you are invited to the department you do have a chance at the job.

How can you maximize your chance of being offered the job? It may help your case if the interviewer knows that you have other offers or interviews. Work this information into the conversation smoothly so it does not appear as if you are dropping names. If you have applied for many jobs, however, and this is your only interview, keep quiet. If asked directly about your other prospects, say something like "I have applied for a number of positions." Period.

Before your interview, obtain a college catalog and find out who teaches which courses. Take the catalog with you, so you can check off the faculty as you meet them. Are there faculty in your field whom you have not been asked to meet during your interview? Find out why.

Depending upon the time of day your seminar presentation is scheduled, you will either start on a round of individual meetings with faculty members or on a round of parties directly after its conclusion. Advice from many women follows.

First, clothing. Do not wear anything that is short, low-cut, tight, uncomfortable, or extreme, no matter how fashionable. You should be comfortable enough in what you are wearing to forget about it. This means something that fits in the setting, as well as something in which you feel comfortable. You are not likely to be at ease in jeans if everyone else is wearing three-piece suits or vice versa.

Second, drinking. Approach the bar with extreme caution. You will be tired, tense, and often hungry. Under these conditions, even small quantities of alcohol may have unexpected effects. If you have any doubts at all, ask for a soft drink. If your hosts insist that you have a drink, they will probably fail to notice that you do not drink it. Use your ingenuity. Remember, the more you like these people, and the more relaxed you feel with them, the fewer chances you will want to take. This caution applies to more than alcohol!

At times during interviews you may feel absolutely exhausted. If you are sitting in the office with someone with whom you feel trust and rapport, you may want to tell him or her everything, including how you felt about the grilling by the person down the hall. *Do not do it*. Never forget that you are being interviewed all the time. Anything you say to anyone is going to be considered and, likely, repeated. No matter what schisms and animosities faculty members may display, they still form a group and are bound to each other by

319

a complex network of ties, while you are still the outsider. You can lose a job because of comments dropped to the undergraduate who drives you to the airport. Never let your guard down or forget that you are being interviewed until you are on the airplane. Also, do not imply that you are relieved or grateful for the interview. Such a stance only makes you appear less desirable: Even if you do get the job, your negotiating power will be reduced.

This advice also applies when changing jobs. In this case, people will ask why you are leaving your present position. Concentrate on how attractive you find the job for which you are interviewing rather than on how awful your current one is. If pressed, you might state that you do not like living in your present location. Any personal reasons you have for wanting to move are none of their business, and any professional ones are far better left unstated. If you are a postdoctoral fellow, the reason for looking for a job should be obvious but, again, do not criticize the university, lab, or people with whom you are working, even to the most sympathetic listener. Complaints cannot possibly help your cause and may label you as a malcontent.

The worst problem most candidates encounter during interviews is exhaustion. There are several ways to partially protect yourself against it. If possible, do not schedule interviews at two institutions back to back. Do your best to stay at a hotel, rather than at a private home. In someone's home, you may find little or no privacy and constant conversation. If a party in your honor looks as if it is going to go on all night, ask the soberest person present (preferably a woman) to take you back to your hotel when you are tired. Be sure to say a polite good-bye to your host before you leave. You will not benefit by staying on to the bitter end. If you desperately need a nap before dinner, say so. Let people know about your scheduling needs in advance. They will be grateful that they do not have to fill every minute of your available time.

You will probably be shuffled from office to office in a series of interviews with individual faculty members and, perhaps, graduate students. There is nothing worse at such meetings than an embarrassed silence. It is up to you to prevent it. If you can, schedule your seminar before these interviews, so it can provide a subject for conversation. On the other hand, some of the faculty will be in fields so far from yours that your seminar will be almost incomprehensible, others will not have liked it, and a few—always—won't be able to make it. These people will still want to talk with you and hear what sorts of questions you ask them.

This is where the candidate who has done her homework will reap the greatest rewards. If you have read the catalog and other literature about the institution, and if you have researched everything you can about the department and its faculty, you will be prepared. You should have intelligent questions ready that will let the faculty know that you are broadly interested in and know about their work. With faculty close to your own interests, look for areas of collaboration and competition. If you do not know the person's area of expertise, ask him/her about latest results.

If you find you have absolutely nothing to discuss with a person, there are still some options. You can ask

◆ for a cup of coffee or a soda

◆ for a tour of the student union or campus

◆ to see a typical undergraduate lab

◆ to see the library, herbarium, greenhouse, etc.

◆ about housing or recreational facilities

The point is to appear interested in this person and the institution. Do not bring up your daycare needs or anything else that makes your situation look even slightly complicated until you have the offer.

At this stage, because the job has not yet been offered to you, do not attempt to settle contractual details. This is a logical time, however, to find out in a general way about the following items:

◆ salary range

◆ available lab space

◆ teaching duties

◆ length of contract

◆ chances at tenure (this may require some clever deduction on your part, rather than outright questioning)

◆ library holdings

◆ laboratory facilities

◆ shared equipment

◆ institutional research funds

Before you arrive, make a list of the major facilities and equipment pieces you require. Do not overlook such items as dishwashers, autoclaves, distilled or deionized water, refrigerated facilities, darkrooms, secretarial help, shop services, etc. Does the library contain your favorite journals? Who pays for postage, photocopying, computer costs, and telephone bills? If you need special culture facilities for your work, check on availability. Does

321

the space you are shown contain adequate water, electricity, gas, on-line air, and vacuum lines? Are there unsafe features such as floor plugs next to the drains? Are the windows clean? Are janitorial services regular and adequate? Must your grant pay for equipment hookup and minor architectural modifications?

Request a short meeting with students. What do most students from this department do after graduation? Does the school provide fellowships or are all students teaching or research assistants? Are they all paid the same amount or do faculty with bigger grants "bid up" the salaries?

The Seminar

You will almost certainly be expected to present a seminar. If you are unclear about it, ask.

Give a superb presentation. If you have worked for years to get good data, a few hours of preparation and practice for your talk will be a good investment. For Heidi B. Hammel's advice on this subject, see pages 233–236.

When you prepare your seminar, remember that it differs from one presented to colleagues in your field in an important way. You are almost certainly being interviewed for this particular job because this department is missing a representative of your field. This means there may be no single person in the entire audience who really understands the details and significance of your work. It is, therefore, worthwhile to include a 10-minute introduction to your particular area for a general audience to point out why your work is new and significant. Some of the most powerful senior faculty will frequently know the least about your field.

The question period following the seminar is another opportunity to show your skills. Some of the questions may be so confused that you may wonder whether the askers were actually present. In other cases, you may feel as if the questioner is hostile and out to get you, but this is unlikely to be true. The point of the question period is to see how well you think on your feet and how self-possessed you are. But even if someone is hostile, give the impression that you are enjoying the challenge. Never show anger or lose control.

In cases where you do not know the answer to a question (or where a factual response does not exist), you can still send several positive messages in reply. For example, you can say, "No, I haven't tried that, but so and so, who published on the same subject in the last issue of *Nature*, showed that . . . etc." Indicate that you keep up with the literature. Or admit, "I really don't know the answer, but I think that problem could be approached using such and such a new technique or system." Show that you consider similar issues and that you can respond quickly.

Never say, "I don't know. That's a hard question" (end of comment). And never suggest that anyone's question was stupid or obscure.

Negotiating a Contract

During the months that follow the interview, before the institution has made its decision, it is wise to keep in touch, taking care not to be pushy or annoying. One ideal way to do so is to send them reprints or preprints of your papers, should you be so fortunate as to have some come out during this time. You will be insuring that they don't forget you or lose your dossier.

Then, one day, you may receive a telephone call from the department chair offering you a job as assistant professor at "x" thousand dollars per year. Of all the institutions at which you interviewed, this was the one that you preferred. Furthermore, the chairperson, as well as all the other faculty members you met, struck you as being decent and honorable. Your initial impulse will be to shout "yes" on the spot, write letters of rejection to all the other positions for which you are currently being considered, and throw a huge party to celebrate. *Do not do it.*

Be prepared for this telephone call, and—resisting the impulse to say yes instantly—tell the chairperson that you are delighted, that you are interested in joining his or her department, and that you think that both of you would be best served at this juncture by your paying the institution another visit. Also be prepared, however, to offer to pay for part or all of the visit yourself. If a second visit is absolutely impossible, you should still resist an immediate yes. Instead, tell the department's representative that, in order to have matters clear from the beginning, you will write a letter stating your understanding of the contractual agreements. In this letter, spell out everything verbally implied or agreed to at the interview necessary to do your job properly and give you the best chance of tenure. Ask the chairperson to sign and return a copy to you.

The letter might go something like this:

Date

Name

Address

Dear _____:

Thank you for. . . . This letter confirms our (telephone) conversation of. . . .

I understand that I shall be free to use the electron microscope at least 15 hours per week. My air-conditioned laboratory space shall be not less than 1,500 square feet. The department will allow me $100,000 as starter money to set up my laboratory. I shall have a computer terminal with access to electronic mail in my office. My salary shall be $35,000 per 12-month academic year, and I shall be expected to teach not more than one undergraduate and one graduate semester-long course per year. . . .

Thank you for offering me the position.

Sincerely yours,

Signature

This confirming letter should be written whether or not you revisit the institution after the offer is made. The major advantage to a second visit is that it is the perfect opportunity for you to check out a number of things which may not have been evident the first time around. Salary, for example, is a sensitive item, and it is difficult to establish the departmental range and median over the telephone.

In numerous cases, candidates have been offered jobs by phone and told that formal offers would follow. After much delay and the appearance of a "problem," the written confirmation failed to follow. The lesson: It is imperative to have the offer in writing, signed by the appropriate institutional official, before you give up other options.

Most schools base all future cost-of-living increases, as well as merit increases, on your starting salary, so it is important to negotiate for the best possible salary. Find out what the range is for someone of your experience and rank. This information is available from the department chair, the department's administrative secretary, or the personnel office. Talk to your recently hired friends in comparable positions to get an idea of salary level. At the very least, hold out for the median. Many people find this sort of haggling difficult and painful.

It is important to remember the following points. The system you are about to enter judges you, at least in part, by your salary. By agreeing easily to a low salary, you are hurting your image in the eyes of your colleagues and supervisors. The higher the price you place upon yourself, the more respect you will command.

After years of graduate school and postdoctoral fellowships, almost any salary may look good. But remember: You will be expected to maintain a different lifestyle, your tax base will change, and your salary may, over the long run, maintain dependents as well as yourself. Many young women justify accepting low salaries on the contradictory grounds either that they are single (and therefore have only themselves to support) or that they are married (and therefore provide a second salary). How many men accept low salaries either because their wives are bringing in money or because they are bachelors?

Since all of your future salaries may depend upon this first one, keep in mind that lack of current dependents does not mean that you will never have them. Your parents or a sibling may require financial support. You may have children. You may also be divorced or widowed or have to support an unemployed or disabled husband. In this country, a high proportion of women are heads of households. So argue for your highest fair salary. You are worth it.

It is also important to check into benefits. These include moving allowances, retirement benefits, health insurance, subsidized housing and childcare. Good benefits add significantly to the value of your salary. Moving allowances can vary, so negotiate.

Try to obtain a copy of the local newspaper. What kind of cultural events are listed? Do the stores advertise things you buy? How much does housing cost? If you have children, does the university have a childcare center, and can you enroll your child? On the second visit, try to look at apartments or houses. This is especially important if you are not familiar with the area where the institution is located: A salary may sound great until you discover the cost of housing, transportation, etc. Write to the local and state chambers of commerce for information.

In many of the more expensive cities, subsidized faculty housing is available. If so, find out how to apply for such housing and how long the waiting list is. Then apply immediately. If you can make subsidized housing a condition of your arrival, you can husband time and energy to set up the lab. If faculty housing exists, you will never need it more than when you first arrive. It often has the additional advantage of having no lease, making it a good place to live while you look at other options.

It is critical to find out what departmental funds are available to help you set up a laboratory. The cost will vary depending on your needs: For example, a top quality microscope and basic molecular biology equipment can easily cost over $100,000. Find out comparable figures for your field. What will the department buy for you? What pieces of existing equipment will they give you? What pieces of common equipment will they let you use?

Common equipment is particularly tricky. For example, your department may be willing for you to have all the time you want on a centrifuge two buildings away from your laboratory. Or the chair may promise you the use of a piece of equipment that another faculty member regards as private property. If you had permission in writing, you could insist on using it, but you would probably end up making at least two enemies. It is this sort of thing that the second visit is intended to uncover. You may find it is better to ask for funds to buy a certain piece of necessary equipment, rather than promise to use old equipment, maybe in disrepair, maybe hard to share.

Ask not only how much square footage you are being given, but also its location. Is it in the basement, far away from every facility and all your colleagues? Be sure to look at the space in case it needs renovation.

Does your department expect you to show up grant in hand? If so, this will not only take your time, but their grants and contracts office will have to process it. What kind of help will they offer you here? When do they expect you to start? If the date seems unrealistically close, know your options. You should be able to ask them to

◆ wait anywhere from six months to a year

◆ have your teaching and committee assignments delayed

◆ help you get your grant proposal ready immediately (and to pay all office costs)

◆ have your laboratory and office ready upon your arrival (with running water and working telephone)

Find out if you will be the first or the only woman staff member. How are female faculty treated? Will you be expected to do counseling or take over all the advising of women students?

All of this may seem overwhelming. Your initial reaction may be that, if you make such requests, the university will simply retract its offer, but this is unlikely. Remember: The department has spent time, effort, and money searching for a colleague. After looking over hundreds of dossiers and as many candidates as they could afford, after sitting through many boring seminars and search committee meetings, after arguing and compromising up and down the institutional hierarchy, they have finally found one person—you. You represent the end of a tiresome, tedious, and expensive search. They want you. You can, therefore, request a few concessions from them now. But make sure to get them in writing, and make sure to request them now. Two months after you are there, your special status will be gone, and you will be one of the herd of assistant professors, trying to make it in academia.

Also remember that being offered a job as an assistant professor does not mean you are professionally secure. You have made it up the ladder, but you are not safe until you have tenure. Insure that you have the facilities (and the time) to do research when you sign this first contract for your first job to be certain that you have done everything possible to allow you eventually to earn tenure.

Many departments may permit you to come to an empty laboratory, put off getting your first grant, carry an unusually heavy teaching load, and accept a surfeit of committee assignments; the same department may then refuse you tenure later because you have not published enough original research papers since arriving.

Do not blame your superiors for this attitude. You are an intelligent adult: You must be aware of what behavior is rewarded and act accordingly. Your first contract period is probably only two or three years long. Making preparations before you even arrive on campus is the only way to accomplish anything within this short time.

At a number of excellent universities it is possible to take a first job but, realistically, not to expect tenure. If you accept this limitation and plan to change institutions in five years, such institutions can offer good job options.

It is important to see how people are paid in the department where you are going. Are technicians' salaries paid during breaks in outside funding? Does the department have money for postdoctoral fellows or graduate students? Have there been recent rearrangements or layoffs? Tenure means nothing if a department disappears, and there is no space and no salary.

Once you have done your homework and all is well, sign the official institutional contract, which will have been countersigned by the dean or president. (The department head has already signed your unofficial contract letter, drawn up by you, and has returned a copy to you.)

Congratulations! You are hired. Now, and only now, telephone or write to the other institutions considering your candidacy, and tell them that you have accepted another position.

By now you are aware of the amount of energy, time, and money that both sides must put into the first contract of a tenure-track appointment. Realizing these expenditures and the economics of the job market should lead you to apply only for jobs that you do want and to accept only the most attractive. No matter what difficulties you have winning your assistant professorship, the fact that you have one implies that you will probably be offered others, and you are probably at your most professionally salable now.

As you grow older and more experienced, you will be able to demand a greater commitment and higher salary from the hiring institution. If you wish to leave your first job when you have achieved the rank of associate professor (or if your institution awards you that rank but denies you tenure), you will be on the job market at the associate rank, which at some institutions carries obligatory tenure. The first contract period before the tenure decision comes up will be a short one, making it difficult for you to show your department what research you can accomplish. Try to make sure that your first academic job is at an institution where you think you would like to stay, and work your hardest, particularly for the first five or six years.

Applying for Jobs Outside Academia

In these days of two-career families, tight funding, and a growing biotechnology industry, many women are considering jobs in business and industry. In fact, unless you cannot imagine life without teaching, there is every reason to do so. Compared to academia, money for equipment, travel, and technicians' salaries is usually generous, giving you a better chance of attracting, and keeping, experienced, first-rate technicians. Salaries are higher and overall support facilities are frequently better and more up-to-date than in academic institutions. More and more, presentations at major meetings and articles in major journals are written or cowritten by people working in industry. This reflects the growing recognition of the importance of first-rate research in industry.

Remember, however, that "industry" provides an extremely diverse group of opportunities ranging from those in giant chemical and pharmaceutical companies to small start-up companies with only 20–60 employees. The experience of working in these places will differ. You need to do a lot of research to get the feel of a place and be very hardheaded about how well you feel you would fit into that particular environment. Industry microenvironments can leave you more isolated than academic institutions. Many industries are still behind academia in providing equal opportunities for women. Overt discrimination is of course illegal in industry, but you may need to be more aggressive about "reminding" people of your existence when job openings or promotion time come around.

You also need to think through what you can bring to industry:

◆ Do you like to work on a number of different projects at once?

♦ Do you enjoy working on team efforts?

♦ Do you like practical problems?

♦ Do you like to be part of a project that is moving fast in a competitive environment?

♦ Do you receive satisfaction from seeing your work put to practical, immediate use?

♦ Would you enjoy having the opportunity to learn more about other aspects of where your work might lead, for example, patent writing or designing clinical trials?

♦ Are you willing to change fields if the company's objectives change?

♦ Would you like to combine any of the above qualities to work on more long-range basic research questions?

If the answer to some of the questions above is "yes," you might enjoy working in industry.

On the other hand, you will have less control over what you work on and with whom you work than you would have as the head of a typical academic lab. Many of the biotech industries sound almost like research institutes when you visit. They are not. Their purpose is to make money, and you should realize that helping them do so would be part of your job. (And having your job next year can depend on how successful they are!) If you cannot cope with this profit motive, do not accept a job in industry.

If, after these caveats, you find yourself interested in working in industry, look for listings in journals and at professional meetings and ask your advisor and friends for the names of people they know who work in industry. Wherever possible, contact these people by telephone, as well as sending in a c.v.

If you are invited to interview, most of the suggestions about academic interviews and seminars also will apply here. Again, it is important to be as knowledgeable and as enthusiastic as you honestly can be about working for that company. The people interviewing you will be evaluating you to see whether you can be depended upon to do your part to see that the company survives (if it is a small company). Much confidential work cannot be discussed outside the company, so it is important that your colleagues are congenial.

If you are being hired as a scientist, your industrial employer will be interested in your general background. And many companies will consider only the best scientists. Learn as much as you can about the science being done in the company. Ask for a list of publications from the department or company. When visiting, ask people what they are doing and what their major interests are. (These may or may not be the same.)

Find out what you will be expected to do, how much time will be allowed to follow your own interests, what the publication policy of the company is, how much space you will have and where, and how many people will be working for you and at what level. If the company takes postdoctoral fellows, how can you get one in your lab? Can you have a joint appointment with a local university, and, if so, do you want to? This is extra work, since you most likely would be asked to teach, but it could make an eventual move back to academia easier.

Investigate the equipment budget and the available shared equipment. Try to learn about the company structure. Find out what the reporting structure is and as much as you can about the person to whom you will be reporting. Ask what other people in the area/department where you are interviewing do with their time. This can vary from doing predominantly basic research to running a service lab (for example, making monoclonal antibodies for other areas of the company). In any case, assume that you will be spending a significant percentage of your time on things of interest to the company. The more you can see what is needed before others do and voluntarily take it on, the more control you will have over how you spend your time and the more you will be seen as valuable. Remember, you will be able to take on more projects because you will not be required to teach (unless you become associated with a university), and you will not have to write grant applications for support.

Finally, learn everything you can about your compensation package. Find out what your title, and grade or rank will be, and obtain a complete listing of the titles and grades along the entire professional ladder. This is especially important in industry since some companies are creative in titles, and, without further information, there is no way of knowing whether a "staff scientist" is equivalent to a postdoctoral fellow or a vice president. Find out the median and range of salary for your position as well as details of the benefits and relocation programs (including possible interest-free or forgivable loans to help you buy a house).

The benefits and hiring package also may include some type of stock program or stock options. If you do not follow the market, especially if the company is small, ask the opinion of a stockbroker, investment banker, or analyst. The stock options may turn out to be worth far more than your salary—or may be worth nothing. As with any investment, bigger and more established companies offer more security, less flexibility, and less potential for a big gain, either financially or through fast promotion, than in a rapidly growing company.

When you have all of this information, negotiate everything. In industry, this seems to be the norm. One can even come back several times with counter offers. Everything from moving expenses to salary to staff should be discussed. Some factors are less flexible than others (stock, for instance, is regulated by the Securities and Exchange Commission), but you need a clear idea of what your options are. There is frequently no contract, but, as with any other job, you can and should have everything in writing. When you interview, you might ask some staff members, discreetly, if they were given what had been promised. This is probably the best guide to what you can expect.

Make up your mind about taking the job speedily but not hurriedly. Request a second visit if you have any doubts. Many companies will bring you out on a "house-hunting" visit after you have accepted and/or will pay for an apartment while you find a place to live. Once you have accepted the job, some companies will want you there in a week. Try to find a reasonable and mutually agreeable time to begin. Finish up as much as you can of paper writing and other commitments before you arrive. You will need to concentrate on your new job and may well find a stack of deadlines waiting for you.

Now that you have a job, this is a perfect time to take a short vacation. You will need it to get through the hectic first year or two, whether you have accepted a job in academia or industry. And good luck!

Not Getting the Award, Grant, or Job? Check Your References*

Association for Women in Science

While overt discrimination against women in graduate school is becoming a thing of the past, many forms of subtle discrimination still exist. One of the most pernicious forms occurs in letters of recommendation. Generally speaking, a graduate student will never see the letters of recommendation written for her by her advisor or by other faculty members in her department. Yet these letters are of extreme importance to the student. They can contain statements that discourage the recipient from thinking the student should get the fellowship or job. Furthermore, advisors can subtly discriminate against female students by writing letters that are less enthusiastic and more critical than those they write for male students.

Below are four *actual* letters of recommendation, all written by the same professor within the same year, and edited only to use a gender-free name [Chris] and to remove gender and some other identifiers. The four students were members of the same laboratory at similar stages of their graduate careers. Two were female and two were male. Can you identify the student's gender in each?

Further information about the students is provided following the letters. In addition, several AWIS members provide their views of these letters.

The Letters

Letter 1:

Chris R. is one of my graduate students working toward a Ph.D. in biology at XYZ University. This student is close to finishing degree work on behavior of [animal species].

Chris is original and multi-faceted, doing thesis research that has a clear central theme, [topic]. Chris has approached this subject with several different techniques of observation and measurement: Behavioral observations, SEM morphology, high-speed video, tracer particles, current measurement, and nest construction studies.

Chris is someone who seeks collaboration in scientific projects. Chris initiated collaborative research with the late [name], with Professor

*This paper first appeared in the 1992, January/February AWIS Magazine, 21(1), 7-12.

333

[name], and with several other professionals who had specific expertise required for different phases of this research. The collaborations extend to working well with junior students and volunteers and allowing them to participate and help with the work. All these associations have been productive. This student has already published several papers in good scientific journals and is a thoroughly competent professional.

One of Chris's greatest strengths is perseverance. Chris emerged victoriously after the thesis committee challenged Chris's performance at an oral exam. It made this student even more determined to succeed: Say it cannot be done, and Chris will try to do it. This attitude of challenge goes together with idealism, conviction, and self-sufficiency. More than likely Chris will accomplish his/her goal. Similarly, Chris has persevered on some tedious observational studies and some difficult technical problems.

Chris writes well and speaks directly and clearly; I enjoy our interactions. Chris is young and brash and also is a concerned human being with a lot of vitality. This energy is valuable and productive. In addition, Chris is a careful administrator. Chris is well organized and can document both scientific work and financial accounts in great and convincing detail.

Chris is well worth the support requested. Since my current research is in [topic], I regret that I have no grant support for Chris.

Letter 2:

Chris S. is one of the most committed and hardest working students I have seen. This student is seriously preparing for a scientific career. Because early college grades were mediocre, Chris has now achieved overcompensation by superb performance in difficult courses and assignments. Chris's enthusiasm is contagious, and Chris's sense of purpose is admirable.

Chris has participated in a number of research projects, including those connected with his/her honor's thesis and master's thesis. In all of these Chris is an excellent student who learns quickly and displays great initiative. Chris's grasp of biological problems is good. This student's research on [topic] is his/her own design, made after some highly successful pilot studies conducted again entirely independently. When [animal] behavioral research became mired in low and unpredictable responsiveness of the animals, Chris decided to develop an alternative behavioral model that could generate data quickly and reliably, so invented the [noun]! It works like a charm. Chris has now carried out research in the field and in the lab and has collected significant amounts of data that seem to demonstrate a most intriguing relationship between [topic] and [topic]. Chris is using novel recording techniques to measure the [topic] with the high resolution required to match [topic] performance.

Chris has carefully thought through the proposed research in [country] with first-rate scientists, both of whom I know and respect greatly.

334

Chris shows great initiative, persistence and drive. This student has matured into a junior scientist and has the characteristics that lead to success anywhere. A foreign country will be a fine challenge.

I recommend Chris highly for a fellowship. I am confident that Chris will use these new opportunities well.

Letter 3:

I write on behalf of Chris T., who has applied for an ABC fellowship. Chris has been my graduate student for almost 4 years. This student entered our program with a DEF fellowship—reserved for the top few applicants to our graduate school. Chris will complete the Ph.D. this summer. In the process Chris has published two papers (both as first author), 10 abstracts (6 as first author), and 5 more papers are being written before this fall. Such intensity and productivity is unusual: Only one other student in this program obtained a postbaccalaureate Ph.D. in 4 years with such an impressive list of publications.

Not only are Chris's publications large in number, they also constitute an important and well-received body of new knowledge. The central theme is the characterization of [topic]. To this end Chris has begun to use [special] techniques used more commonly in the measurement of [topic]. Last year this student won the PQR Award for the best student paper presented at the Annual Meeting of the [organization name]. Chris will be nominated for other awards upon completion of the thesis.

In addition to having talents as a researcher, Chris is an outstanding teacher who has inspired many students and has run several courses— often taking full responsibility. Last year Chris won this department's award for best teaching fellow. This student's success lies in dedication, enthusiasm, energy and a willingness to explain difficult topics to beginning and advanced students (and faculty) alike.

Chris's strength lies in [topic] to [topic] problems. Chris is interested in expanding this expertise into [topics]. Chris is in a good position to make significant contributions to this field. Chris's background in [topic] research will allow Chris to approach the subject with an original perspective. While in [city], Chris has participated in many difficult experiments. There is no doubt that this student has the versatility to enter new fields of scientific investigation. Indeed, it is often the fresh perspectives that lead to new insights and discoveries.

Chris has my full confidence and my highest recommendation for [type of] research.

Letter 4:

Chris U. is a graduate student in my laboratory, working toward a Ph.D. in [topic]. Chris has completed all formal requirements besides the final phase of thesis research and writing. The research deals specifically with the [topics] that are involved in [topics]. Besides several abstracts, Chris has published two full papers, one on the sources of [topic] themselves, and another paper on [topics], within

335

the context of natural [animal] behavior. Chris's final work will be to determine the morphological structures that allow for [topic]. Further manipulations will elucidate the role of [topic] in [topic] behavior and in [topic].

Chris has the observational skills and critical mind required to carry out this behavioral research: Ample experience and publications demonstrate this. Chris is fully committed to do the work and to do it very well. In addition, Chris is a good communicator and exciting teacher. Oral presentations at national meetings and elsewhere demonstrate this student's effectiveness in communicating work and ideas. Chris's enthusiasm is contagious. Chris is always chosen to guide TV and news reporters in (city). Chris's work has been featured in several popular publications.

Chris is well worth the support requested. Since my current research is in [topic], I regret that I cannot provide grant support.

In addition to the scientific merits, I want to mention a peripheral but not insignificant issue. Chris's success would be an important contribution to [item]: This student is at the stage in graduate school where discouragement is common and encouragement most needed. Financial support is an important psychological boost that can propel someone into a higher orbit of self-confidence and productivity. Successful [item] are much needed and Chris has the potential to become one of these.

Analysis

Comments: Anonymous*

The tone of both *1* and *4* is bland, while that of *2* and *3* is highly enthusiastic. The implication from *1* is that the student plods along and will "probably" accomplish what she or he sets out to do (but there is room for doubt).

The student in *4* sounds less confident than those in the other letters. According to the recommender, the world will not be set on fire by either of the students in *1* or *4*. On the other hand, the world will probably be made much richer by the accomplishments of the students in *2* and *3*. Letters *1* and *4* were written for female students; *2* and *3* were written for male students.

Furthermore, the recommender states in *1* that the student is "thoroughly competent," a phrase which is the kiss of death, according to a male colleague, and suggests mediocrity. However, what was not stated is that this student supported herself for her first two years by working full time in industry while completing coursework, by teaching for the next four years, and by working full

---

*The person who submitted these letters and the first set of comments prefers to remain anonymous.

time once again in industry after her teaching fellowships ran out. During that time, she published 4 articles (3 as first author) and 7 abstracts (5 as first author); in addition, she has submitted 2 articles, has 4 more in preparation, and has been asked to contribute 2 book chapters in an upcoming work. None of these publications included her advisor as an author. She has given 8 lectures at outside universities and 8 presentations at organization meetings. Her research expenses, travel, and publication costs were partially supported by 9 small, graduate student grants; the remainder was paid for out of her pocket. She also had to pay four semesters of tuition. As a teaching assistant she received high praise from both her students and the faculty members for whom she worked—this was not mentioned in the letter, nor was she ever recommended for the university's teaching award.

The student in *2* was supported during his tenure as a student by his live-in girlfriend and one teaching fellowship. His research expenses were paid for by the laboratory. He published 6 abstracts (3 as first author) and has 1 paper in press (he is not first author). He gave 3 presentations at organization meetings. His teaching received high praise from his students, but he was not recommended for the university's teaching award.

The student in *3* was also supported during his tenure by a combination of teaching fellowships, research assistantships, and the full-time employment of his wife. As stated in the letter, he published 2 articles (both as first author) and 13 abstracts (6 as first author), and has 3 papers in press, 2 submitted, and 1 in preparation. He gave 4 outside university lectures and 7 presentations at organization meetings. He received one small, university-based, graduate student grant, but his research expenses were paid for out of the lab's budget. He also received awards for teaching and for his thesis—to be eligible for these awards, he had to be recommended by his faculty supervisor and/or his advisor.

The student in *4* received the same university fellowship mentioned in the first paragraph of *3* ("reserved for the top applicants..."), but the mention of this award was somehow neglected by the recommender. She published 3 articles (2 as first author), 1 book review, 6 abstracts, has 1 article in press and 1 accepted. She is the first author on the remaining articles. In addition, she and her work have been featured in several popular science magazines. She has given 8 outside university lectures and 7 presentations at organization meetings. She, too, has had to support herself with a combination of teaching fellowships and part-time jobs. Her research and travel expenses have been supported by 5 small, graduate student grants with the remainder of expenses coming from her pocket. She also has received excellent teaching reviews,

337

but has never been recommended for the university's teaching award.

Clearly, the students in letters *1* and *4* were as productive and qualified as those in *2* and *3*; in fact, they were more productive than the student in *2*. However, their letters indicated that they were not of as high caliber as the male students. Details were left out of the female students' letters that might have helped them in obtaining grants and fellowships and code words ("competent") and negative phrases ("support is a psychological boost that can propel someone into a higher orbit of self-confidence") were used that clearly could harm them. And these letters were written by a male professor who believes himself supportive of his female students! With support like that, who needs enemies?

The *New York Times* (1991, July 14) has reported the use of negative code words for evaluations of female medical students. These same code words were not used when evaluating the male students. This *New York Times* story and the letters reprinted above indicate that the use of code words may be a common method for restricting women to lower paying positions or for keeping them from obtaining positions.

If you suspect that your advisor might not be writing you the best of letters, attempt to replace him/her with someone you trust will highly recommend you. This could be a colleague you see and talk with at national meetings, another professor in your graduate program, or someone for whom you teach. However, you should realize that with some fellowship applications, an explanation is required if you do not use your advisor. Finally, be aware that should a prospective employer know whose student you are, s/he can call your advisor and receive a recommendation over the phone.

If you should find that you are not getting any of the small grants for which you apply, you can also try a little experiment. Send out two grants to two separate groups—such as the American Museum of Natural History or Sigma Xi, (or send them both to Sigma Xi, but at different times for different award periods). Both grants should have the same wording. However, in one of the grants remove the recommender you suspect might not be doing you any good. Leave him or her on the other grant. Then wait and see which grant gets funded. This tactic was used successfully by the student of *1*; since then, both she and the student from *4* have tried to use that particular recommender as infrequently as possible. And they've been more successful at receiving the small grants. Only time will tell about their success in obtaining jobs.

Comments: Edna Kunkel*

The *Handbook of Nonsexist Writing* (Miller, Casey, and Swift, Kate, 1988) offers many suggestions for writing devoid of sexual connotations. In order to analyze these letters, I concentrated on two of the sections on double standards from the chapter on "Parallel Treatment: Trivializing and Passive Constructions." In trivializing, the "language used to describe women's actions often implies that women behave more irrationally and emotionally than men," and "verbs chosen . . . can subtly affect the impression given of the person's effectiveness or forcefulness." Women, "traditionally perceived to be passive," tend to be victims of "this particular form of belittlement more often than men." The following example from Miller and Swift demonstrates the difference between a weak and a strong sentence:

> *Weak*: "Harriet Tubman helped slaves to escape and served as a spy."
> *Strong*: "Harriet Tubman led slaves to freedom and was a spy."

In addition, William Strunk, Jr., and E.B. White (1979) regard passive language as "less direct, less bold, and less concise," whereas the active voice leads to "forcible writing" that is "more direct and vigorous."

The first item that I evaluated was whether the author of the letters was using passive constructions more in the letters for the men or for the women. In each letter, there were passive constructions, but according to my computer's grammar checker the numbers were not above normal for a general document style. The letters did not vary much in their number of passive hits: *1* and *3* each contained 9, *2* had 7, and *4* topped the group with 11.

Further analysis of the letters yielded some direct insight regarding the overall tone of the letters, which varied from convincing and positive (*2*) to discouraging and vague (*4*). It bothered me to see an ambivalent "letter of recommendation." I measured trivialization by categorizing objective terms (adjectives, adverbs, and phrases) either as positive, negative, or neutral. However, my "neutral" category included terms that were either ambiguous (or could be interpreted by a reader as either positive or negative) or redundant (those qualities required for any graduate student in a technical field). Table 1 shows the results.

By this method, *3* is prominently positive (perhaps excessive to a certain extent), a letter that yields a favorable personal evaluation. Letter *4* never should have been written as a recommendation. (If you don't have anything nice to say, don't say anything at all.) Not

---

*Edna Kunkel, Ph.D., is a cartoonist, interviewer, and laboratory scientist.

Table 1

Letter	No. Positive	Negative	Neutral
1	12	1	12
2	17	1	2
3	23	0	0
4	4	1	11

only is it unclear and lacking in substance, but worst of all, it ends with a negative paragraph. The other letters that contained negative hits had them early in the letters, and treated them as challenges already overcome, not as potential barriers to progress.

I rank the letters from strongest to weakest in the following order: 3, 2, 1, 4. Unfortunately and not unexpectedly, the more positive (3 and 2) were written for men.

Comments: Sheila Lukehart*

Lukehart's first reaction was incredulity that an advisor would write letters that were so different for roughly equivalent men and women students. Letter 4 was especially appalling.

For 1, Lukehart observed that the advisor was not an author on any of the student's publications. Given that, Lukehart concluded that something unusual was going on in the student/advisor relationship, and that a less-than-excellent recommendation was probably to be expected. In analyzing 1, Lukehart noted that, unlike the case for 2 and 3, letter 1 damns with faint praise. The writer is not "selling" the student; the letter contains no superlatives.

In terms of advice, Lukehart pointed out that students need to have several people who know them well enough to write good letters, especially if there is a problem with the advisor. However, an advisor who can't write a very positive letter for a student should tell the student and should not offer to write any letter at all.

Comments: Resha M. Putzrath†

It was clear to me which letters were for men and which for women. In my opinion, 3 is the best recommendation, 4 is a kiss of death, and 1 and 2 are roughly equivalent in level of praise. I differentiated between 1 and 2 because 1 seemed to emphasize personality more while 2 seemed to stress accomplishments. As this would be the expected form of discrimination, I correctly identified which letter was for a woman.

*Sheila Lukehart, Ph.D., a past treasurer of AWIS and a research professor in immunology, was interviewed about the letters.

†See also pages 61–65.

This article illustrates how a reference letter that may appear positive can become less so in comparison with other letters. Below are some suggestions that may help you obtain more accurate and positive recommendation letters, especially if omissions of your accomplishments are inadvertent.

◆ Discuss common code words. Some people are unaware that, in this litigious age, a word such as "competent," even with superlative adjectives, may be considered a negative reference, but one that will not cause problems for the author if the reference becomes public.

◆ Try to discuss some of the issues mentioned in this article with the people you are using as references. Indeed, this article could serve as a vehicle for initiating such discussions. After assuring the individuals that you know they would never discriminate, discuss what influences them when they read reference letters. If a recommender states that she looks for an enthusiastic letter, she will be more likely to write one.

◆ Give your recommenders a list of your accomplishments, even if it is under the pretense of having them review the résumé you are sending with the application. Assuming they are trying to write you positive letters, having such information available helps them write better, more specific references for you.

◆ When it comes to references, some of your best friends can be your worst enemies. People who like you may agree to write a reference but, when putting pen to paper, find they are unwilling to rank you among their top students. Without some superlatives, any reference is mediocre.

◆ Realize that phrases such as "gets along well with coworkers" may be interpreted differently for males and females. For men, quality professional credentials may be assumed and congeniality considered an additional asset. For women, this phrase may be interpreted as "she's nice, but isn't very good."

Comments: Barbara Filner*

I read these letters and had an initial impression that *3* was the best, *4* the worst, and *1* and *2* were mixed, with *1* being somewhat more favorable. To help me focus on how the letters communicated these impressions, I highlighted positive comments and negative comments (in pink and blue, respectively!). The color coding revealed

*See also pages 32–34 and pages 219–225.

that *2* was a stronger letter, and a rereading confirmed that impression.

I tried to determine the basis for my incorrect initial impression and I think it has to do with where in the letter the negative comments are placed. Interestingly, the weaker comments in *1* are buried in the middle (paragraphs 2, 3, and 4 of 6) whereas the weaker comments in *2* occur at the beginning and end (paragraphs 1 and 4 of 5). Assuming many reference letters receive a cursory initial reading (for example, when comparing 20 applicants for one position), my observation makes the art of writing and reading a letter even more complicated. The initial and final paragraphs apparently can be disproportionately significant.

I agree with the identification of "competent" as a negative characteristic, with nothing more positive to say. In *1*, other negative phrases were "techniques of observation," because analytic techniques and experimental design skills were not mentioned; "good journals," clearly not the best ones; and "perseverance on tedious observations," as though the student hadn't the intellect to find something more interesting and effective to do. To me, the phrase "hardest working" in *2* also is negative—all this work must be making up for some lack, such as knowledge, skill, or creativity. "Junior scientist" also suggests someone sorely in need of supervision.

I would like to emphasize the notion that the absence of a letter from a thesis advisor is conspicuous and must be explained. I would also add that it is important for all of us to have a number of people who know the content and caliber of our work. When I participate in advice panels for students, I usually say that it is their responsibility as students to be sure that several professors know them well enough to write an informed and supportive letter. It is a mistake (which I see in my work on fellowship programs) to ask a well-known scientist to write a letter unless the person really knows you and your work. An applicant is better off with a more solid, albeit less prestigious, letter.

References

Miller, Casey, and Swift, Kate. (1988). *The handbook of nonsexist writing*, (2nd ed.). New York: Harper & Row.

Female surgeon's quitting touches nerve at medical schools. (1991, July 14). *New York Times*, p. 10.

Strunk, William, Jr., and White, E. B. (1979). *The elements of style* (3rd ed.). New York: Macmillan.

Index